Minimalist Parsing

Minimalist Parsing

Edited by
ROBERT C. BERWICK
AND
EDWARD P. STABLER

OXFORD
UNIVERSITY PRESS

OXFORD
UNIVERSITY PRESS

Great Clarendon Street, Oxford, OX2 6DP,
United Kingdom

Oxford University Press is a department of the University of Oxford.
It furthers the University's objective of excellence in research, scholarship,
and education by publishing worldwide. Oxford is a registered trade mark of
Oxford University Press in the UK and in certain other countries

First Edition published in 2019

Impression: 1

Published in the United States of America by Oxford University Press
198 Madison Avenue, New York, NY 10016, United States of America

British Library Cataloguing in Publication Data
Data available

Library of Congress Control Number: 2019939273

ISBN 978-0-19-879508-7 (hbk.)
ISBN 978-0-19-879509-4 (pbk.)

Printed and bound by
CPI Group (UK) Ltd, Croydon, CR0 4YY

Contents

Preface

The chapters in this volume grew out of a workshop on Minimalist Parsing held at MIT on October 10–11, 2015. So far as we know, they represent the first workshop devoted solely to this topic. They draw on ongoing work originating from Noam Chomsky in the early 1990s through the present day, leading to perhaps the dominant approach in contemporary generative grammar, the Minimalist Program (MP). This approach left open a central question: how can we build computer programs that map from *external* sentences back to *internal* representations that follow MP linguistic theories, comprising part of the broader program of viewing linguistic theory as fully integrated into human computational cognitive (and biological) science? The aim of this book is to answer this question.

A central tenet of the MP is that accounts of human language ought to be grounded on the simplest possible logically necessary set of assumptions. For example, hierarchical syntactic structure need only be binary-branching, rather than ternary-branching, since empirically, binary-branching seems to suffice; further, this property itself can be seen to follow from more basic principles, as a corollary of the basic combinatory operations of Minimalist Grammars. However, despite this apparent simplicity, building parsers for such systems turns out not be not so simple. In fact, it is one of the great surprises of the modern study of human language that, as the Introduction that follows explains, the standard computational toolkit for parsing the structure of, say, programming languages *fails* outright when applied to the "simpler" case of human languages.

Most of the chapters that follow describe the ways in which we must extend our computational toolkit to cover human language. The rest extend these insights to other staples of computational cognitive science, such as integrating such parsers into models of human sentence processing behavior, even down to the level of brain activity.

In this regard it is important to stress that the MP is indeed a *program*, a particular methodological approach to generative grammar and human language, not a *theory*. Moreover, it is a still-developing program. In practice this means that there can be several distinct strands or choices in how to realize the basic "simplicity" tenets of the MP. The reader will see this reflected in the distinct ways the authors have approached implementation—some formal, some not, but all within the general spirit of minimalism. We hope that the resulting diversity and the success in tackling the thorny computational issues inspire a new generation of researchers to continue to explore how linguistics and computation can be made to fit together.

Robert C. Berwick
Edward P. Stabler

October, 2018

Acknowledgements

We would like to thank the Director of the Laboratory for Information and Decision Systems in October 2015, Professor Munther Dahleh, and the generous funding by the MIT Department of Linguistics and Philosophy under the leadership of Professor David Pesetsky. We would also like to thank our student volunteers, especially Sagar Indurkya and Beracah Yankama, for their invaluable technical support, and Lynne Dell for her unequaled logistical support.

List of abbreviations

ABS	absolutive
BOLD	blood-oxygen-level-dependent
CFG	context-free grammar
CI	Conceptual-Intensional
DC	doubling constituent
DET	determiner
DLT	Dependency Locality Theory
DP	Determiner Phrase
EF	Edge Feature
EPM	External Pair Merge
EPP	extended projection principle
ERG	ergative
ESM	External Set Merge
EX	Extraction
GEN	genitive
IM	Internal Merge
ISM	Internal Set Merge
LIFG	left inferior frontal gyrus
LPTL	left posterior temporal lobe
MG	Minimalist Grammar
MLC	Minimal Link Condition
MP	Minimalist Program
Nom	nominative
NTC	No-Tampering Condition
OBJ	object
OBL	oblique
P&P	principles and parameters
PC	Phase Completion
PIC	Phase Impenetrability Condition
prt	participle
RATL	right anterior temporal lobe
ROI	region of interest
SBJ	subject
SG	singular
SMC	shortest move constraint
SO	syntactic object
SPE	*The Sound Pattern of English*
T	Tense
TH	Thematization
TOP	topic marker
uCase	unvalued Case

uF	unvalued feature
uGen	unvalued gender
uNum	unvalued number
uPerson	unvalued person
uPhi	unvalued phi-features
VPE	verb phrase ellipsis
WS	Workspace
!F	unvalued feature

List of contributors

Robert C. Berwick Professor of Computer Science and Computational Linguistics, Department of Electrical Engineering and Computer Science, Massachusetts Institute of Technology, USA

Sandiway Fong Associate Professor of Linguistics and Associate Professor of Computer Science, University of Arizona, USA

Jason Ginsburg Associate Professor, Department of Educational Collaboration, English Communication Course, Osaka Kyoiku University, Japan

John Hale Professor, Department of Linguistics, University of Georgia, USA

Tim Hunter Assistant Professor, Department of Linguistics, University of California, Los Angeles, USA

Gregory M. Kobele Professor, Institut für Linguistik, Universität Leipzig, Germany

Jixing Li Postdoctoral Researcher, Neuroscience of Language Laboratory, NYU Abu Dhabi, UAE

Edward P. Stabler Senior Principal Research Scientist, Nuance Communications, and Professor Emeritus, Department of Linguistics, University of California, Los Angeles, USA

Kristine M. Yu Associate Professor, Department of Linguistics, Amherst, Massachusetts, USA

1

Minimalist parsing

Robert C. Berwick and Edward P. Stabler

The Minimalist Program has inspired diverse studies of parsing with diverse goals: to clarify the commitments of particular informally presented linguistic theories; to explore how different theories fit together; to make explicit the fundamental mechanisms of minimalist theories; and to identify a range performance mechanisms that could be relevant for psycholinguistic models. All of these goals are represented in the contributions to this volume.

This diversity of goals is not surprising. The Minimalist Program is a loose collection of linguistic theories inspired by the work of Noam Chomsky and many others beginning in the mid-1990s. While "parsing" in this context refers to the assignment of linguistic structure to sentences, it is important to distinguish what, exactly, this means. An interest in parsing could address diverse questions: how linguistic theories define structure; how algorithms can assign structure to acoustic or perceived representations of what has been heard; or how structure can be assigned in models of human linguistic abilities. And when we refer to linguistic structure, we could mean all analyses compatible with the grammar, or we could mean just those analyses that would be (or would probably be) assigned by a competent speaker in a particular discourse context. So when the title of this volume is unpacked even slightly, we see that it covers a wide range of research projects, some of which are represented here. Nevertheless, all the different goals mentioned above overlap. In these diverse proposals there are overarching themes, with an intelligible history and a promising future. It is easy to forget that common ground in our daily skirmishes, so a perspective uniting many of these projects is sketched here.

A foundational, unifying perspective is provided in the next section. This volume extends that perspective in various ways, briefly overviewed in the section 1.2. And section 1.3 provides some additional formal details, with attention to translating between some of the various notations used.

1.1 A perspective on language and parsing

This section presents a sketch of how some some familar linguistic results relate to parsing. Focusing on what is most relevant for situating the contributions of this volume in a rough and ready way, very many important aspects of current linguistic theory are put to one side, and we can be quite brief.

Minimalist Parsing. First edition. Robert C. Berwick and Edward P. Stabler (eds.) This chapter © Robert C. Berwick and Edward P. Stabler 2019. First published 2019 by Oxford University Press.

Hierarchy. The arithmetic term $2 + 3 * 4$ is conventionally assumed to denote the same thing as $(2 + (3 * 4))$, and parsers for calculators and other systems using arithmetic are typically expected to find the parenthesized structure. Note that the structure is hierarchical, with one arithmetic term inside of another, and, in this case, the structure branches to the right, with the more complex subconstituent on the right side.[1] A substantial mathematical theory in computer science addresses the question of how this kind of parsing problem can be solved, mapping the symbol sequences of context-free languages to appropriate hierarchical structures.[2] To say that the infinite language of arithmetic has a context-free grammar (CFG) means that the categorization of expressions needed for arithmetic is finite; the rules of combination need to know only which of finitely many categories an expression falls into. The set of well-formed hierarchical CFG derivations for sentences of arithmetic is "regular" (modulo a simple renaming of categories) in the sense that it can be recognized by a simple finite-state tree automaton (Thatcher 1967; Comon et al. 2007). From this sort of global perspective, a perspective that is probably more familiar to the computer scientist than the linguist, it is not hard to show that the context-free languages that are the yields of these regular tree languages are closed with respect to regular string transductions.[3] That is, when the strings of a context-free language are altered by a finite state transducer, the resulting language can also be defined directly by a CFG.

Turning to human language, for a competent English speaker, the sentence *Bo praises Cal* is usually assumed to have a hierarchical structure *(Bo (praises Cal))*. As in the arithmetic case, this structure has a phrase within a phrase, and again it happens that the more complex subterm is on the right. One might think that the algorithms for parsing context-free languages would carry over immediately to deliver the structures for human languages, but in a perhaps surprising discovery, this does not work, as noted in Chomsky (1957; 1955) and very many other studies. Human language presents many essential features not found in simple artificial languages like arithmetic or even programming languages.

Movement. One prominent, even basic, feature of human language not reflected in artificial languages is that phrases with particular grammatical roles can appear in various structural positions. For example, in the topicalized sentence *Cal, Bo praises*, many of the grammatical relations are the same as in the previous example, so the latter

---

[1] To be sure, this is not necessary. Obviously we could define a higher order function f such that, for any x, y, the value $f(x, y)$ is a function that maps another argument z to $x + (y * z)$. Since this is exactly the result obtained by the traditional calculation, why not find the structure $f(x, y)(z)$, which has the more complex subterm on the left? Certainly, by definition, the latter approach is fine if the goal is simply to denote the intended value, but there is a reason that math teachers instruct children to do a calculation that corresponds to the right-branching calculation. Not only is f in a higher type than $+$ and $*$, but also, although both approaches involve two function applications, unpacking the definition of f involves more function applications involving $+$ and $*$. So it is easy to identify various senses in which the former structure is *simpler*. This in turn invites a longer discussion of how the notion *simplicity* might be cashed out in cognitive terms—perhaps "simpler" means easier to parse, produce, or learn. And if we are modeling what humans do, there is an empirical question about which account better fits the facts. We will, however, leave this important discussion for another occasion.

[2] See e.g. Aho and Ullman (1972); Valiant (1975); Nijholt (1980); Sippu and Soisalon-Soininen (1988; 1990); Leermakers (1993).

[3] The yield of an ordered tree is the sequence of its leaves (its terminal elements), in order.

structure may be something like *(Cal (Bo (praises ~~Cal~~)))*, using the strike-out to indicate that the constituent *Cal* is pronounced only in its first appearance, now at the root and pronounced on the left, but still the object of the verb. One core idea of Minimalism, aiming for the simplest account possible (Chomsky 1995a), is that the operation that builds this latter structure may be just like the operations building *(Bo (praises Cal))*, except that an additional step selects something already in the structure (namely, *Cal*), merging it again on the left, at the root.

Is there a simple way to extend formal grammars and parsers to allow operations like that? The minimalist grammars (MGs) of Stabler (1997) start with a category-based merge operation—similar to a context-free rule but applied bottom-up—and extend it to allow a constituent already in the derivation to move from its original site to merge at the root.[4] These grammars preserve some fundamental properties of CFGs: parsing with MGs is formally tractable even in the worst case (Fowlie and Koller 2017; Harkema 2000); the categorization of expressions needed for any MG is finite; and the set of derivation trees for any MG is regular (Kobele et al. 2007). The MG derivation tree languages also have the more surprising property that they are (modulo a simple category renaming) closed not only with respect to regular transductions on their yields but also with respect to intersection with other regular sets of trees (Kobele 2011; Graf 2011). Of course, MGs are a very simple approximation to what we are aiming for, but they provide a useful starting point, allowing elegant modular descriptions of phenomena. It is conceivable that at least some of their fundamental properties will continue to hold as we move closer to human language.[5]

Biolinguistics. The idea that the theory of linguistic structure and parsing provides the basis for a cognitive science, as a component of human psychology and biology, is a another distinctive strand of the Minimalist tradition (Chomsky 1965; 1995b; 2015a; Berwick and Chomsky 2011; 2017). There is evidence that a competent English speaker's understanding of a sentence involves recognizing hierarchical relations similar to those that our grammars define. Time-course studies and memory interference effects confirm, as one would expect, that the continuous and dynamical mechanisms for storage and computation in human cognition are rather different from the discrete tapes, stacks, queues, and matrices that computer scientists usually assume in their parsing algorithms, but the neural architecture must realize something similar to our

---

[4] Details are provided in section 1.3, or see e.g. Stabler (2011) for a more thorough overview.

[5] Since dependency parsing is currently so popular in natural language processing, it is worth noting that if by "dependency grammar" we mean a grammar that specifies for any two pronounced heads whether one can depend on the other, then dependency grammars are expressively equivalent to CFGs (Gaifman 1965). Those grammars can be extended to a form that is equivalent to LCFRSs and hence to MGs (Kuhlmann and Möhl 2007). And if "dependency grammar" is used in a looser sense to refer to any grammar whose derivations can be exactly represented by dependencies between heads, then MGs are dependency grammars too (Stabler 1999; Salvati 2011a; Boston et al. 2010). The dependency representation of MG is sometimes useful. But there is also "data-driven" dependency grammar, a linguistic tradition which typically uses very few types of dependencies and leaves parsing to a statistical model that typically uses a very large set of features—see e.g. de Marneffe et al. (2014) and references cited there. These projects mainly aim to find useful statistical models that are simple enough to be easily trainable with available technologies and available data, deliberately ignoring performance of the model on data that is not relevant to application goals. The engineering success of this last tradition is really what has brought dependency grammar into the limelight, while seemingly putting aside the traditional concerns of explanatory adequacy in terms of fixing the proper structural relationships of sentences or accounting for language acquisition.

parsing strategies. We know rather little about the needed neural mechanisms, but there are some speculative proposals.[6]

Efficiency, determinism, and locality. For precisely defined formal grammars and parsing problems, there are empirical questions about where they fail as accounts of human languages. But they define precise parsing and acquisition problems. For example, evidence seems to suggest that, at least in a wide range of cases of fluent language understanding, each word is integrated into a single structure as soon as it is heard. So we can ask whether, given our current approximate but formal grammars for human language, whether the parsing problem presented by a precisely defined grammar makes that kind of human ability expected—or is it surprising? That is, is the parsing problem for our approximation simple enough that it should be solvable in the linear time allowed for each word, or is it more difficult than that? The question is still vague, especially because it is not quite clear which aspects of human language understanding count as part of the parsing problem. We can make some preliminary observations about the issue, based on the simple formal models already mentioned. First, it is well known that for any CFG we can calculate all possible parses (representing them compactly in a "chart" or "matrix") in just less than cubic time in the worst case. That is, we can calculate the chart for an n-word sentence using no more than $O(n^{2.37})$ basic computational steps. MG languages can be parsed in at worst $O(n^{2k+3})$, where k is the number of licensor features.[7] These complexity results may seem discouraging. If, when we use an adequate grammar of the language, the number of steps required to parse examples that are readily comprehensible even when the examples are fairly long grows cubically or worse with the length of the sentence, that could be hard to fit with our apparent ability to identify syntactic relations on a roughly word-by-word basis. But for unambiguous context-free languages like arithmetic (either with parentheses or with rules about operator priority), parsing requires only linear time, and similarly for MG languages. If the parsing steps are deterministic (or nearly so), linear time suffices.[8]

Some attention has been given to the idea that human parsing, in a disambiguating context, is also deterministic, building a single syntactic structure with a sequence of steps that never deletes any earlier assigned structure. Marcus (1980) and Berwick and Weinberg (1984) propose that deterministic parsing for human languages is possible if a certain kind of lookahead is allowed, a lookahead that is not finitely bounded in the string but that is nevertheless finitely bounded in terms of the number of structural elements it needs to consider at any point. Furthermore, they explore the possibility that that this bounded lookahead provides a functional explanation of locality restrictions on displacement operations. These proposals face empirical

---

[6] E.g. beim Graben and Gerth (2012); Gerth and beim Graben (2009); Cho, Goldrick, and Smolensky (2017); Hale and Smolensky (2006).

[7] The different kinds of features used by MGs are defined and related to various notations in section 1.3.

[8] Note that MG parsing does not specify binding relations and other aspects of language that are known to be significantly more complex—see e.g. Ristad (1993); Barton et al. (1987). Graf and Abner (2012) point out that although problems incorporating the full range of binding phenomema may be complex, a certain subset of them remain tractable and enforceable in an MG framework.

problems, as all current accounts of locality do,[9] but some basic architectural features of these systems find their way into almost all modern theories.

It is no accident that the assumption of a finitely bounded domain for movement operations in those earlier works has a close analog in MGs. The proposal in Stabler (1997) is that at most one licensor of each type can be the first feature of the heads in an MG derivation. This is called the *shortest move constraint* (SMC) because it means, for example, that a wh-phrase must move to the nearest +wh landing site, predicting certain kinds of wh-islands. Since the total number of licensor types is finitely bounded in any grammar, the SMC immediately entails that only finitely many possible movement operations are possible at any point in a derivation. The consequences of this assumption for deterministic parsing with lookahead have not been fully explored,[10] but as with earlier proposals about bounds on movement, we can see immediately that the SMC faces empirical problems. For example, how can the SMC allow attested cases of multiple wh-movement? There are possible responses to that particular challenge (Gärtner and Michaelis 2010; 2007), but the correct analysis is still unclear, and for all linguistic theories, many puzzles about locality restrictions on movement remain.[11] Salvati (2011a) has established, though, that if the SMC is simply removed, the parsing problem for MG languages becomes substantially harder—as difficult as provability in multiplicative exponential linear logic, which is intractable (Lazić and Schmitz 2014).

1.2 This volume

Fong and Ginsberg describe not a parser but an implemented system that computes derivations according to a blend of proposals from Chomsky (2001), Pesetsky and Torrego (2001), Gallego (2006), Kayne (2002), and Sobin (2014), a system which is able to provide sophisticated treatments of a wide range of examples from the literature. Compared to the spare basics of MGs, their system may seem complex, at least at first. Internal and external merge are assumed to form sets with two elements instead of trees with two daughters, and a third case of merge is used to form not simple sets with two elements but an ordered pair. Agree and probe-goal operations that value features, a labeling operation, theta-marking and feature inheritance can apply.[12] Letting these operations apply freely to a set of lexical items would produce many results that should be filtered out, so the operations are tightly restricted in a machine that acts on a on a triple comprising a syntactic object (SO), a stack (!FStack) of unvalued features, and a list (LIs) of lexical items and other LIs, where embedded LIs contain the parts of subconstituents to be derived, putting the results back into the

---

[9] See e.g. Fodor (1985) for a critical review of those proposals.
[10] Kallmeyer and Maier (2015) explore LR parsing for LCFRSs, an expressively equivalent grammar formalism that is precisely related to MGs by Michaelis (1998).
[11] Overviews are presented in e.g. Szabolcsi (2006), Boeckx (2012), den Dikken and Lahne (2013).
[12] Features are valued by unification. See e.g. Adger and Svenonius (2011).

containing list. Finally, an oracle (the linguist) initially puts the elements into an order that allows each derived SO to combine with the first element of LIs, and a decision procedure P decides which groups of operations should apply at each point. Fong and Ginsberg dispense with the feature checking idea of early minimalism in favor of constraint-driven and free displacement, to be filtered by possibly external conditions downstream from the merge steps, including for example requirements of a "Labeling algorithm at Transfer" which is not fully described here. The mechanisms introduced by **Fong and Ginsberg** are deployed in linguistic analyses described by **Ginsberg and Fong**, with particular attention to expletives, that-trace effects, and relative clause constructions with properties that are explained in part by economy conditions.

Of all the constraints proposed in the Minimalist Program, the trans-derivational economy conditions – those that rule out one analysis based on the possibility of another one – seem most computationally difficult, and most unlike anything in the MG formalism. Nevertheless, Graf (2013) shows that, in spite of appearances, most economy conditions proposed by linguists are in fact tractable and consistent with MG assumptions. Many trans-derivational constraints can be reformulated so that they achieve exactly the same effect without comparing derivations. Quite a few constraints of this kind are analyzed by Graf (2013), but not the particular set adopted by Fong and Ginsberg, so the complexity of these remains an open question.

This clarification of theoretical proposals in work like Fong and Ginsberg's is an essential prerequisite to assembling a rigorous formal model of the theory, a formal model that would allow conclusions about which kinds of languages are definable, and one that would pose definite parsing problems whose complexity and implementation we can study. So for the (possibly rare) reader who studies this volume from beginning to end, it is good to begin with these two studies that start close to the linguistic theory; they remind us of the distance we need to go from simpler formal models to complete linguistic descriptions.

Yu observes that recent work continues to confirm the observation from Chomsky and Halle (1968) that prosodic domains do not coincide with syntactic constituency, and so she proposes a working model of the syntax/prosody interface, based on MGs for the syntax and using the optimality-theoretic MATCH constraint of Selkirk and others for the mismatched prosody. This might seem like a difficult marriage, but Yu shows how it might work. She observes that, if the prosodic and MATCH constraints can be enforced with only finite counting (as it seems they can be), then the effect of the OT interface can be represented with a finite-state string transduction. That transduction can be integrated into standard bottom-up MG parsing in such a way that syntactic/prosodic mismatches are penalized but allowed when no better analysis survives.

Kobele observes that ellipsis seems to involve the deletion of unbounded amounts of material, and so it could seem that adding any such operation to MGs or any other formalism would make parsing intractable. But using a pro-form theory, where the pro-forms at "deletion" sites take MG derivation antecedents, the syntactic and semantic effects of antecedent material can be predicted, while efficient parsing is preserved. To set the stage, he presents a kind of sequent calculus for hypothetical reasoning about

MG expressions. A hypothesis introduces a kind of hole in a derivation. When the derivation containing the hole is silenced—all phonetic contents deleted—we define a mapping from assumptions with certain features to an expression with certain, usually different, features. These mappings are the possible ellipsis operations. He adds finitely many of these operations to MGs. As Kobele says of these pro-form operations, "Building up an expression, and silencing all of it except for some moving pieces, is reconceptualized as building an expression which is missing some parts, and silencing all of it." When the new operations are interpreted by antecedent derivations with the right features, then we obtain an appropriate interpretation of the ellipsis construction, as was proposed more informally in Kobele (2015). With this approach, the parsing problem is to determine whether a given sequence of lexical items has a parse (i.e. any positive number of parses of the specified "start" category) using the basic MG operations supplemented with the finitely many ellipsis operations that the grammar allows. With this approach, it is easy to see how parsing stays efficient.

Hunter begins with a review of psycholinguistic studies supporting the intuitive idea that when a possible trace or gap site is encountered—the original positions of internally merged ("moved") elements—the listener engages in a gap-filling process that takes some effort. After considering a top-down parser for MGs that does not predict that effort, Hunter proposes to formulate a left-corner parsing strategy for MGs. The basic left-corner idea is that the first constituent of a phrase is processed bottom-up, but then its sisters, if any, are predicted top-down. This may sound simple, but it is tricky to define left-corner parsing operations that are sound and complete for MGs—"sound" in the sense that any derivation found is, in fact, a derivation allowed by the grammar, and "complete" in the sense that, if the grammar allows a derivation, there is a sequence of parser operations that will find it. Hunter takes some first steps towards such a parser here, and shows how it has the potential to model the "active gap-filling" strategy that psycholinguists have proposed.

Li and Hale describe a more abstract perspective on the effort of human parsing, asking which linguistic structures and parsing strategies predict the effort indicated by fMRI studies. They define a wide variety of parser time-course complexity metrics, and then use a stepwise regression to fit a model to fMRI timecourse results from Brennan et al. (2016). Examining the coefficients for the linguistic predictors of fMRI activity, they find a number of connections, including an effect of what they call "bottom-up node counts" in MGs, over and above the node counts of similar CFG formulations—where the bottom-up node count is the number of parsing steps between successive words in bottom-up parsing. The active regions support a model in which temporal lobe processing is involved in both phrase structure syntax and in the recognition of distributional semantics.

1.3 Minimalist-inspired formalisms

For readers who want to understand the contributions of this volume in complete detail, this section provides a little background and keys to translations between the various notations. We use Stabler (2011) as a starting point because the notation there is among the simplest, and that notation is adopted by several of the chapters here. Some readers may want to skip this section, possibly returning to it as needed for clarifications.

MG features in Stabler (2011). An MG is given by a finite lexicon, which associates each phonetic form with a sequence of features. The basic features come in four types:

categories = {D,N,V,A,P,...}
selectors   = {=D,=N,=V,=A,=P,...}
licensees = {-wh,-topic,-focus,-case,...}
licensors = {+wh,+topic,+focus,+case,...}

For each category X we have the correponding selector feature =X, and for each licensee feature −x we have the corresponding licensor feature +x. And to specify a language, a set of strings, a particular "start category" is chosen; the language is the whole set of sequences of phonetic forms that have completed derivations that include that category feature.

Example MG1. Consider the following minimalist grammar, a lexicon with twelve elements, where complementizer C is the start category. We indicate each pairing of phonetic form with a features sequence with two colons :: for readability:

(MG1)	Cal :: D	praises :: = D = D V	ε :: = V C
	Bo :: D	knows :: = C = D V	ε :: = V +wh C
	student :: N	the :: = N D	ε :: = V +foc C
	teacher :: N	which :: = N D −wh	ε :: = D D −foc

We will refer to each lexical item by its phonetic form. In the right column, the ε indicates phonetically empty elements, so we will call them C, C_{+wh}, C_{+foc}, and D_{-foc}, respectively.

In this grammar, the lexical item *praises* has three features. That sequence of three features indicates that *praises* will merge with two phrases of category D (which we can think of as its object and subject, respectively) to complete a phrase of category V. And, again reading the features from left to right, the lexical item *which* selects an N to form a phrase of category D, and the additional feature −wh indicates that it can be licensed in a +wh position. Finally, ε is the empty sequence, used to indicate the silent elements in the right column.[13] An example derivation, just below, will illustrate how all these features work together to define a set of structures whose leaves form a set of sequences of heads, a language.

MG merge in Stabler (2011). Rather than imposing linear order on a derived structure with separate principles (though that can easily be done), let's specify it as a side-effect of the single basic combinatorial operation, merge. A first-merged element is always attached to the right of the selecting head (as the "complement"), and subsequent merged elements are attached to the left (as "specifiers"). In the formal

---

[13] Empty categories are familiar in Chomskyan syntax but are often misunderstood by other traditions, even though other linguistic traditions often have some form of type-changing rules with similar effects.

specification of the merge rule, it is convenient to separate the cases of external merge and internal merge, where internal merge ("movement") is distinguished by the fact that it selects something already merged. The stage has been set for this by dividing the category features from the licensees. Two elements can merge only if the head features of the first begin with a selector =X or licensor +x, and the head features of the second begin with the corresponding category X or licensee –x. When two elements merge, instead of putting the two together in a set, we will put them into a tree with an arrow at the root that points to the selecting element, and we will delete the features involved in the merge step. (For reasons that will be irrelevant here, in derived structures, Stabler (2011) changes the double colon :: pairing notation to a single colon.) To impose a kind of economy, the SMC, mentioned above, restricts internal merge to just those structures in which no two feature sequences begin with the same licensee. Finally, a derivation of category X is *complete* if X is the only feature left in the structure. The language defined by the grammar is the set of yields of the completed derivations of a specified category (the "start category"). That completes the specification of minimalist grammars.

Note that while external merge has a different effect depending on whether it is a first merge or non-first merge, internal merge has no first-merge case, because it requires a structure in which things have already been merged. And while external merge is binary, internal merge is a unary function. The structural effect of internal merge is identical to non-first external merge, but the single argument of internal merge already contains the phrase to be merged.

Example derivation from MG1. Notice that since *Cal* only has one feature, it is already a completed derivation of a D. But let's construct a complete derivation of a structure of category C to illustrate how merge works. Since the features of *which* begin with the feature = N, and since the features of *student* begin with N, we can merge them, deleting the features = N and N:

(1)   m(which, student) =

$$
\begin{array}{c}
< \\
\text{which:D –wh}\quad\text{student}
\end{array}
$$

Here we write m for merge. Note that the head of structure (1)—indicated by the arrow at the root—has a sequence of two features left, namely: D –wh. Since structure (1) has first feature D, it can now be selected by *praises*, deleting the =D and D. Note that this is again a "first-merge" for the selecting head *praises*:

(2)   m(praises, 1) =

$$
\begin{array}{c}
< \\
\text{praises: = D V}\quad < \\
\text{which:–wh}\quad\text{student}
\end{array}
$$

Our next step is a non-first merge, so the merged element is placed on the left of the selector:

(3)   m(2, Bo) =

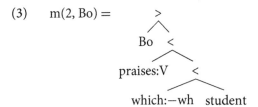

We perform another first merge, checking and deleting the category feature V:

(4) $m(C_{+wh}, 3) =$

```
                            <
                          /   \
                ε:+wh C      >
                           /   \
                         Bo   <
                            /   \
                       praises   <
                              /   \
                      which:−wh  student
```

Note that the head of structure (4) begins with a licensor feature, and there is exactly one corresponding licensee feature, so we can take the maximal projection of the head with the licensee feature and merge it to the root, checking and deleting +wh and −wh:[14]

(5)   m(4) =

```
                          <
                     /         \
                  <              <
                /   \          /   \
         which   student   ε:C    >
                                 /   \
                               Bo   <
                                  /   \
                             praises
```

Since the first feature of (5) is now the category feature C, it can be selected by *knows*, and then the result can select the external argument *Cal*:

(6)   m(knows, 5) =

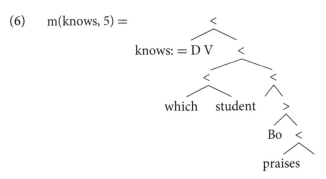

---

[14] Notice that we leave just an empty node, a trace, in the original position of the moving element, but it would not affect anything later in the computation if the original phrase were left there, but without pronounceable material and without any active syntactic features.

(7)   m(6, Cal) =

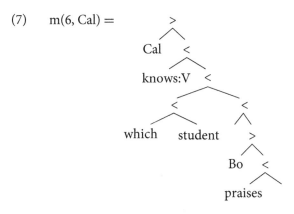

(8)   m(C, 7) =

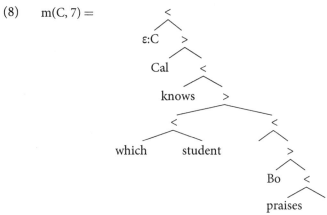

The structure (8) is complete, since it contains only one feature, namely C. Recapitulating the 8 steps succinctly, what we have shown is:

m(C,m(m(knows,m(m(C$_{+wh}$,m(m(praises,m(which,student)),Bo)))),Cal)) = (8)

and clearly

yield(8) = *Cal knows which student Bo praises* ∈ L(MG1).

Obviously, the language L(MG1) is infinite, since, for example, it also includes *Cal knows Cal knows which student Bo praises*, and so on. We also get the simple examples mentioned in section 1.1:

yield(m(C,m(m(praises,Cal),Bo))) = *Bo praises Cal*
yield(m(m(C$_{+foc}$,m(m(praises,m(D$_{-foc}$,Cal)),Bo)))) = *Cal Bo praises*

Obviously, this tiny artificial grammar MG1 has no way to predict the "comma intonation" of the last example, but a more complete grammar together with a prosodic interface of the sort studied by Yu (Chapter 4 this volume) should eventually be able to do that.

With this definition of MGs, the set of minimalist languages is exactly the class generated by MCFGs and LCFRSs (Seki et al. 1991; Michaelis 1998). This class of languages is "mildly context-sensitive" in the sense proposed by Joshi (1985). A range of standard parsing algorithms (bottom-up, top-down, etc.) are known, and they are provably sound, complete, and tractable for any MG.[15] So these simple grammars and parsers provide a useful starting point, and now we would like to move toward something closer to human language. A range of variants and extensions has been formally explored in prior literature; of particular interest are variants that add covert movement, head movement, copying, adjunction, asymmetric feature checking, coordination, and more.[16] These extensions are mainly well understood; we know their expressive power, we have parsers for them, and we know the complexity of their parsing problems. The chapter in this volume extend this basic picture.

Fong and Ginsberg use slightly different basic operations: set merge and pair merge. The differences between these operations and the MG operations are quite clear and easy to track precisely. Notice that sets can be represented with trees, where the arcs represent membership.[17] So where MGs derive the tree on the left, below, external set merge derives the structure on the right, where the bullet represents the set that contains its children:

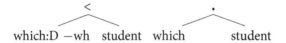

And for internal merge, where MGs derive the tree on the left, internal set merge derives the tree on the right:

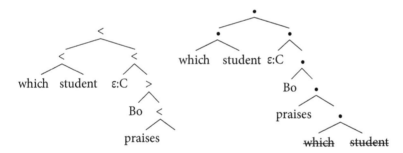

Unlike set merge, **Fong and Ginsberg** say that their pair merge results in an ordered structure, always putting the adjunct on the right. The ordered pair that results is like our ordered tree, except while MG trees are linearly ordered by time, this pair merge has a different order, adjunct-last.[18] After a merge, a labeling operation determines headedness, which converts a simple set into a set with its head indicated—like an MG-derived tree but without linear precedence.

Although MG-derived trees have linear order, none of the MG operations depends on that linear order of constituents in the derived tree, and so the switch to set-based

---

[15] See e.g. Harkema (2001); Stabler (2013); Fowlie and Koller (2017).

[16] See e.g. Stabler (1997; 2011); Michaelis (2001; 2005); Kobele (2005; 2006); Kobele and Michaelis (2005; 2009; 2011); Torr and Stabler (2016); Fowlie (2017).

[17] In the literature, the reason for representing standard sets as trees is usually to set the stage for more complex non-standard membership relations (Aczel 1988; Collins and Stabler 2015). Here, the connection between standard set notation and tree representations is made just to emphasize the similarity between the set notation and the tree-like structures used elsewhere in linguistic theory.

[18] MGs have been extended with various kinds of adjunction operations before – see e.g. Frey and Gärtner (2002); Gärtner and Michaelis (2003); Fowlie (2017).

structure-building operations is inconsequential. Much more important than these small changes is the manipulation of features, the differences in the conditions on operation application, and the spell-out of the syntax. Taking feature manipulations first, we see in example (1) in **Ginsberg and Fong**, Agree(X,Y) applies when Y is in the c-command domain of X, and the operation can change both X and Y. If the domain of feature values is finite, an expressively equivalent formulation could simply list all the pairs of values that could agree; so this is essentially a finite checking step, and it is easy to see that it could be implemented with a tree transduction, rewriting the original features to their new values, even with blocking conditions of the sort given in **Ginsberg and Fong**'s "Economy" condition (16). The other economy conditions used in the paper are more complex though. As noted above, the particular challenge posed by the extensive use of economy conditions is one that has been anticipated by Graf (2013), but open questions remain about the particular set of assumptions adopted by **Ginsberg and Fong**. Also, note that while Ginsberg and Fong's structure building operations are similar to those in MGs, it is unclear that anything like the SMC follows from their assumptions, and so one anticipates complexity problems in parsing until additional factors tie things down more tightly.

Yu uses the MG notation for lexical items introduced just above, adding prosodic annotations to the phonological representations of strings so that OT constraints on syntax/prosody alignment can be enforced. The difference is that she displays derivation trees rather than derived trees. Just above, we diplayed a derivation of *Cal knows which student Bo praises* like this:

$$m(C,m(m(knows,m(m(C+wh,m(m(praises,m(which,student)),Bo)))),Cal)) = (8)$$

But in Yu's notation for derived trees, we write Move for internal merge, and the feature cancelled in each step is shown in brackets. So in her notation, our derivation with eight merge steps has eight internal nodes, with lexical items at the leaves, and looks like this:

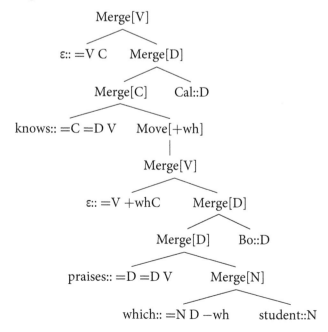

At each node, there is one and only one MG operation that could apply, but this tree is easy to read because it reminds you what the operation is and what feature is checked.

Kobele stays close to the notation introduced above, but assumes a Select operation that introduces lexical elements, and adds new ellipsis operations. He separates the elements of each lexical feature sequence with dots. Kobele does not use a non-first external merge step, but uses internal merge (which he calls "Move") to get phrases into specifier position on the left; determiners are assumed to have a feature –k that triggers an EPP movement. To illustrate, let's modify our lexicon above as follows, eliminating the transitive verbs in favor of the intransitive *laughs*, to keep things simple:

(MG2)   Cal :: D.–k   laugh :: = D.V   will :: = V.+k.T
        Bo :: D.–k   know :: = C.=D.V   should :: = V.+k.T
        student :: N   the :: = N.D.–k   ε :: = T.C
        teacher :: N   which :: = N.D.–k.–wh   ε :: = T.+wh.C

Using our earlier notation for derivations and our earlier merge operation, we would say that the yield of m(C,m(m(will,m(laugh,Cal)))) is *Cal will laugh*, but Kobele uses slightly different operations. Intuitively, his $Merge_1$ is our external first merge. His $Merge_2$ is a merge with a moving element. $Move_1$ is like our internal merge, and $Move_2$ is an internal merge of an element that will continue moving. So for him, the derivation of *Cal will laugh* is:

$Merge_1(Select(C),Move_1(Merge_1(Select(will),Merge_2(Select(laugh),Select(Cal)))))$,

depicted in a tree like this:

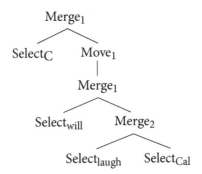

It is easy to show that MG2 defines a language that also includes *Cal should know which student will laugh* and infinitely many other sentences.

As mentioned above, Kobele's ellipsis operations are defined in a calculus that is similar to MGs, a kind of meta-MG that serves just to define these operations. To keep this calculus clearly distinct from the MGs themselves, after introducing a lexical item with Select, Kobele uses the standard angle bracket notation for pairs, and he uses ⊢ to indicate a derives relation – as is done in sequent presentations of logic (Sundholm 1984). So then, in Kobele's notation, the derivation of *Cal laughs*, which uses no hypothetical reasoning, becomes this, with the leaves at the top:

$$
\cfrac{
\cfrac{\varepsilon::=T.C}{\vdash \langle \varepsilon,=T.C\rangle}\ \text{Select}
\qquad
\cfrac{
\cfrac{
\cfrac{will::=V\ +k\ T}{\vdash \langle will,=V.+k.T\rangle}\ \text{Select}
\qquad
\cfrac{
\cfrac{laugh::=D.V}{\vdash \langle laugh,=D.V\rangle}\ \text{Select}
\qquad
\cfrac{Cal::D.-k}{\vdash \langle Cal, D.-k\rangle}\ \text{Select}
}{\vdash \langle laugh,V\rangle,\langle Cal,-k\rangle}\ \text{Merge}_2
}{\vdash \langle will\ laugh,+k.T\rangle,\langle Cal,-k\rangle}\ \text{Merge}_1
}{\vdash \langle Cal\ will\ laugh,T\rangle}\ \text{Move}_1
}{\vdash \langle Cal\ will\ laugh,C\rangle}\ \text{Merge}_1
$$

With this approach, an Axiom can be used instead of a lexical item, creating a derivation with a "hole", one that can be related to an antecedent of the right syntactic type. The new notation and operations are presented tersely but clearly in Kobele's chapter, so the presentation is self-contained.

Hunter's notation is essentially the one from Stabler (2011) introduced in the beginning of this section. And while **Li and Hale** mention minimalist grammar derivations, they do not show the lexical features, instead depicting an MG derivation in a standard X-bar format familiar to linguists.

1.4 Conclusion

Although there are many strands of research on minimalist parsing not collected in this volume, the following chapters illustrate a broad engagement with linguistic and computational issues. A remarkable expressive power and simplicity has been found in mathematical frameworks close to current research, as phenomena that once seemed complex are disentangled to reveal their essentials. In all the proposals about parsing here, we find a striking transparency in the use of the grammar, as one might expect since the grammar plays a role in various kinds of linguistic abilities (Berwick and Weinberg 1984). Grammar is aptly regarded as "the epicenter of all language behavior" (Bever 1970). As the mechanisms of grammar are revealed, we also discover the grammatical basis of linguistic performance.

2

Towards a Minimalist Machine

Sandiway Fong and Jason Ginsburg

2.1 Introduction

With respect to computational modeling, the Minimalist Program (MP) (e.g. Chomsky 1995b; 2001 and thereafter), has not lent itself to straightforward formal characterization. MP models have undergone a series of methodological and theoretical shifts in the continual search for a better characterization of the language faculty. Although computational efficiency is of central concern in cognitive models, a so-called "third factor" principle, this does not imply that theoretical improvements will necessarily make for more efficient implementation, as will be discussed in this chapter.[1] However, it is important to recognize the computational implications of these shifts, evaluate the challenges, and adopt appropriate computational architectures. This chapter describes an efficient architecture that has been implemented and tested on a wider variety of syntactic phenomena than any comparable system that we know of. We discuss in detail the reasons for, and consequences of, our architectural choices.

2.2 Free or feature-driven movement

Let us begin with a concrete example of a theoretical shift: movement, or Internal Merge (IM) in MP terms, has been alternately characterized as being "driven" (e.g. Chomsky 1995b; 2001) or "free" (e.g. Chomsky 2013; 2015b). By "driven", we simply mean that preconditions are placed on movement. The EPP, or Edge-feature (Chomsky 2001), is an example of a mechanism that can drive and limit displacement. A general requirement for grammatical feature-matching during IM can also serve the same purpose. In these theories, no movement may take place without featural approval. The Minimalist Grammar (MG) formalism (Stabler 1997; and much work since) codifies this feature-driven approach. Note that explicit feature checking is not the only way to condition displacement; for example, the Minimal Link Condition (MLC) and the Last Resort rule (Chomsky 1995b) are economy-based conditions that do not

---

[1] According to (Chomsky 2005), there are three factors that enter into the growth of the language for the individual: (i) genetic endowment, (ii) experience, and (iii) principles not specific to the faculty of language.

involve (explicit) feature checking.[2] The Antilocality proposal of Bošković (2016) is yet another. Pesetsky and Torrego's T to C movement is an interesting case of economy that we will discuss in detail in this chapter because it involves a combination of feature checking and operation counting. By "free" we simply mean that there are no preconditions on IM; i.e. by default, constituents are free to displace anywhere without checking first for permission. Within this framework, a theory that can dispense with EPP/Edge and other non-substantive features (perhaps invented solely for the purpose of constraining displacement) carries less "technical baggage" to burden acquisition or biological endowment. Obviously, since not all possible derivations are admissible; structural constraints that filter out uninterpretable or ill-formed syntactic objects (SOs) must appear somewhere "downstream" from Merge. Ideally, these independently- motivated constraints would originate from language-external factors, e.g. the need to reformat SOs to meet the requirements for exchanging relevant information with external systems, or from limits on general cognitive architecture. For example, at the Conceptual–Intensional (CI) interface, Merged objects must be explicitly labeled (Chomsky 2013; 2015b). Thus, Labeling limits possible phrasal movement. Third factor considerations could also limit the range and depth of structures computed.[3]

Let us turn our attention to computational issues for the two types of theories outlined above. First, a feature-driven model, if sufficiently constrained, can result in an "efficient" implementation in the sense that SOs can be derived with few, or no, choice points. Suppose the possible syntactic operations are limited to the following three: (i) External Set Merge (ESM), (ii) Internal Set Merge (ISM), (iii) External Pair Merge (EPM).[4] In the model described here, a machine state (SO, LIs) will consist of a current SO and an ordered list of (unmerged) lexical items (LIs).[5] ESM will merge the first LI H with the current SO α, forming $\{H, \alpha\}$. More succinctly, we can write $(\alpha, [H, ..]) \mapsto (\{H, \alpha\} [..])$. (We use the notation $[H, ..]$ to represent a list (or stack) with first (or top) element H. [..] represents the remainder of the list once H is removed.) ISM identifies a sub-constituent β in α, forming $\{\beta, \alpha\}$; i.e. $(\alpha, [H, ..]) \mapsto (\{\beta, \alpha\}, [H, ..])$. (We will write $\beta \subset \alpha$ to indicate that β is a proper sub-constituent of α.) In principle, β could be any subconstituent of α; however, we use featural identification and locality to limit our choice to just a single β. For example, the interrogative complementizer C_Q will seek a $\beta[wh]$, where wh is a feature. We may limit ISM to the closest available $\beta[wh]$.[6] Finally,

---

[2] The decision procedure P (described later) contains an implementation of the Last Resort rule.

[3] For example, without constraints on IM, we can select any sub-SO for displacement, so the combinatorics of SO growth becomes a problem. One third-factor hypothesis that can be investigated is that cognitive computation not only does not support, but actively suppresses, the creation of infinite loops. Further exploration of this issue falls outside the scope of this chapter.

[4] We put aside a possible fourth type of operation, Internal Pair Merge (IPM). See Richards (2009) and Epstein, Kitahara, and Seely (2016).

[5] Our implementation assumes an Oracle that turns a set of LIs into a properly ordered list. This convenient simplification is purely for efficiency's sake.

[6] Of course, by "closest" we mean the nearest structural constituent as defined by the c-command domain, rather than the nearest compatible constituent in terms of linear order.

EPM will form <*H*, α>, with H as adjunct.[7] Using the notation introduced above, this is (α, [H,..]) ↦ (<H, α> [..]). These are the choices available to the machine. (We put aside for now the situation that obtains when H is not a simple head, but instead a complex SO formed earlier in a lower workspace (WS) and placed at the front of the LIs.)

Suppose the machine has a decision procedure P that deterministically selects the right operation in order for the derivation to converge. If P exists, by always making the right choice, all other candidate operations can be pruned immediately. This is the optimal situation from the point of computational minimalization, in terms both of memory demand and of the number of operations required to converge on the desired SO. Should P make a wrong choice, the derivation crashes, i.e. fails to converge on a single SO. In the case where we intend a crash, e.g. to show a SO is underivable from some particular initial list of heads (LIs), the machine containing P need not show that there is no combination of available operations to circumvent failure; it simply needs to fail to advance its derivation at some point (perhaps as early as possible). An empirically adequate P will produce convergent derivations without backtracking when started with appropriate LIs, and crash when not. Ideally, P will be able to also cite a grammatically relevant reason for a crash, not just simply halt.

The Oracle-like knowledge encoded in P will be a combination of well-motivated linguistic principles, e.g. minimal search, plus (irreducible) ad hoc stipulations.[8] Let us define a simple, or "minimal," P as one that decides on the right operation solely on the basis of current state. A more powerful P, e.g. one that employs lookahead (by precomputing future machine states) or considers prior machine states, e.g. in Markovian fashion, to decide on the right move, will be deemed architecturally non-optimal. We describe such a minimal P in the following sections.

A free Merge model cannot entertain the level of determinism described above for feature-based systems. If Merge is unrestricted, the operations ESM, ISM, and EPM are active and available at all relevant stages of the computation. Irrelevant operations must be blocked somewhere downstream. For example, consider a transitive verb construction {T, {SBJ, {v*, {V, OBJ}}}}, where the subject SBJ is first Merged at the edge of v*P. In typical feature-based theories, tense T has an EPP (or Edge) feature. Assuming minimal search, this triggers ISM to raise SBJ to the surface subject position (in preference to the object OBJ). In the free Merge framework, there is no EPP feature; therefore both {SBJ, {T, {S̶B̶J̶, {v*, {V, OBJ}}}}} (raising) and {T, {SBJ, {v*, {V, OBJ}}}} (no raising) will be put forth to be Merged with the complementizer C.[9] We must rely on the Labeling algorithm at Transfer to the CI interface to rule out the illicit English structure

---

[7] Convention: in this chapter, in the ordered pair <α, β>, the first element α always represents the adjunct, and β the head.
[8] We speculate (without experimental evidence) that the ad hoc component potentially could be acquired. In terms of the decision procedure P, currently, we manually sort the available operations: ESM, ISM, and IPM. (Learning to more efficiently assemble SOs through experience would be the driving principle.) If so, an individual actually has no ad hoc P to begin with. Instead, it might be created through error-driven exposure to data.
[9] Notation: strikethrough will be used throughout this chapter to indicate displacement.

{C, {T, {SBJ, {v*, {V, OBJ}}}}}, as in Chomsky (2013; 2015b).[10] This non-determinism results in combinatorial explosion that minimal P avoids by design.[11]

2.3 Computational cyclicity

Cyclicity also has important consequences for implementation. First, the notion of incrementally assembling SOs in strict bottom-up fashion has not always enjoyed unqualified support in the MP. For example, although it seems to violate the No-Tampering Condition (NTC) of Chomsky (2008), the notion of syntactic head-to-head movement (after phrasal movement) reappears from time to time. For example, Chomsky (2015b) indicates that the root R should raise in {v*, {R, OBJ}} and form the amalgam [R-v*], realized as a reverse-ordered Pair-Merged head-head structure. In short, from {v*, {R, OBJ}}, we non-cyclically create {<v*, R>, {R, OBJ}}.[12] Simultaneous (or parallel) IM operating at the Phase level, as in (Chomsky 2008), is another proposal that seems to violate the idea of the strict cycle at the single-Merge level of granularity. Let us discuss each of these in turn with implementation of minimal P in mind.

Commitment to a strict version of the cycle results in the simplest possible scheme for scheduling operations. For example, suppose a head gets just one (and only one) opportunity, at the time of its first Merge to the current SO, to probe, value, and have its features valued. Once a head is submerged into a larger SO, the system "forgets" and never resurrects the "now buried" head for further probing duties. More precisely, given machine state (SO, [H ..]), Set Merge of H and SO proceeds by first having (the features of) H probe its intended c-command domain SO, and possibly carry out operations such as Agree(H, β), where $\beta \subset$ SO. (Recall that SO is the current syntactic object and H is the first in the list of LIs.) If successful, the new machine state will be ({H, SO}, [..]). We consider H "buried", and the machine never digs into the current SO to have buried heads (re-)probe. (Note this does not prevent H from subsequently being a goal targeted by operations like Agree.) The proposed scheme is the simplest possible because otherwise it would require the system to organize and maintain a list of delayed-past-Merge probe-goal operations. Bookkeeping of this nature requires additional memory and computational resources, so we do not consider it for our minimal P. In fact, whenever we have opportunities to bookkeep, we will pass on

---

[10] An attempt could be made to make a minimal P-type device available in a free Merge model. However, it is not clear whether this would be technically feasible (or deducible from assumptions) in all possible scenarios or computational states. Even in our small example above, to forestall speculative (non-)movement, this would involve building in the knowledge that {T, {SBJ, {v*, {V, OBJ}}}} cannot be labeled unless ISM of something that shares identical φ-features with T happens next (but not ESM or EPM). We must also deduce that the possibility of ESM is ruled out because φ-features in an external constituent cannot satisfy the identity requirement. Finally, EPM must be ruled out on the grounds that the canonical φ-feature sharing configuration would not be achieved.

[11] Note that in free Merge, we find echoes of Move-α, a concept in the earlier Principles-and-Parameters (P&P) framework (see Chomsky 1981). Move-α implies that syntactic objects of any category may, in principle, undergo IM. However, the EPP is very much part of the P&P framework; there is no EPP in free Merge.

[12] Obviously, the timing of head-to-head movement is critical if the operation is to meet the conditions of strict cyclicity. See also Epstein et al. (2016) and Collins and Stabler (2016) for relevant discussion.

them. (However, as will be explained later, this does not prevent the implementation of Multiple Agree (Chomsky 2001).)

Consider example (1a): as discussed in Chomsky (2008), both phrases [..]$_1$ and [..]$_2$ must simultaneously raise from the post-verbal object position in (1b) in order to sidestep a possible violation of the subject island condition. (Compare (1a) with (1e).)

(1) a. Of which car was the driver awarded a prize   = (7ii) (Chomsky 2008)

   b. [[of which car]$_1$ was [the driver of ~~which car~~]$_2$ awarded [~~the driver {of which car}~~$_\text{I}$]$_2$ a prize]

   c. {C$_Q$ {T, {.. {award, the driver of which car}}}}

   d. {[the driver of which car]$_2$, {T, .. {award, [~~the driver of which car~~]$_2$ a prize}}

   e. *Of which car did the driver cause a scandal   = (6ii) (Chomsky 2008)

If we take the pre-IM structure to be (1c), it should be apparent that the raising of *the driver of which car* to the Edge of T is counter-cyclic. Note that the naïve version, i.e. raising to the Edge of T first, and forming (1d) before merging interrogative C$_Q$, does not work. Merge of C$_Q$ will trigger probing, but the closest *of which car* is inside the subject island. In our implementation, a stack data structure originally introduced for computational efficiency saves the analysis.

The machine stack K operates as follows:

(2) (i) In machine state (α[!F], [H, ..]), where !F denotes an unvalued feature F and α[!F] denotes a SO α with unvalued feature F, α[!F] is pushed onto K if α is no longer the current SO, i.e. stacking is triggered when something is merged with α[!F].

   (ii) When a probe requires a matching goal, it must be found on K, i.e. only the stack is consulted.

Given (2), if we apply ESM to machine state (α[!F], [H, ..]), we obtain a new machine state ({H, α[!F]}, [..]), and unvalued feature !F is buried inside the SO ({H, α[!F]}. To avoid a possibly deep (and expensive) search of the current SO each time a probe is first Merged, we simply look to the stack for candidate-matching goals. In a probe-goal model, because the stack (by definition) only contains constituents with unvalued features, we can be confident we have all the candidates of interest without examining the current SO. Finally, for maximal computational efficiency, i.e. eliminating SO search, we can demand that the top element of the stack always contains the right goal.[13]

Returning to example (1a), *which car was the driver awarded a prize*, the DP *the driver of which car* lacks Case when it is first Merged as object of the verb root *award*,

---

[13] Probes search for a particular unvalued feature. If the stack top has cached the right element, there is no search, and the data structure proposed is maximally efficient. If it does not, the next element down in the stack can be tested, and so on. A "cache miss" is non-optimal, but a convergent derivation can still be obtained. In informal testing on our corpus, the first stack element is nearly always the one we want.

creating SO {award, DP}. Since the DP is no longer the current SO, it goes on the stack. Proceeding in strict cyclic fashion, we obtain {T, {v, {.. {award, DP}}}}. In our grammar, T has an Edge feature, and hence the DP raises to form {DP, {T, {v, {.. {award, D̶P̶}}}}}. Next, C_Q merges and probes the SO; but as we have outlined above, it actually grabs the DP initially left on the stack, and the derivation proceeds.[14] To be clear, the stack we have just introduced is not a conceptually necessary component of the architecture. The notion of a machine stack is not normally part of the formal vocabulary of the linguist; therefore, it requires some additional justification. We have introduced it as a computational efficiency measure, largely to sidestep goal search. It happens also to facilitate parallel Merge of the sort discussed in Chomsky (2008).

At this point, a remark on maintaining computational cyclicity in the face of paradigmatic shift is in order. Grammatical operations need not always operate in "lockstep" with the core Merge implementation as sketched above. Although Merge is the driving force in our implementation—i.e. operations such as Agree and probe-goal are triggered immediately at first Merge of a head—this "first wave" approach may not be desirable, or even necessary, from the point of view of empirical coverage or efficient implementation. An example is Labeling of the sort discussed in Bošković (2016), where he exploits differences in the timing of Labeling for various phrases to account for a variety of effects.[15] Computationally speaking, choices exist here; for example, we can choose to always label a phrase as soon as possible, e.g. as in Ginsburg (2016), or delay labeling for some phrases, as in Bošković (2016). Immediate Labeling is Merge-driven and respects the strict cycle. Delayed Labeling, e.g. until Transfer as proposed in Chomsky (2015b), can be viewed as non-cyclic, as Labeling is triggered only on completion of a Phase. Determining the label of deeply buried phrases long after Merge seems, at first glance, to be computationally inefficient. This is true for largely deterministic models, but in the case of free Merge, delaying Labeling may actually be a computational win, simply because large numbers of candidate SOs (introduced non-deterministically) will be ruled out early anyway. In short, why bother to label for Transfer if most candidate SOs won't make it there?

In the system described here, we do not implement algorithmic Labeling; instead, P deterministically assign a label to each syntactic object at Merge-time. Updating to a loosely coupled labeling algorithm poses a challenge to our model of quickly-evaluate-and-forget. One way to reconcile the two paradigms for future implementation is to place Labeling in a "second wave" of cyclic operation. Under this proposal, Labeling proceeds cyclically but exhibits variable latency; i.e. it is simply delayed, and not forced

---

[14] For (1e), *of which car did the driver cause a scandal, there is a Phase boundary (v*P) separating C from the initial Merge of *the driver of which car* to the Edge of v*. Since Phase boundaries are pushed onto the stack in our implementation, we could make use of this to rule out (1e). However, the actual implementation makes use of an i-within-i-style stacking constraint: "if [$_A$ .. [$_B$ ..]] is pushed onto the stack, and [$_B$ ..] from a substream is already on the stack, A subsumes B and renders B unavailable on the stack." This means the stack element for *the driver of which car* blocks the required stack element (*of*) *which car*, and thus (1e) cannot be formed.

[15] By "not in lockstep" we mean that SOs need not be Merged and labeled in complete synchronicity; in particular, the label for a SO can be determined post-Merge (cf. Label Accessibility Condition (LAC): Chomsky 2000).

to make a decision about the label of the result of every Merge. These and other shifts pose concrete challenges to settling on a particular theory to implement, never mind settling on a particular formal or mathematical framework such as minimalist grammars (Stabler 1997).

2.4 Architecture overview

Let us review the components of the implementation introduced so far: we have defined a machine state as consisting of a current syntactic object (SO) and an ordered list of heads (LIs). We have also argued earlier for an unvalued feature (!F) stack. Therefore, the components of the machine state are now as given in (3):

(3)   (SO, !F Stack, LIs)

Operations, to be defined below, map machine states to machine states. Let us note that operations have severely limited access to each of the components identified above for computational efficiency reasons as follows:

A.   The current syntactic object (SO) is opaque except for access to top-level grammatical features. We assume that features percolate upwards according to the headedness of constituents of the SO. In other words, the features of $\{\alpha, \beta\}$ will be determined by P, selecting recursively from the features of α (or β). In more contemporary terms, our model integrates Labeling tightly with Merge P, with P deciding on the label of $\{\alpha, \beta\}$ immediately.[16]

B.   The unvalued feature stack (!F Stack) is accessed for all probe-goal operations. No access is made to the current SO. The first matching stack element is retrieved. However, Phase boundaries are also registered on the stack. Since access cannot proceed beyond a Phase boundary, and stack order equals hierarchical distance, the Phase Impenetrability Condition (PIC) (Chomsky 2001) and the MLC are largely accounted for.[17]

C.   As discussed earlier, we assume the list of heads (LIs) is pre-ordered for convergent computation. Operations can only access the first element of the list; i.e. there can be no operation that selects e.g. the 3rd, LI to be merged with the current SO.

2.5 Fundamental operations

Operations are defined below in terms of machine state. First, let us formally define the fundamental Merge operations (introduced earlier):

---

[16] Deterministic immediate Labeling will not always be available, e.g. Set Merge of XP and YP creates $\{XP, YP\}$. P will be forced to create a choice point producing both $[_{XP}$ XP, YP] and $[_{YP}$ XP YP].

[17] These MP conditions largely supersede earlier P&P framework concepts such as Government, Subjacency, Barriers (Chomsky 1986), and Relativized Minimality (Rizzi 1990).

(4)   a. External Set Merge (ESM):

        (α, K, [H, ..]) ↦ ({α, H}, K', [..])

        stack: K' = K, i.e. unchanged, unless α[!F]; if so push α onto K to create K'

    b. Internal Set Merge (ISM):

        (α, K, [..]) ↦ ({βα}, K, [..]), β ∈ K

    c. External Pair Merge (EPM): (α, K, [H, ..]) ↦ (<H,α>, K, [..])

(Recall that machine states, given in (3), are triples of the form (SO, K, LIs). Operations define mapping (↦) of states to states. Mathematically speaking, operations need not be functions, as will be discussed later. In (4a), α refers to the SO, K refers to the !F Stack, and [H, ..] refers to the input stream of LIs with H as the first element.)

ISM in (4b) selects a sub-SO β of α from the stack K. This means that there must (originally) be some unvalued feature F accessible in β[!F]. ISM is thus a feature-driven operation with one exception. Suppose a feature !F is valued on β, then the question arises whether we should delete it from the stack. It may come as a surprise to the reader that we do not remove anything from the stack. As a result, stack items remain available for further (Merge) operations. To search for and remove inactive stack elements is a bookkeeping task that incurs a computational penalty. We always skip these chores. Also, by not deleting valued stack elements, it is possible to implement movement such as topicalization and rightwards displacement without resorting to the invention of non-substantive unvalued features for the sole purpose of keeping a stack element "active" (necessary in a strict feature-checking model).

We also model Leftwards Thematization/Extraction (TH/EX) (Sobin 2014), making use of already stacked DPs.[18] In the expletive construction shown in (5a), the object *a book* raises leftwards over *taken,* the verbal past participle (cf. (5b)). In our grammar, an invisible light verb v~ (following Sobin) attracts an already stacked sentential object (with unvalued Case), as v~ possesses an Edge feature. In the corresponding active sentence, (5c), there is no v~, and *a book* does not raise.[19]

(5)   a. There was *a book* taken   = (27c) (Sobin 2014)

    b. *There was taken *a book*   = (27b) ibid.

    c. John took *a book*

A second group of fundamental operations involve the shifting of Workspaces (WS). Associated with a WS is a current SO plus stack and input list, and a single stream of operations (determined by P) that empties the input list and converges on a single SO. Consider the sentence (6a) below. There are two DPs that must be independently

---

[18] It can be argued that stylistic phenomena such as TH/EX should not be within the purview of narrow syntax: see Chomsky (2001). It is not clear to us how this can be accomplished at the PF interface, as it seems to involve the displacement of entire DPs. Hence, we have chosen to model it as part of syntactic movement, following Sobin (2014).

[19] Another way to implement apparent leftwards movement would be to add features to move the verb around instead of the object DP. However, in our model this would require potentially stacking all verbs.

assembled. In our model, we pre-load the input list as shown in (6b). (Note that there are two distinct *uncomplicated* LIs shown: these are not copies.)

(6)   a. An uncomplicated man makes uncomplicated plans
      b. [*plans, uncomplicated, make*, v^*, [*man, uncomplicated, an*], T, C]

In the current model, sub-LIs may be pre-inserted at strategic locations within the main input list. Sub-LIs induce WS management operations. A sub-LI specifies both an independent stream of LIs to be assembled and also the position of the computed sub-SO in the main stream. In the example above, [*man, uncomplicated, an*] is placed at the position where we want the DP to be inserted back into the main stream after sub-stream computation completes. Since it is a sentential subject, we specify it should be inserted between the verbal categorizer v^* and tense T. The machine proceeds from left to right, and recursively merges *plans, uncomplicated, make*, and v^* in one uninterrupted sequence of operations to form the intermediate SO {v^*, {*make*, {*uncomplicated, plans*}}}. The corresponding machine state is shown below in (7a).[20]

(7)   a. ({v^*, {*make*, {*uncomplicated, plans*}}}, _, [[*man, uncomplicated, an*], T, C])
      b. (*man*, _, [*uncomplicated, man*])
      c. ({*an*, {*uncomplicated, man*}}, _, [])
      d. ({v^*, {*make*, {*uncomplicated, plans*}}}, _, [{*an*, {*uncomplicated, man*}}, T, C])
      e. {{*an*, {*uncomplicated, man*}}, {v^*,{*make*, {*uncomplicated, plans*}}}}, _, [T, C])
      f. ({C, {DP, {T, {DP, {v^*, {*make*, {*uncomplicated, plans*}}}}}}}, _, [])

In state (7a), the machine encounters the sub-LI [*man, uncomplicated, an*] next. This signals the machine to enter a sub-WS and begin a new sub-stream computation. The sub-WS has *man* as the first SO and remaining LIs [*uncomplicated, an*], as in (7b). This computation ends when a single SO {*an*, {*uncomplicated, man*}}, a DP, is formed and there are no more LIs left ([]), as in (7c). The machine then terminates the sub-stream, and pops back up to the saved main-stream machine state, but with the newly computed DP inserted at the front of the LIs, as given in (7d). ESM of the SO with DP = {*an*, {*uncomplicated, man*}} creates {DP, {v^*, {*make*, {*uncomplicated, plans*}}}}. The derivation then converges with {C, {DP, {T, {DP, {v^*, {*make*, {*uncomplicated, plans*}}}}}}}, as shown in (7f).

   More generally, we can define the two WS shift operations shown in (8a,b):

(8)   a. Down WS (DWS): (α, K, [[H, ..], ..]) $\mapsto$ (H, [], [..])
      b. Up WS (UWS): (β, _, []) $\mapsto$ (α, K, [β, ..])

In (8a), the first element of the input itself is an input stream ([H, ..]), and H becomes the new initial SO of the sub-WS. Note that α, K, and the rest of the input stream are temporarily forgotten, and restored only in (8b). β is transferred from the sub-WS to be the first element of the higher input stream. (8a,b) represent a serial view

---

[20] Notation: an underscore placeholder is used for the stack to indicate that its value is not relevant to this discussion.

of computation implied by the presence of sub-LIs. In a highly deterministic model such as the one described here, a serial implementation is a reasonable choice. In a free Merge model, where non-determinism dominates the computational landscape, separately forming all sub-SOs associated with sub-LIs first, and then substituting the completed SOs back into the LIs before beginning main-stream computation will always be the more computationally efficient choice.[21]

2.6 The decision procedure P

The decision procedure P is at the heart of our model. In fact, one can argue it is actually the "brains" of the model, in the sense it decides which operation should issue given any particular machine state. As mentioned in an earlier section, correct decision-making requires oracle-like powers. We have aimed for a minimal P that is as deterministic as it is practical. The system does compute multiple SOs in some cases— we return to consider an example of this in a later section; but by and large, it is locally deterministic, issuing one fundamental operation (defined in the above section) per machine state. Further, we claim our machine produces correct derivations for a wide variety of examples from the literature. (For space reasons, we cannot list the examples or their derivations. However, we can demonstrate the veracity of our claim.[22]) The question then arises as to how we came up with this particular decision procedure P. The short answer to this important question is simply by inspection (and trial and error) as we incrementally introduced examples to the system. This is also the reason why we stated earlier that P has an ad hoc component (see also note 8).

The following groups of actions are presented in strict order and constitute ad hoc P; i.e. only the first matching action will be triggered. As a result, ad hoc P is largely deterministic. (Cases where P is non-deterministic will also be discussed.) Each action makes use of the following template:

(9)   (SO, Stack, LIs) $\mapsto$ (SO', Stack', LIs')
      [*Preconditions on* SO, Stack, *and* LIs]
      stack: [Stack' *derived from* Stack]
      [*Labeling for constructed* SO']

(Recall that machine states have signature (SO, Stack, LIs).) We construct machine state (SO', Stack', LIs') from (SO, Stack, LIs) if stated preconditions are met. The last two lines will specify stack operations and Labeling for the new current SO, respectively. For each action, we will briefly list an example that motivates its inclusion; however, the reader

---

[21] The reason is that the results of sub-LI computation can be shared (and not repeated) within separate threads of execution in the case of non-determinism. This way memorization is achieved for free, but discussion of the details and its effects would take us beyond the scope of this chapter.

[22] Full step-by-step derivations are provided for all the examples that we cover in http://elmo.sbs.arizona.edu/sandiway/mpp/mm.html.

is referred to Ginsburg and Fong (Chapter 3 this volume) for derivation walkthroughs and further details.

We begin with the only actions that do not follow the template introduced in (9):

(10)   Phase Completion: $(\alpha, [\beta,..], [..]) \mapsto (\alpha, K', [..])$
        if phase(α), where α is current SO,
        stack $K' = [\beta, ..]$ with inactive(SOs) fronted

Basically, this states that completion of a Phase will result in stack visibility changes. First, some background: in the case of syntactic pronominal Binding, we employ a Kayne (2002)-style doubling constituent (DC).[23] In the case of a sentence like (11a), we begin its derivation with the LIs listed in (11b).

(11)   a. John$_1$ thinks (that) he$_1$ is smart
        b. [john, d, he, d, smart, v_{be}, T, c_e, think, v_{unerg}, T, c]
        c. {smart, {d!case, {he, {d!case, John}}}}
        d. [$_{CP}$ (that) he$_1$ is smart]
        e. *John$_1$ praises him$_1$

In (11b), the prefix [*john*, d, *he*, d, ...] produces the DC {d, {*he*, {d, *john*}}}. This is a DP with an internal DP; we will refer to the entire DP as a DC. At the interface, DC [$_d$*x* [$_d$ *y*]] will mean that *x* and *y* are coreferential. (We assume noun phrases are DPs; however, we will sometimes abbreviate a DP using just the head noun.) Since the r-expr *John* is in a subsidiary position within the DC, it will have to undergo IM to a theta-position, and get its Case feature valued.

Since the DC contains unvalued Case, it will be stacked when the adjective *smart* is merged in (11c), in accordance with (2i). (We assume the locus of unvalued Case (!case) to be the D head.) Although *John* is buried inside the DC, since it also has unvalued Case, it must also be stacked. However, we stipulate that the subsidiary DP must be stacked with status "inactive", meaning it is rendered inaccessible to search. Activation of inactive stack elements falls to the PC actions in (10).

Upon completion of a Phase, e.g. (11d), (10) fronts previously inactive *John* in the stack, and activates it. As a result, {d!case, John} becomes visible to IM, and !case to probe-goal. *John* then takes up the matrix subject position. Note that the requirement of activation at a phase boundary is necessary in order to block (11e). If *John* is available upon initial stacking, (11e) would be predicted to be grammatical.

(12)   Halt: $(\alpha, [..], [])$

(12) is the simplest action: if there are no more LIs ([]), the machine halts, and SO α is the result. If α contains any unvalued features, the machine crashes.[24]

The next mini-group of actions concerns merger of a determiner (d) from the LIs:

---

[23] For further details about modeling of Kayne (2002), see Fong and Ginsburg (2012a).

[24] Although our machine halts in this state, in theory additional IM operations may be possible, e.g. topicalization. We do not explore this option.

(13)   Action Group: D Merge

    i. $(n, K, [d ..]) \mapsto (\{n, d\}, K', [..])$

      in $d[!n]$ and $n[!d]$, $!n$ and $!d$ are valued

      stack: K' = push n and/or d onto K if n or d have unvalued features

      d labels $\{n, d\}$

    ii. $(d_1, K, [d_2 ..]) \mapsto (\{d_1\ d_2\}, K, [..])$

      d's share $!$case and $!n$

      d_1 labels $\{d_1\ d_2\}$

External Set Merge of *d* from LIs to the SO *n* in (13i) is accompanied by mutual uninterpretable feature valuation for $!n$ and $!d$. This seems redundant: i.e. why not simply merge *d* and *n* without checking off $!n$ and $!d$? The answer is: in our grammar, some determiners, e.g. d_{rel}, used for relative clauses, do not value uninterpretable $!d$. We derive (14a) from the LIs in (14b). The object DP $\{d_{rel}, book!d\}$ will contain *book* with unvalued *d* (viz. *book*!d). After constructing the clause headed by c_{rel}, *book*!d raises to form (14c). Since *book*!d is a head, it also labels (14c).[25]

(14)   a. the book (that) I read

    b. [book, d_{rel}, read, v^*, [i, d], T_{past}, c_{rel}, the]

    c. $\{book!d, c_{rel}P\}$ ($c_{rel}P$ derives "(that) I read")

    d. $\{the, \{book, c_{rel}P\}\}$

In the final step for the construction of the relative clause, the determiner *the*, a head that is generally able to value $!d$, merges with (14c), creating (14d). The new head *the* values $!d$ on *book*. This completes our discussion of action (13i).

    Action (13ii) was created for the case of exclamatives, such as in (15a):

(15)   a. What a silly book!

    b. $\{what, \{a, \{silly, book\}\}\}$

In our grammar, both *what* and *a* are analyzed as determiners. Since Case on the DP in (15a) will be valued just once, we have *what* and *a* sharing unvalued features ($!$case and $!n$).

(16)   Doubling Constituent (DC) Merge:

    $(\alpha, K, [\beta ..]) \mapsto (\{\alpha, \beta\}, K', [..])$

    if β is a DC $[_d x\ \gamma]$

    stack: $K' = K + \beta[!F_1] + $ inactive $\gamma[!F_2]$

    SO α labels $\{\alpha, \beta\}$

    Earlier, we introduced Kayne's notion of a DC for pronominal Binding. Action (16) will stack both the entire DC (β) and the subsidiary DP(γ) (inactivated) from a lower

---

[25] In a more elaborate theory, *book* in (13) would actually be composed of a root *book* + categorizer *n*, a functional head. A root R would not be able to label {R, XP}. Another strategy will be needed. The details are beyond the scope of this chapter.

WS. Both β and γ have unvalued Case; γ also has an unvalued interpretable θ-feature. See earlier discussion of sentence (11a).

(17)   Action Group: Merge to Edge of T
　　　　i. (T[!Edge], K, [EXPL,..]) ↦ ({T, EXPL}, K', [..])
　　　　　　first(LIs) is EXPL, e.g. *there*
　　　　　　stack: K' = K + β if β[!F], otherwise K' = K
　　　　　　SO T labels {T, EXPL}

　　　　ii. T[!Edge], K, [..]) ↦ ({T, β}, K, [..])
　　　　　　β ∈ K
　　　　　　SO T labels {T, β}

In action group (17), we find a potential conflict between the two actions listed: however, (17i) precedes and blocks (17ii). In more detail, (17i), i.e. ESM of an expletive to the edge of tense T, is preferred over (17ii), i.e. ISM of an argument from the stack. In either case, T[!Edge] means that T must have an unvalued uninterpretable Edge feature (!Edge) for the action to fire.[26]

Consider the expletive construction in (18a) and the machine state in (18b):

(18)   a. There is a train arriving
　　　　b. ({T, ..{arrive, {a, train}}}, _, [*there* C])
　　　　c. A train is arriving

At machine state (18b), the correct move is to merge expletive *there* from the LI input, rather than to raise the DP {a,*train*}. Hence, (17i) must come before (17ii). Note that (17ii), not (17i), must be triggered in the derivation of (18c). (The crucial difference is that expletive *there* will not be present at the LI input in the case of (17c).)

(19)   Theta Merge:
　　　　(XP[!θ], K, [Root,..]) ↦ ({Root, XP}, K', [..])
　　　　if Root is V (or A)
　　　　Root values !θ on XP
　　　　stack: K' = K + XP if XP[!F], otherwise K' = K
　　　　Root labels {Root, XP}.[27]

In action (19), we find the basic case of a verbal (or adjectival) Root merging with an object. The Root assigns a θ-role to the object XP. In our grammar, potential arguments will have an unvalued interpretable θ-feature. Note that structural Case is not valued here. In Chomsky (2000; 2001), functional heads v* and T probe and value

---

[26] Edge of T is the classic EPP feature. After Merge obtains, the uninterpretable Edge feature is valued, and cannot be used again. This feature-driven approach is a weak point in our system: should the theory be updated to allow multiple merges to the edge of T, we would require multiple Edge features.

[27] In algorithmic Labeling, e.g. Chomsky (2013; 2015a), roots are too "weak" to label, and must be strengthened in the configuration {XP, {R, X̶P̶}}, where XP and R share identical φ-features. Thus, Object Shift becomes obligatory. We do not model Object Shift in this system.

accusative and nominative Case, respectively.[28] If XP[!F] obtains, i.e. XP has some uninterpretable feature such as !Case, it is pushed onto stack K, and can be accessed by ISM or probe-goal.

(20) Internal Theta Merge to P:
      $(XP[!\theta!case], K, [P, ..]) \mapsto (\{P, XP\}, K', [..])$
      P values $!\theta$ and !case on XP
      stack: $K' = K + XP$ or $K + \{P, XP\}$ if XP[!F], otherwise $K' = K$
      P labels {P, XP}

Action (20) is very similar to action (19) (but see also action (22) below). In (20), a preposition P selects for an object (XP). The two significant differences are that: (i) P values uninterpretable Case for XP, and (ii) XP may be stacked.[29] To accommodate pied-piping, either the object (XP) or the PP {P, XP} may be pushed onto the stack.[30] This non-determinism allows the generation of either (21a) or (21b) from the same list of LIs (21c):

(21) a. Of which car did they find the driver? (adapted from Chomsky 2008)
      b. Which car did they find the driver of?
      c. [car, which, of, driver, the, find, v*, [they, d], T_{past}, c_Q]

(22) Action Group: External Theta Merge to P:
      i. $(PP[!Edge], K, [XP[!\theta],..]) \mapsto (\{XP, PP\}, K', [..])$
         $PP = \{P, YP\}$
         P values !case and $!\theta$ on XP
         stack: $K' = K + XP$ if XP[!F], otherwise $K' = K$
         P labels {XP, PP}

      ii. $(PP[!Edge], K, [..]) \mapsto (\{XP, PP\}, K, [..])$
         $XP[!\theta] \in K$
         P values !case and $!\theta$ on XP
         P labels {XP, PP}

Action (22i) permits the merger of an external argument XP to a preposition that supports one. The PP, abbreviated {P, YP} in (22i), must have an unvalued Edge feature. P also values interpretable $!\theta$ on XP, as well as assigning Inherent Case. Dyadic theme/goal *to* is an example of such a preposition; see example (23a), with our analysis given in (23b). Note that XP, from the LIs in (22i), is not a head, and therefore must

---

[28] Except, in later theories, e.g. Chomsky (2008; 2013), v* simply transmits its inflectional features to the verbal root. The verbal root then is responsible for valuing accusative Case. This has architectural consequences. In an earlier section, we stated that, for simplicity and efficiency, a head gets only a single chance, i.e. at ESM time, to probe and value. But in {v*, .. {V, OBJ}}, V cannot probe and value until it receives the inflectional features from v*. But this does not happen until v* is ESM'd, a situation that could be ungenerously viewed as a NTC (or strict cycle) violation.

[29] In action (19), V does not directly assign Case; instead, the higher functional head v* does. In action (20), P directly assigns Inherent Case. But see also note 30.

[30] The actual code is a bit more complicated. In our grammar, some prepositions may be empty, i.e. have no spellout. Following Pesetsky (1995), such prepositions may be used to analyze double object constructions, e.g. I gave [p [DP Mary] [[p][DP a book]]]. There is no choice point generated in these cases.

have been formed in an WS earlier. (It must then have been uplifted to the LIs using operation (8b).)

(23)   a. John gave a book to Mary
       b. {{d, John}, {v*, {give ,{{a, book}, {to, {d, Mary}}}}}}

Action (22ii) differs from (22i) in that it grabs the external argument XP off the stack. This is to permit the subsidiary DP in a Doubling Constituent (DC) to θ-Merge. Consider sentence (24a):

(24)   a. I showed John₁ himself₁ in the mirror
       b. [john, d, he, self, G, [mirror, the, in], show, v* [i, d], T_past, c]
       c. {self!case, {he, {d!case, john}}}
       d. {G, {self!case, {he, {d!case, john}}}}
       e. {{d!case, john}, {G, {self!case, {he, {d̶,̶ ̶j̶o̶h̶n̶}}}}}

(24b) is the list of lexical heads needed. The prefix [john, d, he, self, ..] forms the DC given in (24c). In our grammar, we assume *himself* = *self* + *he*, and therefore [_d *himself*, [_d *john*] is the relevant DC.[31] Following Pesetsky (1995), G is a dyadic preposition with the DC as object. *John* does not yet have Case or its θ-feature valued; hence *John* will be stacked upon Merge of G.[32] Action (22ii) will trigger at stage (24d) to form (24e).

(25)   External Theta Merge to D:
       (DP[!Edge], K, [XP[!θ!case], ..]) ↦ ({XP, DP}, K', [..])
       DP = {d YP}
       D values !case and !θ on XP
       stack: K' = K + XP if XP[!F], otherwise K' = K
       D labels {XP, DP}

   Action (25) is very similar to action (22i), the crucial difference being that we ESM to DP (instead of PP). Action (25) is triggered for possessives in English; e.g. example (26a) receives the simplified analysis given in (26b):

(26)   a. his dog
       b. {{d, he}, {'s, {d, dog}}}

In (26b), *'s* is treated as a dyadic determiner with internal subject *he* and object *dog*. We assume that *he* + *'s* = *his*.[33]

---

[31] See also discussion of example (11a).

[32] Given the discussion of example (11e), the reader might reasonably expect *John* to be stacked inactive, and therefore inaccessible to action (22ii). However, in our grammar, the reflexive *-self* is analyzed as the head of the DP *himself*, and it permits active stacking by being a Phase head (a lexical stipulation). On completion of the DP headed by *-self*, it activates any inactive stack items in its domain, in accordance with the Phase Completion (PC) actions defined in (10). Thus, examples like *John₁ praises himself₁* and (24a) are ruled in.

[33] The analysis given in (26b) is the simplest case. We make use of a Doubling Constituent (DC) for pronominal *he* for examples like *John₁ likes his₁ dog*. In other words, *he+'s dog* should be {{d, {he, {d, john}}}, {'s, {d, dog}}}. See also discussion of example (11a).

(27) Action Group: External Theta Merge to v*

    i. (vP[!Edge], K, [XP[!θ], ..]) ↦ ({XP, vP}, K', [..])

      vP = {v*, YP}

      stack: K' = K + XP if XP[!F], otherwise K' = K

      v* labels {XP,vP}

    ii. (vP[!Edge], K, [..]) ↦ ({XP, vP}, K, [..])

      vP = {v*, YP}, XP[!θ] ∈ K

      v* labels {XP,vP}

Actions (27i,ii) parallel (22i,ii). The essential difference is we θ-merge to the Edge of transitive verbalizer v* in (27). Since (27i) precedes (27ii), we have expressed a preference for external Merge over IM. The situation in (28b) represents the crucial case:

(28) a. John$_1$ knows Peter realizes that Mary likes him$_1$

    b. {v*, {realize, .. {d, {he, {d, john}}}..}}

    c. Peter knows John$_1$ realizes that Mary likes him$_1$

In the case of example (28a), *Peter* must be externally Merged at stage (28b). However, the DC analysis of pronominal Binding means that *John* is also a candidate for Merge. The DC is [$_d$ he [$_d$ john]], and *John* will be stacked as initially inactive (see earlier discussion of (11)). On completion of the Phase [$_{CP}$ that Mary likes him], *John* will be activated and compete with *Peter* (from the input stream) for the subject position of v*-*realize*. The correct decision in this case is to take *Peter* from the input stream (external Merge) over *John* from the stack (IM).

Comparing (28a) with (28c), it is clear that we must take *John* from the stack in (28c). However, we have only the appearance of a reversal of choice. For (28c), *Peter* will be further downstream in the LIs, and therefore unavailable at stage (28b). Our preference of Merge over Move can be maintained.[34]

(29) Merge v and VP:

    (VP, K, [v, ..]) ↦ ({v, VP}, K', [..])

    v probes K: Agree(v, G) if goal G ∈ K

    stack: K' = K + v

    v labels {v, VP}

Action (29) triggers probe-goal for categorizers that need to value Case, e.g. v*. We assume that all verbal roots (V) must have some categorizer v. However, not all categorizers need probe. For transitive sentences such as (30a), v* must probe and value Case on the object (see (30b)). However, for intransitives like (30c), v in (30d) does not probe.

(30) a. John likes Mary

    b. {v*, {like, {d!case, mary}}}

---

[34] In the case of action group (22), we have the same preference encoded when merging to the subject position of P. The crucial example(s) for that group are: *John$_1$ gave Peter$_2$ his$_{1/2}$ book.*

c. John runs

d. {v, {run}}

In some situations, the v probe itself could be a goal downstream. Since all probe-goal operations consult the stack, we stack v. For our grammar, the probe-as-goal scenario occurs in cases of auxiliary verb movement to C, such as (31a). In our grammar, auxiliary *will* is a v, a light verb stacked on v*, as shown in (31b).

(31)   a. What will Mary buy?

b. {will, {{d, Mary}, {v*, {buy, {d, what}}}}} = *will*P

c. {T, *will*P}

d. {will, {T, *will*P}}

e. {c$_Q$, {{d, Mary}, {will, {T, *will*P}}}}

f. {{d, what}, {T, {will, {c$_Q$, {{d, Mary}, {will, {T̶, *will*P}}}}}}}

Merge of T in (31c) results in T probing not only with the purpose of Agree(T, *Mary*) but also for a unvalued v-feature present on auxiliaries like *will*. We stipulate that when this situation obtains, T attracts v in the sense of Pesetsky and Torrego (2001; hereinafter abbreviated to P&T). Suppose we assume that when a head x attracts another head y, y must raise to the edge of x. In the case of (31a), *will* raises to the edge of T, forming (31d).[35] Next, Mary raises to the surface subject position at the edge of T. Then interrogative head c$_Q$ is merged. c$_Q$ probes and attracts *wh*-item {d, what}. However, adopting the T to C story of P&T, c$_Q$ also has an unvalued uninterpretable T feature. In the case of (31a), unvalued T on c$_Q$ can be valued by attracting T. Therefore T raises to the edge of c$_Q$. Pied-piping ensures that *will* also raises to the edge of c$_Q$.[36] Assuming Spellout operates by only pronouncing the highest copy, auxiliaries appear in C in interrogatives.[37]

(32)   Merge T and vP:

(vP, K, [T,..]) ↦ ({T, vP}, K, [..])

T probes K: Agree(T, G) if goal G ∈ K

T labels {T, vP}

Action (32) encodes the T counterpart to v* of action (29). Some instances of T, e.g. T$_{past}$ (present in many of the examples above), will probe and value Nominative Case on a matching goal from the stack. Others, such as non-finite T embedded in *Peter likes to eat*, will not.

(33)   Merge C and TP:

(TP, K, [c, ..]) ↦ (CP, K, [..])

c$_Q$ probes K: CP = {G$_1$ ..{G$_n$, {c$_Q$ TP}}..} for some goal(s) G$_i$ ∈ K

c$_{rel}$ probes K: CP = {G, {c$_{rel}$, TP}} for some goal G ∈ K

---

[35] Note that *will* does not label {*will*, {T,vP}}. It is attracted to the edge of T, so T still labels.

[36] We assume transitivity of attraction here: i.e. if x attracts y, and y attracts z, then z also raises to x.

[37] "The simplest assumption is that the phonological component spells out elements that undergo no further displacement—the heads of chains—with no need for further specification" (Chomsky 2001).

c_e probes K: CP = {G, {c_e, TP}} for some goal G ∈ K
c does not probe: CP = {c, TP},
c labels CP

Action (33) encodes merge of the complementizer C to the current SO TP. Interrogative c_Q triggers *wh*-phrase probing. As described in detail for example (31), this may also trigger a cascade of concomitant IMs to the edge of c_Q. In our grammar, non-interrogative C is relatively inert; it has no Edge feature, and IM is not permitted.[38] (We will return to consider the cases of c_{rel} and c_e later.)

(34)   Pair Merge:
       (α, K, [β, ..]) ↦ (<β, α>, K, [..])
       α and β both non-heads
       α labels <β, α>

Action (34) is deliberately situated as nearly the last possible action of ad hoc P. If none of the previous actions match, and α and β both are phrases, Pair Merge is permitted to apply. As currently defined, the adjunct comes from the input stream side only. This means the order of LIs supplied is crucial.

(35)   a. John read a book in the gym
       b. [book, a, [gym, the, in], read, v*, [john, d], T, c]
       c. ({a, book}, ⌐, [{in, {the, gym}}, read, v*, [john, d], T, c])
       d. <{in, {the, gym}}, {a, book}>
       e. {read, <{in, {the, gym}}, {a, book}>} = VP
       f. {c, {{d, john}, {T, {{d, john}, {v*, VP}}}}}
       g. [gym, the, in, [book, a], read, v*, [john, d], T, c]
       h. ({in, {the, gym}}, ⌐, [{a, book}, read, v*, [john, d], T, c])
       i. <{a, book}, {in, {the, gym}}>

Consider sentence (35a). (35b) is a possible input stream for (35a). After constructing the object *a book*, the machine builds *in the gym* in a lower WS, and injects the PP back into the main stream just in front of the verb *read*. This machine state in given in (35c). Action (34) applies, and (35d) is created. The verb root *read* is merged next, forming (35e), and the derivation can proceed to converge as (35f). With regard to probe-goal search and further Merge operations, (35d) is identical to {a, book}.[39] The adjunct *in the gym* is opaque to further inspection.[40]

---

[38] See also note 29. We do not implement syntactic feature transmission. In recent accounts, e.g. Chomsky (2008), inflectional features are transmitted from C to T, and from v* to verbal root R. R is the proxy for v* that initiates Agree. In our grammar, T in the lexicon comes with the necessary inflectional features, and v* carries out Agree directly. One disadvantage of our approach is that we need to list multiple T-s in the lexicon. On the other hand, we get to preserve our simple computational model of (first) Merge probe only, thus avoiding extra search and bookkeeping.

[39] The adjunct *in the gym* can be adjoined at a higher level, e.g. to the verb *read*, to obtain a different reading for sentence (35a).

[40] Note pair merge should crash if <β[!F], α> results. Since the adjunct is opaque to the machine, the unvalued feature F can never be valued. *β[!F] (unimplemented) should precondition (34).

If we swap *book* and *gym*, as in (35g), (35h) would be the equivalent machine state, producing (35i), with the adjunct *in the gym* incorrectly identified as the head of the pair-merged phrase.

(36)   Relabeling:
$(\alpha, K, [d,..]) \mapsto (\{d,\{n,\alpha\}\}, K, [..])$
head $n \in K$
in $d[!n]$ and $n[!d]$, $!n$ and $!d$ are valued
n labels $\{n,\alpha\}$, and d labels $\{d,\{n,\alpha\}\}$

Action (36) is designed solely to fire in the case of relative clauses, and is an example of an experimental construction-specific rule.[41] Consider example (37a):

(37)   a. the book which I read
       b. *the book which that I read
       c. [book, which$_{rel}$, read, v*, [i, d], T$_{past}$, c$_{rel}$, the]
       d. { which$_{rel}$, book!d}
       e. {c$_{rel}$ {{d, i}, {T$_{past}$, {{d̶, i̶}, {v*, {read, {which$_{rel}$, book!d}}}}}}}
       f. {{which$_{rel}$, book!d}, {c$_{rel}$ {{d, i}, {T$_{past}$, {{d̶, i̶}, {v*, {read, {w̶h̶i̶c̶h̶$_{rel}$, b̶o̶o̶k̶}}}}}}}}
       g. {the, {book, {{which$_{rel}$, b̶o̶o̶k̶} c$_{rel}$P}}}

In (37c), the object DP *which book* will be relativized. To trigger this, we preselect *which*$_{rel}$, instead of regular determiner *which*, for the input stream. The determiner *which*$_{rel}$ has some special properties: (i) unlike regular *which*, it cannot check unvalued *d* on the noun (see (37d)); and (ii) it can check unvalued T, which will become useful at the sentential level.[42] When (37d) is formed, *book* has an unvalued feature, and so it is stacked. We proceed to build the clause headed by c$_{rel}$, shown in (37e). The head c$_{rel}$ possesses both unvalued T and Rel features, and probes into the TP complement domain. IM of *which book* will satisfy both unvalued T and Rel on c$_{rel}$ (due to the special properties of *which*$_{rel}$). (37f), = c$_{rel}$P, is formed. At this point, action (36) kicks in: it first raises previously stacked *book*!d to head {*book*!d, c$_{rel}$P}; this is the relabeling step. Then *the*, the last item on the input stream, is merged to form (37g).

Let us now consider (37b): why is this blocked? Following P&T (2001), the complementizer *that* is the spellout of T to C movement. T to C movement arises when a C, with unvalued T, attracts T. We have mentioned that c$_{rel}$ possesses both unvalued T and Rel features; so c$_{rel}$ could value these features by first attracting T to C (to value T), and then {which$_{rel}$ book} (to value Rel).[43] However, derivational economy blocks this

---

[41] This action should be expanded and replaced by a more general rule governing IM of heads. Relabeling is currently only permitted for nouns for the sole purpose of forming relative clauses. Even in a tightly constrained feature-checking system, such as the one described here, the action should be generalized (with respect to constructions and categories).

[42] Relativization was also discussed earlier with respect to action (13).

[43] For dialects of English that do permit (37b), we must: (a) turn off economy, and (b) make sure *which book* is raised last to block *the book that which I read*. If there are dialects that allow all three versions, we need not worry about the order of raising.

option in favor of the single operation of IM of {which$_{rel}$ book} to simultaneously satisfy both features. Hence (37b) is ruled out.

To summarize, we have presented a list of structure-building actions that all follow the template in (9). We have attempted to justify the inclusion of each one from theory and example.[44] Taking a step back, the listed actions can also be viewed as just "ground" instances, in terms of particular lexical and functional categories, of the fundamental operations listed in (4) and (8). For actions where we are reasonably sure the preconditions are deducible from theory, we can make a case that (that part of) P is not ad hoc. However, the order of the actions presented involves manual curation, and thus is wholly ad hoc.

2.7 Non-determinism revisited

We have already seen an example of non-deterministic behavior for cases of pied-piping such as in (21a,b), implemented using action (19). We have also seen above how Pesetsky and Torrego's economy condition can be extended to eliminate competing derivations in relative clause formation. Turning to examples (38a,b) we will now describe how P&T's condition can also lead to productive non-determinism in action (33).

(38) a. Mary thinks that Sue will buy the book
      b. Mary thinks Sue will buy the book
      c. [book, the, buy, v*, Sue, will, T, c$_e$, think, v$_{unerg}$, Mary, T, c]
      d. { c$_e$, {Sue, {T, {~~Sue~~, {v*, {buy, {the, book}}}}}}}
      e. {Sue, { c$_e$, {~~Sue~~, {T, {~~Sue~~, {v*, {buy, {the, book}}}}}}}}
      f. {T, { c$_e$, { Sue, {T, {~~Sue~~, {v*, {buy, {the, book}}}}}}}}

Both (38a) and (38b) have the same starting input stream, (38c), in the system described here.[45] We first form the embedded clause, (38d), headed by c$_e$, using the prefix [*book, the, buy,* v*, *Sue, will,* T, c$_e$, ..]. We assume the complementizer c$_e$ has unvalued T (and an Edge) feature. Hence, c$_e$ must probe, and action (33) is engaged. There are two ways to value T in P&T's framework: (i) by attracting a Nominative Case-marked subject, as in (38e); and (ii) by attracting T, as in (38f). In both cases, the attracted constituent moves to the edge of c$_e$.[46] Continuing (38e) with the suffix

---

[44] Examples given in this chapter are all from the English side. Fragments of Arabic, Japanese, and Persian have also received some attention. As a result, there are a few implemented actions, including some dealing with mood and scrambling, that are not listed here. (The webpage mentioned in note 23 also contains links to a small inventory of derivations of non-English examples.)

[45] We have replaced [d, *sue*] and [d, *mary*] by *Sue* and *Mary*, respectively, in (38c). This is purely for convenience of exposition; *Sue* (and *Mary*) should not be treated as heads in the derivation.

[46] In (38e), *Sue* has moved from the edge of T to the edge C. Already, at the edge of T, both of *Sue's* unvalued features, Case and θ, have been valued. Although the stack is initially stocked with constituents with unvalued features, as discussed earlier, we do not prune away constituents that no longer possess unvalued features. One reason is that it is a chore. The second is that there is a need to keep stack items around for further non-feature-driven movement, e.g. (38e).

[.., *think*, v_{unerg}, *Mary*, T, c] will derive (38b). Assuming T to C in (38f) spells out as *that*, (38f) will lead to (38a).

2.8 Computational cyclicity revisited

Long-distance agreement can be a challenge for our notion of computational cyclicity described earlier, in which Merge is closely tied to head probing. To recap, a head from the input stream gets just a single chance to probe, value features, and have features valued: precisely when it is first Merged with the current SO. Consider (39a,b):

(39) a. There seem to have been several fish caught (Chomsky 2001)
      b. There seems to have been only one fish caught
      c. [fish, several, catch, PRT, v~, there, perf, v, T_{inf}, seem, v_{nop}, T, c]
      d. {catch, {several!case, fish}}
      e. Agree(PRT!case!φ, {several!case, fish})
      f. Agree(there, {several!case, fish})
      g. Agree(T_{inf} {several!case, fish})
      h. Agree(T, {several, fish})

(39a,b) shows that long-distance φ-feature agreement obtains between the matrix verb and the object of the embedded clause. (See Figure 2.1 for the detailed parse computed by the model.[47]) In either case, matrix T is a probe that needs to have its unvalued uninterpretable φ-features valued by *several/one fish*. The initial input stream for (39a) is given in (39c), and (39d) is produced by repeated ESM using the prefix [*fish, several, catch*,..].

Next, the passive participle PRT will be merged. According to Chomsky (2001), PRT has both unvalued uninterpretable φ and Case features. Hence, PRT must probe, and finds *several fish*. For Agree, as in (39e), *several fish* can value PRT's φ-features, but as both of them are unvalued for Case, PRT cannot have its Case feature valued at first Merge time. This poses a problem for our model because we would prefer not to have to search out PRT to probe again (after *several fish* receives Case from matrix T). Instead, following Fong (2014), suppose Agree can "unify" Case features. In the current model, the representation of unvalued uninterpretable Case is a term case(V), where V is an open variable. A valued Case feature is one with the open variable bound to a particular value, e.g. Nominative or Accusative. Suppose PRT and *several fish* are associated with case(V_1) and case(V_2), respectively. Then we simply unify V_1 and V_2. Essentially, they become identical but remain unvalued. When one of them is valued, the other is valued simultaneously because they have been made identical

---

[47] We will not explain Sobin (2014)'s v~ here, except to mention that v~ triggers leftwards TH/EX that raises *several fish* above the verb *catch*. Instead, we refer the reader to Ginsburg and Fong (Chapter 3, this volume) for the details.

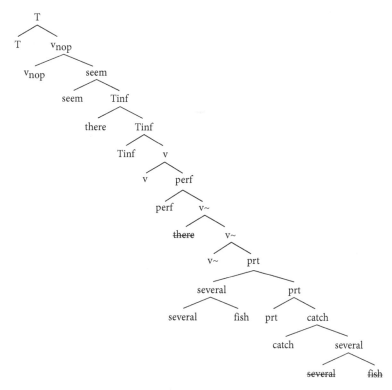

Figure 2.1 There seem to have been several fish caught

Continuing with the derivation, expletive *there* has unvalued φ-features.[48] If *there* is a head, it must probe, and we compute (39f), valuing the expletive's φ-features. Next, we need to consider Merge of non-finite T, T_{inf}. Should T_{inf} have unvalued φ-features, we compute (39g).[49]

Finally, Merge of finite matrix T triggers (39h). To produce the analysis in Figure 2.1, we have computed (up to) four separate Agree operations, (39e) through (39h). With unification, we have no need to search out and relaunch the most deeply embedded Agree operation. Thus, strict computational cyclicity and simplicity of the computational cycle can be maintained.

2.9 Further remarks and conclusions

We believe that building a "realistic" model of linguistic theory should be an important goal of computational modeling. Let us define "realistic" computational modeling as including automatically deriving in full detail the examples that linguists typically use. However, there is considerable scope for variation on the degree of automation. In

---

[48] In Chomsky (2001), expletive *there* has only unvalued person.
[49] T_{inf} seems to be able to value nullCase for PRO subjects, and so perhaps it should have φ-features too. V_{nop} is a dummy light verb that simply categorizes root *seem*.

our current model, we manually pre-assemble the LIs; the model is solely responsible for automatically converging on desired SOs (and rejecting those we deem illicit) in a timely manner, without going into an infinite loop, or requiring manual intervention or guidance. In a free Merge model, some of these simple goals may prove to be impractical due to the combinatorics of the problem. In the case of our model, we have a decision procedure P that is responsible for pruning the search space by selecting the right operation to perform at all possible machine states. A highly deterministic model such as the one described here is unlikely to encounter real-world limits on computational resources. The non-determinism described here is empirically productive, i.e. it is needed to generate multiple licit examples. Then it is just an empirical question whether single-action P can be maintained.

In at least two aspects, computational modeling can potentially provide useful tools that are currently unavailable. First, through detailed tracing of the operations performed, we can retrieve and compile complete step-by-step analyses (available online). Should an action or fundamental operation be modified, automation permits us to quickly and systematically determine the examples that will be affected.

Second, by bringing together theories and tweaking them to be mutually compatible, we believe we have strengthened those individual accounts. The snapshot of the MP that we have chosen to model and describe in this volume is a "mash-up" of the probe-goal framework of (Chomsky 2001), overlaid with Pesetsky and Torrego's (2001) economy-driven model of T-feature checking, a modified account of Gallego's (2006) theory of relativization—a syntactic Binding theory that extends Kayne's (2002) theory of doubling constituents—and Sobin's (2014) syntactic account of leftwards TH/EX. Space does not permit us to fully describe the modifications made, but see Ginsburg and Fong (Chapter 3 this volume) for a summary and highlights of the linguistic aspects of the implemented theory.

Acknowledgements

We are grateful to Yuan-Lu Chen and the participants of the Workshop on Minimalist Parsing for the useful comments.

3

Combining linguistic theories in a Minimalist Machine

Jason Ginsburg and Sandiway Fong

3.1 Introduction

Theoretical syntacticians, working within the framework of Generative Grammar, investigate the nature of the human grammatical system (i.e. Universal Grammar). Most of this work involves developing theories that predict and explain the structures and well-formedness/ill-formedness of constructions found in natural language. Theoretical linguists generally do not use computer models to test the validity of their theories. In this chapter, we show how a computer model can be a useful tool for combining components of different theories into a single unified model, which also clarifies the inner workings of the target theories.

We have developed a Minimalist Machine that automatically constructs detailed derivations of over 140 examples from recent important work in the Minimalist Program. We discuss particular modifications that are necessary to combine the target linguistic theories into a single unified model. This is an important and necessary step towards making the Minimalist Machine viable because there is no guarantee that theories in the same framework are indeed compatible; for example, they might rely on contradictory assumptions.

This Minimalist Machine is a useful tool for finding and overcoming problems that arise in minimalist theories. In order for the Minimalist Machine to construct the successful derivation of a target sentence, all operations must converge successfully. Inconsistencies in the model will cause a derivation to crash, or the computer program to halt, and thus, problems that otherwise might be difficult to notice become immediately apparent. In a derivational theory, both crashes and computation convergence are key components of the framework that communicate important information about grammar. Convergence will admit valid examples. Crashes are used to rule out illicit examples. In other words, one can use this system to figure out why a particular derivation does or does not converge. Hence, it is important to demonstrate that the grammar does "compute."

The Minimalist Machine has the unique property of demonstrating how minimalist theories work in extreme detail, beyond what is normally possible via typical paper-and-pencil linguistics. This model automatically constructs detailed step-by-step

Minimalist Parsing. First edition. Robert C. Berwick and Edward P. Stabler (eds.) This chapter © Jason Ginsburg and Sandiway Fong 2019. First published 2019 by Oxford University Press.

derivations of target constructions that can be read in a web browser. This output displays charts and tree diagrams that show all core feature-checking operations, Merge operations, and Spell-Out operations (see http://elmo.sbs.arizona.edu/sandiway/mpp/mm.html). This model is thus useful for clarifying exactly how derivations work, as well as for elucidating problems within target minimalist theories, so this work can benefit theory development in linguistics.

The notable components of this probe-goal model[1] are as follows. The model utilizes feature unification, which simplifies cases of multiple agreement, in which a single probe must Agree with multiple goals. The model incorporates a low-Merge position for the expletive *there*, thus accounting for how *there* is licensed in certain core expletive constructions. To account for thematization/extraction, we utilize a light verbal head that must be checked via Agree with a theta-bearing DP. Edge Features, specified for various functional heads, play a role in driving movement. Economy also plays a role in derivations, so that simpler operations block more complex operations—if multiple features on a head can be checked via Agree with a single goal vs. Agree with multiple goals, the more economical Agree relation with the single goal is required. Economy plays an important role in accounting for *that*-trace effects and the presence/absence of *that* in relative clauses.

We demonstrate how this model implements the following types of target constructions in a unified manner: expletives and multiple agreement (Chomsky 2001), thematization/extraction (Chomsky 2001; Sobin 2014), *that*-trace effects and subject vs. object *wh*-movement (Pesetsky and Torrego 2001), and relative clauses (Pesetsky and Torrego 2001; Gallego 2006). We point out certain problems that arise in previous work on these types of constructions, and we explain how we resolved these problems in our computational implementation. Also, it is important to note that we created a single computational implementation that can account for the structures of all of these types of sentences, as well as others (which we do not have space to discuss).

3.2 Multiple Agree (Chomsky 2001)

Chomsky (2001) develops an account of language in which agreement between a probe and a goal is crucial. In Chomsky (2001), however, problems arise with respect to multiple agreement—cases in which a probe must Agree with more than a single goal.

Agreement works as follows. A probe, which is the root of a Syntactic Object (SO), has an unvalued feature (uF) that searches for a goal with a matching valued feature (F). Crucially, the probe must c-command the goal. Case checking results as a reflex of a phi-feature-checking relation. A probe with unvalued phi-features (uPhi) Agrees with a goal that has valued phi-features (Phi) and unvalued Case (uCase). Agreement checks the uPhi on the probe and the uCase on the goal. For example, as shown in (1),

---

[1] This model does not incorporate the recent labeling-based framework of Chomsky (2013; 2015a). For discussion of labeling-based models, see Ginsburg (2016) and Fong and Ginsburg (in preparation).

given a probe X that has uPhi and the ability to check Case as nominative (Nom), and given a goal Y that has Phi and uCase, Agree between X and Y results in checking of the uPhi on X. As a reflex of this Agree relation, the uCase on Y is valued as nominative.

(1) $\text{Agree}(X_{[uPhi,Nom]}, Y_{[Phi,uCase]}) \rightarrow X_{[\cancel{uPhi},Nom]}$ and $Y_{[Phi,Case:Nom]}$

Certain issues arise with respect to checking of uCase on a participle. Chomsky (2001: 17), citing the fact that certain past participles show agreement in languages such as Icelandic, takes the position that a past participle requires Case. Thus, in the passive (2), the participle *-ed* (which combines with *award*) must obtain Case.

(2)   Several prizes are likely to be awarded. (Chomsky 2001: 7)

The relevant portion of the derivation of (2) is shown in Figure 3.1. A participle, indicated as prt, has a defective set of uPhi, containing unvalued number (uNum) and unvalued gender (uGen), as well as uCase. The prt is defective in that it does not have a complete set of uPhi, as it lacks uPerson. Prt Agrees with the object *several prizes*. The uNum and uGen of prt are checked by the valued number and gender, Num and Gen, of the object *several prizes*. The uCase on prt remains because the object, also an argument, cannot check uCase. The non-finite T, *to*, is defective. It has an EPP feature and an incomplete set of uPhi, which Chomsky (2001: 7) suggests is uPerson. Non-finite T, being defective, cannot check uCase. The non-finite T Agrees with *several prizes*, resulting in checking of uPerson (indicated as uPer) on *to*, and an EPP on *to* forces the object to remerge in embedded subject position. The matrix T has uPhi and can check Case, which it values as nominative. In this case, T forms a

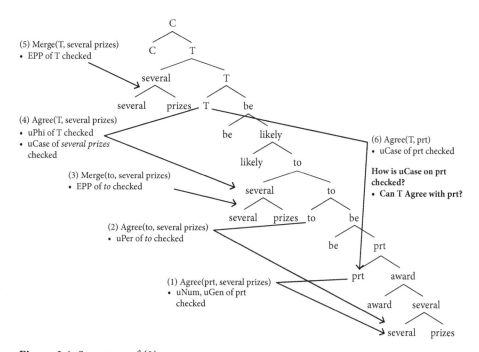

Figure 3.1 Structure of (2)

probe-goal Agree relation with *several prizes*, resulting in uPhi of T being checked. As a reflex of this phi-feature agreement relation, the uCase of *several prizes* is checked and valued nominative. An EPP feature on T also forces *several prizes* to remerge in subject position.

This derivation, however, faces a problem with respect to the participle—it is not clear how the uCase of the participle is checked. In order for uCase on prt to be checked, the matrix T must form an Agree relation with prt, shown in step (6) of Figure 3.1. But the uPhi on T are already checked via Agree with the higher object *several prizes*, shown in step 4. Thus, after T forms an Agree relation with *several prizes*, T has no reason to continue probing and further Agree with prt. Even if T were to Agree with prt, it is notable that the only phi-features that prt has are checked number and gender, raising the question of whether or not checked uPhi of prt are capable of further phi-feature agreement with T.

In order to generate an example such as (2), in which there is multiple agreement, it is necessary to determine exactly how the uCase of prt is checked. To this end, we implemented feature unification. If a probe with a uF Agrees with a goal with an identical uF, the uFs unify.

(3)   *Feature unification*
      uFs of the same type unify.

With feature unification, checking of uCase on prt is no longer a problem. The derivation of (2) proceeds as shown in Figure 3.2. An Agree relation established between prt and *several prizes* results in checking of uNum and uGen of prt by the

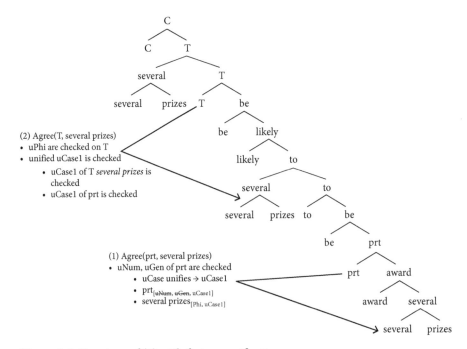

Figure 3.2 Structure of (2) with feature unification

Phi of *several prizes*. Note that both prt and *several prizes* have uCase. Thus, the uCase of prt unifies with the uCase of *several prizes*, indicated as uCase1. This is shown in step (1) of Figure 3.2. When the matrix T is Merged, shown in step (2), T Agrees with the object *several prizes*, resulting in checking of uPhi (which includes uNum, uGen, and uPer) on T and checking of uCase1 on *several prizes*. Crucially, checking of uCase1 on *several prizes* also results in checking of the unified uCase1 on prt. Thus, feature unification crucially does away with the need for T to probe after it is licensed. In our Minimalist Machine model, we implemented feature unification in this manner.

3.3 Expletives (Chomsky 2001)

Expletives raise some problems for Chomsky's (2001) account. According to Chomsky (cf. p. 16), the expletive (Expl) *there* is a defective argument that has uPerson features and that lacks uCase. The Expl is also Merged directly in the Spec position of T and the uPerson feature of *there* is checked via Agree with T. Several issues arise in (4), with the structure shown in Figure 3.3, in which *there* appears in subject position. First, Agree between uPhi of T and uPerson of *there* checks the uPerson of *there*. Note that this Agree relation holds between uFs (uPhi of T and uPerson of Expl), but it is not clear how a uF can check a uF. Second, when T is Merged, T should form a probe-goal Agree relation with the object *a train*. Crucially, this Agree relation between T and *a train* is formed before *there* is Merged in Spec position. Thus, after agreement with the object, T should not have any uPhi available for Agree with *there*. One possibility, pointed out by Chomsky (2000: 128), is that the Expl *there* probes and Agrees with T, but it isn't clear if the checked uPhi on T could check the uPerson of the Expl. Another issue that arises is whether or not a non-root node can probe. The root node of the SO is T, so if Expl probes from Spec position, then there is probing from a non-root node. Richards (2007) points out that probing from a non-root node is problematic—permitting both root and non-root nodes to probe is more complex than limiting probing to a root node. Richards also points out that probing by Expl would go against Chomsky's (2008) proposal that only phase heads can probe.

(4)   There arrived a train. (Sobin 2014: 386)

   The feature-checking and probing problems raised by expletive constructions are resolved if (a) we assume that an expletive is Merged below T and (b) we utilize feature unification, as described in (3) above. We follow Richards (2007), who, in order to avoid the problem of probing from a non-root node, proposes that *there* is Merged below T.[2] The successful derivation is shown in Figure 3.4. Assume that *there* is Merged as the specifier of a light v projection below T. We assume that this v has an Edge Feature (EF) that requires it to have an element Merged in specifier position.[3] Then when T is

---

[2] This view is also adopted by Sobin (2014), among others.
[3] An Edge Feature (EF) is akin to an EPP feature, and is checked via Merge with any argument (Chomsky 2008).

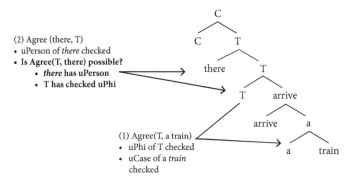

(2) Agree (there, T)
- uPerson of *there* checked
- **Is Agree(T, there) possible?**
  - *there* **has uPerson**
  - **T has checked uPhi**

(1) Agree(T, a train)
- uPhi of T checked
- uCase of *a train* checked

Figure 3.3 Problems with (4)

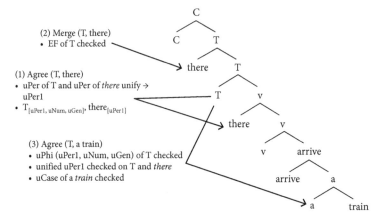

(2) Merge (T, there)
- EF of T checked

(1) Agree (T, there)
- uPer of T and uPer of *there* unify → uPer1
- $T_{[uPer1, uNum, uGen]}$, $there_{[uPer1]}$

(3) Agree (T, a train)
- uPhi (uPer1, uNum, uGen) of T checked
- unified uPer1 checked on T and *there*
- uCase of *a train* checked

Figure 3.4 Structure of (4) with low Merge of Expl and feature unification

Merged, uPerson of T Agrees with uPerson of *there*, resulting in feature unification, so that T and *there* have unified uPerson features, indicated as uPer1 in step 1 of Figure 3.4. Since *there* is defective, it cannot check any uPhi of T. Thus, T continues to probe and Agrees with the object *a train*. Agree results in checking of the uPhi on T. Crucially, in addition to uNumber and uGender, the uPhi includes the unified uPerson feature. Thus, when the uPerson feature of T is checked, the unified uPerson on *there* is also checked. As a reflex of this Agree relation, uCase on the object is also checked. Note that only T probes, so there is no probing from a non-root node. Since the uPerson of *there* is checked via feature unification, there is no need to rely on uPerson of *there* being checked via Agree with T. Also note that an EF of T forces *there* to raise to the Spec position of T.

3.4 Thematization/Extraction (Th/Ex) (Chomsky 2001; Sobin 2014)

Chomsky (2001: 20) presents the following example in (5), in which the direct object "is extracted to the edge of the construction by an obligatory thematization/extraction rule Th/Ex." The direct object *several packages* undergoes Th/Ex to a preverbal position, as can be seen in (5b). Note that if the object remains in its base position, the result is ill-formed, as shown in (5c), indicating that Th/Ex is obligatory.

(5)   a. There were several packages placed on the table. (Chomsky 2001: 20)

   b. There were [several packages] placed ~~[several packages]~~ on the table.

   c. *There were placed several packages on the table.

Chomsky suggests that Th/Ex is phonological, writing "Th/Ex is an operation of the phonological component" (2001: 21), without offering specifics about how Th/Ex would work as a PF (Phonological Form) phenomenon. However, we follow Rezac (2006) and Sobin (2014), who take a syntactic approach to Th/Ex. Sobin, following Rezac (2006), writes: "Th/Ex positions are the specifier positions of those functional v heads that are θ-open and allow an argument to appear in them" (2014: 398).[4]

Sobin's approach relies on a Split-EPP feature, which has Agree and Merge sub-features. In order for a Split-EPP feature to be fully checked, the Agree and Merge subfeatures must be checked. The Agree subfeature can take the form of uCheckTheta (6), which is checked via Agree with a theta-bearing DP. The Merge subfeature is checked via Merge of an element in specifier position, and can have the form uD_{Mrg}, shown in (7), which requires Merge of any type of DP (an expletive or a theta-bearing DP are fine).[5]

(6)   *Agree subfeature*
   uCheckTheta—checked via Agree with a theta-bearing DP

(7)   *Merge subfeature*
   uD_{Mrg}—checked by Merge of a DP

Adopting Deal's (2009) proposed default verbalizing head v~ that appears in unac-cusative, passive, and progressive constructions, Sobin proposes that English v~ has the EPP subfeatures shown in (8). It has a uCheckTheta, so it must Agree with a theta-role bearing DP, and it also has a uD_{Mrg} feature, so a DP must Merge with it in specifier position. Crucially, uD_{Mrg} can be checked by any type of DP, including an Expl.

---

[4] See Rezac (2006) for discussion of why Th/Ex is syntactic. For example, Rezac argues that Th/Ex positions can be iterated, which requires Th/Ex to apply before PF, as a derivation is constructed. Also, in Swedish, a passive participle shows agreement with an argument that appears to have undergone Th/Ex. Assuming that agreement is syntactic in nature, then this too suggests that Th/Ex is not a PF phenomenon.

[5] We only include the Agree and Merge subfeatures that are relevant for the examples presented in this chapter. The full set of Agree and Merge subfeatures utilized by Sobin are as follows.

(i)   Agree subfeatures
   a. u CheckTheta—checked via Agree with a theta-bearing DP
   b. uD_{Agr}—checked via Agree with a DP (any DP is okay, including expletive)

(ii)   Merge subfeatures
   a. uD_{Mrg}—checked by Merge of a DP
   b. uTheta$_{Mrg}$—checked by Merge of a theta-role bearing DP
   c. $uD_{MrgExpl}$—checked by Merge of an Expl

Sobin proposes that light verbs can have different combinations of the Agree and Merge subfeatures. See Sobin (2014) for further details.

(8)   v~ has [*u*CheckTheta, *u*D$_{Mrg}$] (Sobin 2014: 393)

    a. *u*CheckTheta is checked via Agree with a theta-bearing DP

    b. *u*D$_{Mrg}$ is checked via Merge of a DP

The v~ head provides a way to account for Th/EX in English.

    The split-EPP feature of v~ accounts for the possibility of either the Expl *there* or the object *a train* appearing in subject position in (9a,b).

(9)   a. There arrived a train.

    b. A train arrived. (Sobin 2014: 393)

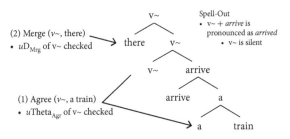

Figure 3.5 Derivation of (9a)

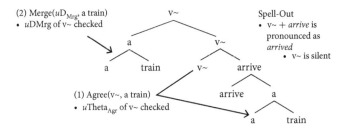

Figure 3.6 v~ in (9b)

In (9a) as shown in Figure 3.5, when v~ is Merged, its *u*CheckTheta subfeature Agrees with the theta-role bearing object *a train*. Then, when the Expl *there* is Merged, the *u*D$_{Mrg}$ subfeature of v~ is checked. Note that *u*D$_{Mrg}$ can be checked via Merge of any DP, regardless of whether or not it bears a theta-role. Thus, Expl is sufficient.

    The structure of (9b) is shown in Figure 3.6. Assume that there is no Expl available for Merge. Thus, both the *u*Theta$_{Agr}$ and *u*D$_{Mrg}$ subfeatures of v~ are checked by the same object, *a train*. In this case, the need to check the *u*D$_{Mrg}$ subfeature of v~ results in the object *a train* undergoing Th/Ex.

    Note that in (9a,b), the v~+*arrive* complex is pronounced as *arrived* (assuming that a past-tense T is Merged). The v~ has no pronunciation, which turns out to be an issue, since v~ is pronounced in other examples (see below).

    The progressive construction with an expletive (10) has two instances of v~, as shown in Figure 3.7, where prog represents a progressive head that combines with v~ and a verbal root to form an *-ing* construction. The lower v~1 has both its *u*Theta$_{Agr}$ and *u*D$_{Mrg}$ subfeatures checked by *a train*. Checking of the *u*D$_{Mrg}$ subfeature forces *a train* to remerge in specifier position of v~1, and thus undergo Th/Ex. The *u*CheckTheta subfeature of the higher v~2 then is checked via Agree with *a train*. Then Merge of an Expl with v~2 satisfies the uD_{Mrg} subfeature of v~2, thus also preventing *a train* from moving higher.

(10)   a. There is a train arriving. (Sobin 2014: 399)
       b. A train is arriving.

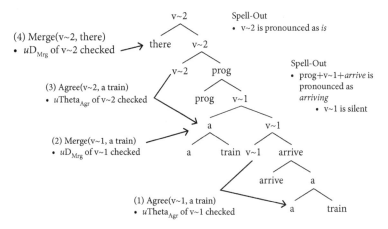

Figure 3.7 v~ in (10a)

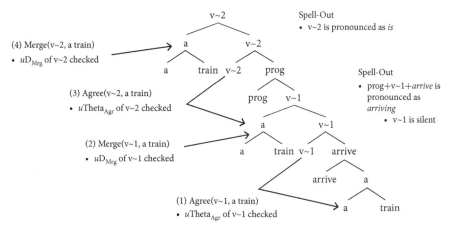

Figure 3.8 v~ in (10b)

If the derivation lacks an Expl, then the structure shown in Figure 3.8 results. In this case, the object *a train* moves all the way to matrix subject position, due to the lack of an Expl, to check the uD_{Mrg} subfeature of v~2. Thus, *a train* checks the $uTheta_{Agr}$ and uD_{Mrg} features of both v~1 and v~2.

Note that pronunciation of v~ in (10a,b), as shown in Figures 3.7 and 3.8, is complex because the higher v~2 is pronounced as *is* but the lower v~1 lacks any pronunciation, assuming that the progressive head Prog and v~ are pronounced as *arriving*. But it isn't clear how to distinguish the pronunciations of v~.

Sobin's analysis also accounts for the impossibility of (11), as shown in Figure 3.9. In this case, the uTheta$_{Agr}$ of v~1 is checked via Agree with the object *a train*, and the uD$_{Mrg}$ feature of v~1 is checked by Merge of the Expl *there*. A problem then arises when v~2 is Merged because the Expl blocks the uTheta$_{Agr}$ subfeature of v~2 from Agreeing with *a train*; since an Expl lacks a theta-role, it cannot check uTheta$_{Agr}$. Sobin (2014) argues that this type of example is ruled out because a phase boundary intervenes between v~2 and its potential goal. But even if there were no phase boundary, this could be ruled out as an intervention effect caused by the Expl.

(11)   *There is arriving a train.

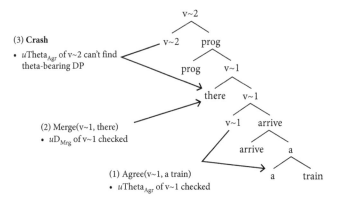

Figure 3.9 Structure of (11)

While Sobin's analysis accounts for Th/Ex of an object to preverbal position, as well as for the distribution of the Expl in English, there are some issues that arise with respect to Spell-Out. In (10a,b), as shown in Figures 3.7 and 3.8, the higher v~1 is pronounced as *is* but the lower v~2 lacks any pronunciation, as it combines with *arrive* and the progressive, to form *arriving*. Thus, sometimes v~ is pronounced, and other times it is not, as shown in Figure 3.10. If both of these are identical v~ elements, then the question arises of how the Spell-Out component determines the correct pronunciation of v~. Another problem arises from the placement of *a train* in constructions such as (10a), in which *a train* undergoes Th/Ex to preverbal position. As a result, *a train* intervenes between the progressive head prog and the lower v~1, which need to combine to form *arriving*, as shown in Figure 3.10.

These Spell-Out problems are resolved in our model as follows. First, since sometimes v~ is pronounced and other times it is not, we propose that there are actually two different types of v~. One type, (12a), which we refer to as v~, is simply a light verb that is pronounced as a form of *be*, (12a). Another type, (12b), which we refer to as v~unacc, Merges with an unaccusative verbal root, and lacks any pronunciation. Both types of v~ have the same Agree and Merge features, (12c). We utilize CheckTheta, which is essentially the same as Sobin's uTheta$_{Agr}$, to refer to a feature that is checked by a theta-bearing argument. Instead of uD$_{Mrg}$ we simply utilize an Edge Feature (EF). To deal with the affix-hopping problem, in which an object intervenes between the progressive and v~, we assume that the progressive head (prog) has an EF, (13). Thus, the EF on

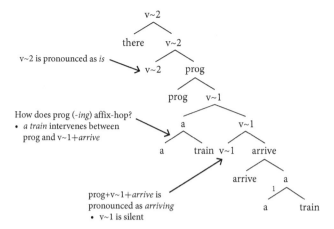

Figure 3.10 v~ pronunciation in (10a)

prog forces an object to move to the edge of prog, which enables affix-hopping to occur without an intervening overt argument.

(12)   v~ types

   a. v~ is pronounced as *be*

   b. v~unacc has no pronunciation (v~unacc Merges with an unaccusative verbal root)

   c. v~ and v~unacc have CheckTheta and EF

(13)   prog has an EF

   With these proposals, we next explain how we implemented Sobin's v~ analysis with our computer model. The derivation of (10a), as generated by our model, is shown in Figure 3.11. This construction contains a v~unacc and a separate v~. The CheckTheta feature of v~unacc is checked via Agree with the object *a train* and the EF feature of v~unacc is checked via remerge of *a train*. Then the higher prog head is Merged, and prog has an EF that forces *a train* to remerge again in specifier position of prog. Note that because the object moves to the Spec of the prog projection, it no longer intervenes between prog and the v~unacc+*arrive* complex, so that prog can affix-hop onto v~unacc+*arrive*. Then the higher v~ is Merged, and the CheckTheta of v~ is checked via Agree with *a train*, which is in the Spec of the next lower projection, and thus is accessible. The EF of v~ is checked via Merge of the Expl *there*. The Expl has uPhi (unvalued Phi), indicated as !phi in the figure. These uPhi are eventually checked via Agree with a higher T. The final structure and Spell-Out steps are shown in Figure 3.11b. Crucially, the higher v~ is pronounced as a form of *be* and the lower v~unacc is silent, and prog affix hops onto v~unacc+arrive, forming *arriving*.

   With our assumptions about v~ combined with our previous assumptions about feature unification, we can now account for the core examples of Chomsky (2001), including those with Th/Ex.

   The derivation of (2), repeated below as (14), is shown in Figure 3.12.

(a)

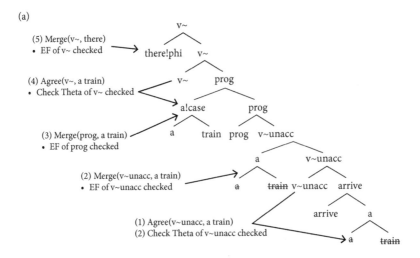

(b)

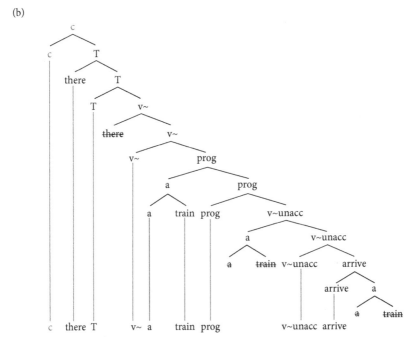

Spell-out:
there -s be a train -ing arrive (after morpheme realization)
there be -s a train arrive -ing (after affix-hop)
there is a train arriving

Figure 3.11 Derivation of (10a)

(14)   Several prizes are likely to be awarded. (Chomsky 2001: 7)

When prt is Merged, Agree between prt and *several prizes* results in unification of uCase of prt and *several prizes*, as well as checking of uNumber and uGender of prt. An EF of prt forces *several prizes* to remerge in Spec position. Then when v~ is Merged, the CheckTheta feature of v~ is checked via Agree with the theta-role bearing *several prizes*. An EF on v~ also forces *several prizes* to remerge in Spec position. Next, the

(a)

(8) Merge(T, several prizes)
• EF of T checked

(7) Agree(T, several prizes)
• uPhi of T checked
• unified uCase1 checked on
    • *several prizes*
    • prt

(6) Merge(v_{be}, several prizes)
• EF of v_{be} checked

(5) Merge(Tinf, several prizes)
• EF of Tinf checked

(4) Merge(v~, several prizes)
• EF of v~ checked

(3) Agree(v~, several prizes)
• Check Theta of v~ checked

(2) Merge(prt, several prizes)
• EF of prt checked

(1) Agree(prt, several prizes)
• uNum, uGen of prt checked
• uCase of prt and uCase of *several prizes* unify

(b)

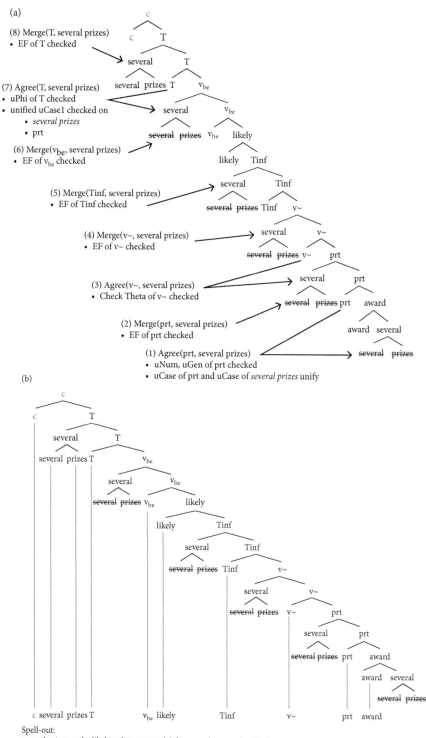

Spell-out:
several prizes -re be likely to be -en award (after morpheme realization)
several prizes be -re likely to be award -en (after affix-hop)
several prizes are likely to be awarded

Figure 3.12 Derivation of (14)

non-finite Tinf has an EF that forces *several prizes* to remerge in Spec position. The higher light verb *be*, v_{be}, also has an EF that forces remerge of *several prizes*. When the matrix T is Merged, T Agrees with *several prizes*, resulting in checking of the uPhi of T and the uCase of *several prizes*. Crucially, the uCase of *several prizes* is unified with uCase of prt, so the unified uCase of prt is also checked. Then an EF of T is checked by reemerge of *several prizes* and the derivation eventually converges. The final tree and Spell-Out are shown in Figure 3.12b.

We next explain how we extended this model to account for completely different types of examples (*that*-trace effects, *wh*-movement, and relative clauses).

3.5 *That*-trace effects and subject vs. object *wh*-movement (Pesetsky and Torrego 2001)

Pesetsky and Torrego (2001), hereafter P&T, present an analysis that accounts, in a unified manner, for the English subject/object *wh*-movement asymmetry and the *that*-trace effect. We explain how we implemented their proposals.

P&T's analysis relies on the idea that certain C heads have a uT feature that must be checked in the most economical manner. P&T propose that a uT feature on C can be checked by T or by nominative Case, which is checked uT on D, as summarized in (15). Nominative Case can check uT because Nominative is a checked uT feature.

(15)   Certain C heads have a uT feature
    a. uT can be checked by T
    b. uT can be checked by Nominative Case

P&T also propose that T in C is pronounced as *that*. Thus, when *that* appears in an embedded clause, T has checked a uT feature on C. In a *wh*-question, they assume that an interrogative C has uWh and uT features that need to be checked in order for a derivation to converge. From the perspective of economy, Agree between an interrogative C and a single goal that can check both uWh and uT features is most economical. This is stated in (16), where we utilize uQ instead of uWh; we assume that a *wh*-phrase is headed by Q (cf. Hagstrom 1998; Cable 2007) and it has an iQ feature that checks a uQ feature on an interrogative C. If the option of checking both uT and uQ features is not available, then it is possible for C to form two separate Agree relations, one which checks the uT feature and one which checks the uQ feature.

(16)   *Economy*
    Given $C_{[uQ,uT]}$, if goal X can check uT but not uQ, and goal Y can check both uQ and uT, then Agree with Y blocks Agree with X.

This analysis accounts for the optionality of *that* in embedded clauses, as in (17).

(17)   Mary thinks (that) Sue will buy the book. (P&T 2001: 373)

The embedded clause is shown in Figure 3.13a. The embedded non-interrogative C is indicated as C_e (our notation). P&T assume that C_e has a uT feature. Thus, one option is for the uT feature to be checked via Agree with the subject *Sue*, in which case Nominative Case of the subject checks the uT feature. P&T assume that uT has an EPP subfeature that forces remerge of whatever uT Agrees with. We utilize an Edge Feature (EF), assuming that whatever Agrees with C_e must remerge with the C_e projection to check the EF. Thus, an EF of C_e forces the subject *Sue* to remerge. Since the subject is in C_e, there is no pronunciation of *that*, as can be seen in the final structure, shown in Figure 3.13b. Note that the matrix clause contains what we refer to as v_{unerg}, which occurs with a verbal root such as *think* that takes a clausal complement. This v_{unerg} is an unergative light verb that assigns a subject theta-role, but does not check Case or have uPhi.[6]

Another possibility is for *that* to be pronounced in (17), as shown in Figure 3.14. In this case, the uT feature of C_e is checked via Agree with T and an EF forces T to raise to C_e.[7] T in C is pronounced as *that*, as shown in Figure 3.14b.

We next demonstrate how P&T (2001) account for *wh*-movement in an example such as (18). Although P&T do not discuss this exact example, it is important for demonstrating the need for a verbal element to raise to T.

(18)   What will Mary buy?

Initially, shown in Figure 3.15a, after T is Merged, the modal *will* raises to T, which is necessary so that the modal can eventually raise to C. We implemented this movement by giving T an unvalued v feature, uv, that requires checking by the closest verbal head. The interrogative C, which we indicate as C_Q, has uQ, uT, and EF features. The EF feature forces whatever Agrees with C_Q to remerge with C_Q. Initially, C_Q forms an Agree relation with T, resulting in checking of uT. An EF on C_Q then forces T to remerge. Furthermore, the modal *will* is pied-piped with T. This has the desired effect of bringing the modal into pre-subject position. Thus, we assume that the highest verbal element raises to T (to check a uv feature) and that when T raises to C_Q, this verbal element also raises. While movement of the verbal element to T may seem like an imperfection, this is necessary to account for the correct word order. If T alone were to move to C, without the highest verbal element, then the result would be the ill-formed (19) in which *will* remains below the subject, and T in C is pronounced as *do*.

(19)   *What does Mary will buy?

If there is no overt auxiliary/modal that can raise to T, then the default *do* is inserted. Continuing on, the uQ feature of C_Q is checked via Agree with the Q-phrase *what*, and an EF of C_Q forces *what* to remerge. Note that two operations are required to check the uT and uQ features of C_Q. The derivation then converges as shown in Figure 3.15b.

---

[6] Another possibility is that if v* doesn't assign Case to an argument, then its uPhi don't have to be checked. Also see Epstein et al. (2016) for an account that relies on pair-Merge.

[7] For P&T, an EPP subfeature of uT forces raising.

(a)

(b)

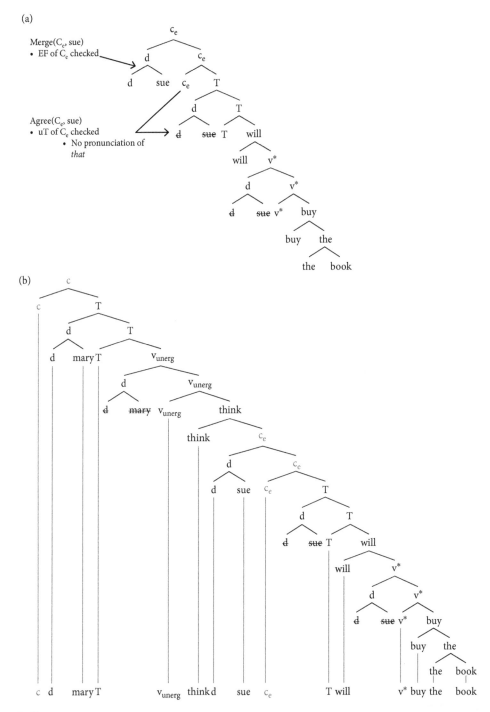

Spell-out:
mary -s think sue -s will buy the book (after morpheme realization)
mary think -s sue will -s buy the book (after affix-hop)
mary thinks sue will buy the book

Figure 3.13 Derivation of embedded clause of (17) without *that*

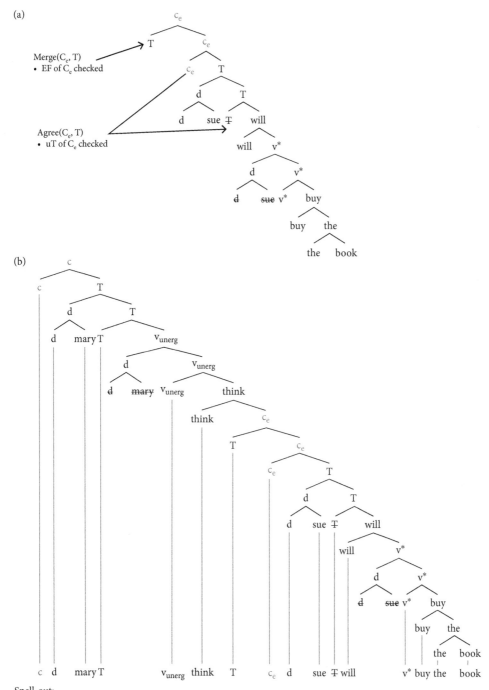

Spell-out:
mary -s think that sue -s will buy the book (after morpheme realization)
mary think -s that sue will -s buy the book (after affix-hop)
mary thinks that sue will buy the book

Figure 3.14 Derivation of embedded clause of (17) with *that*

(a)

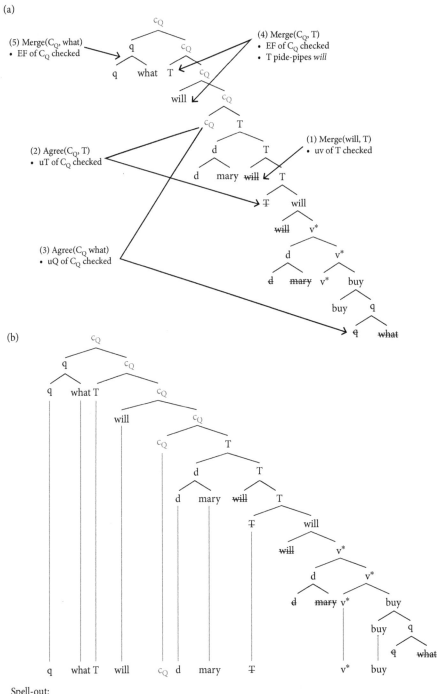

(b)

Spell-out:
what -s will mary buy (after morpheme realization)
what will -s mary buy (after affix-hop)
what will -s mary buy (after morpheme realization, stage 2)
what will mary buy

Figure 3.15 Derivation of (18)

P&T (2001) present an economy-based account for the subject/object *wh*-question asymmetry, exemplified in (20a–c). When the object *what* undergoes *wh*-movement, *did* is pronounced (generally considered to be an indication of T to C movement), but when the subject *who* undergoes *wh*-movement, *did* is not permitted, as in (20b,c).

(20) a. What did Mary buy?
      b. Who bought the book?
      c. *Who did buy the book? (unless *did* is focused) (Koopman 1983, per P&T: 357)

The relevant portions of the derivation of (20)a are shown in Figure 3.16. As with the previous example, the highest verbal element, in this case v*, remerges with Tpast (past tense). An Agree relation between C_Q and Tpast checks the uT feature of C_Q and an EF forces Tpast to remerge. When Tpast remerges, v* is also pied-piped. Then C_Q forms a second Agree relation with the Q-phrase *what*, resulting in checking of the uQ feature of C_Q, and an EF forces *what* to remerge. In this case, Tpast in C_Q is pronounced as *did*, assuming that when T in C_Q lacks a phonological form, a form of *do* is required. As in the previous example, separate Agree operations are required to check the uQ and uT features of C_Q.

The subject *wh*-question in (20)b has the structure shown in Figure 3.17. In this example, the subject *who* is a Q-phrase, and thus it can check a uQ feature. Furthermore, the subject has Nominative Case, which it obtains from T. When C_Q Agrees with *who*, both the uT and uQ features are checked. Then an EF of C_Q forces remerge of *who*. The other option would be for the uT feature of C_Q to be checked by Tpast, and then for the uQ feature to be checked via a separate Agree relation with *who*. But P&T argue that this latter derivation is ruled out by economy. Since the uQ and uT features of C_Q can be checked via a single Agree relation formed with *who*, the less economical derivation involving two separate Agree relations is blocked. As a result, T cannot move to C, and (20b) is ruled out.[8]

We next explain how we implemented P&T's account of the *that*-trace effect, as found in (21a,b).

(21) a. Who did John say will buy the book?
      b. *Who did John say that will buy the book? (P&T: 371)

The embedded clause contains what we refer to as C_{eQ}, which is an embedded non-interrogative C that hosts a *wh*-phrase. C_{eQ} contains uT and uQ features, but it cannot fully license a Q-phrase. Rather, it hosts a Q-phrase that undergoes movement from an embedded clause to a higher clause. The embedded clause of (21a) is shown in Figure 3.18a. Assume that a Q-phrase has an unvalued scope feature, uScope, which is

---

[8] Note that according to P&T's analysis, a subject can also check uT on C_Q, as in (i) in which the subject *Mary* checks the uT, but this is ruled at Spell-Out for reasons of interpretation—only an exclamative subject (not a *wh*-phrase) can appear in a specifier of a C_Q resulting in an exclamative. Thus, P&T rely on what is essentially a conceptual interface well-formedness condition to block (i).

(i) *What Mary bought (P&T: 358)

(a)

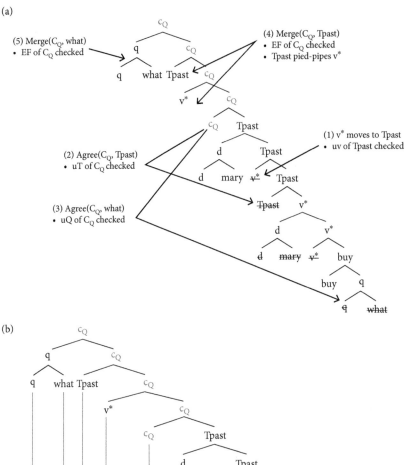

(b)

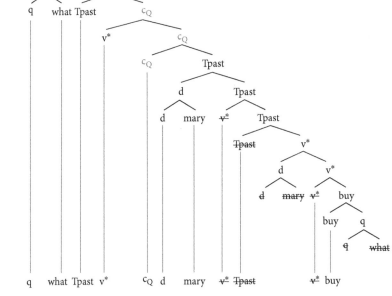

Spell-out:
what -ed(sg) do mary buy (after morpheme realization)
what do -ed(sg) mary buy (after affix-hop)
what did mary buy

Figure 3.16 Derivation of (20a)

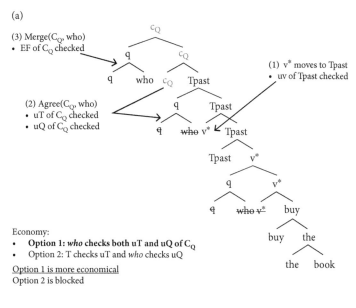

(a)

(3) Merge(C_Q, who)
- EF of C_Q checked

(1) v* moves to Tpast
- uv of Tpast checked

(2) Agree(C_Q, who)
- uT of C_Q checked
- uQ of C_Q checked

Economy:
- **Option 1: *who* checks both uT and uQ of C_Q**
- Option 2: T checks uT and *who* checks uQ

<u>Option 1 is more economical</u>
Option 2 is blocked

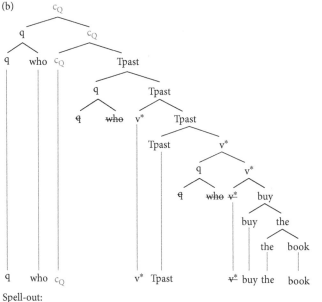

(b)

Spell-out:
who -ed(sg) buy the book (after morpheme realization)
who buy -ed(sg) the book (after affix-hop)
who bought the book

Figure 3.17 Derivation of (20b)

indicated as !scope in Figure 3.18a. This uScope is not checked via Agree with C_{eQ}—uScope must be checked by a truly interrogative C_Q. As in the previous example, C_{eQ} forms an Agree relation with *who*, thereby checking the uT and uQ features via a single Agree relation, since *who* can check a uQ feature and the Nominative Case of *who* can check the uT feature. The other option of checking the uT feature via Agree with T,

(a)

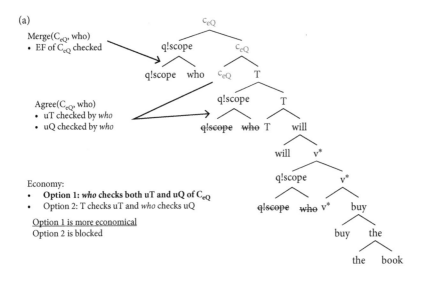

Merge(C_{eQ}, who)
- EF of C_{eQ} checked

Agree(C_{eQ}, who)
- uT checked by *who*
- uQ checked by *who*

Economy:
- **Option 1: *who* checks both uT and uQ of C_{eQ}**
- Option 2: T checks uT and *who* checks uQ

Option 1 is more economical
Option 2 is blocked

(b)

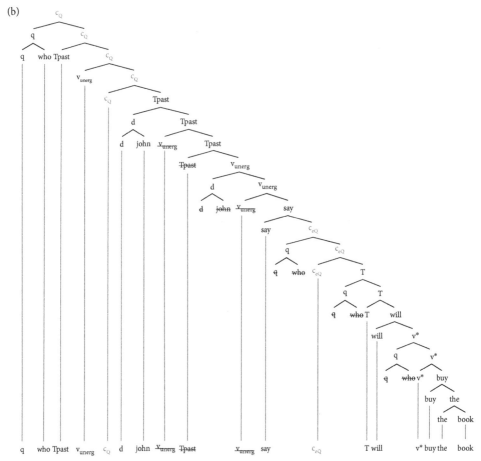

Spell-out:
who -ed(sg) do john say -s will buy the book (after morpheme realization)
who do -ed(sg) john say will -s buy the book (after affix-hop)
who did john say will buy the book

Figure 3.18 Derivation of (21a)

which would result in pronunciation of *that*, and the uQ feature via Agree with *who*, is less economical, and thus banned. Therefore, the ill-formedness of (21b) is blocked due to economy. The final output and Spell-Out are shown in Figure 3.18b. Note that in the matrix clause, the uT feature of C_Q is checked via Agree with T, assuming that the Nominative Case of *who*, from the embedded clause, is not available to check uT in the matrix clause.

In a construction such as (22a), there is no *that*-trace effect because economy is not an option for checking the uT and uQ features of the embedded C_{eQ}, since there is no single element that can check both uT and uQ features.

(22)   a. What did John say that Mary will buy?
        b. What did John say Mary will buy? (P&T: 370)

In (22a), as shown in Figure 3.19a, the embedded C_{eQ} forms an Agree relation with T, which checks the uT feature. As a result, an EF of C_{eQ} forces T to remerge, and T in C is pronounced as *that*. In (22b), as shown in Figure 3.19b, C_{eQ} forms an Agree relation with the subject *Mary* instead of T. Thus, *Mary* remerges with C_{eQ} to check an EF. Since there is no T in C, there is no pronunciation of *that*. In both examples (22a,b), C_{eQ} also forms an Agree relation with the object *what*, which checks the uQ feature of C_{eQ} and forces *what* to remerge.

We have thus demonstrated how we implemented the core proposals of P&T. We changed a few of the formalisms of P&T (e.g. we used an EF instead of EPP subfeatures, and uQ instead of uWh). We also had to implement raising of a verbal element to T in matrix interrogative clauses, which, although not discussed by P&T, is crucial for producing the correct outputs. Our model thus demonstrates that P&T's proposals can be successfully implemented; and this implementation is not in conflict with the constructions, involving multiple agreement and expletives, presented in the preceding sections. We next explain how we extended this model to account for relative clauses.

3.6 Relative Clauses (Pesetsky and Torrego 2001; Gallego 2006)

Gallego (2006) proposes an analysis of relative clauses that follows P&T's (2001) views about economy and feature checking. Therefore, it is natural for us to extend our analysis to utilize Gallego's insights. Gallego proposes that a relative C has uRel and uT features. Following P&T, the uT feature can be checked by T or by a nominative subject. The uRel feature, however, must be checked by a relative DP. Gallego also assumes that there is a c head above C that has uPhi (cf. Bianchi 2000 for a similar proposal), and N raises to c to check uPhi. Furthermore, these uRel, uT, and uPhi features can have EPP subfeatures, although there is some variation with respect to when an EPP subfeature is present. We explain how Gallego accounts for subject relative clauses, discuss some problems, and then explain our implementation.

English subject-relative clauses permit *who* but not *who that*, as show in (23a,b).

(23)   a. the man who loves Mary
        b. *the man who <u>that</u> loves Mary (Gallego 2006: 156)

(a)

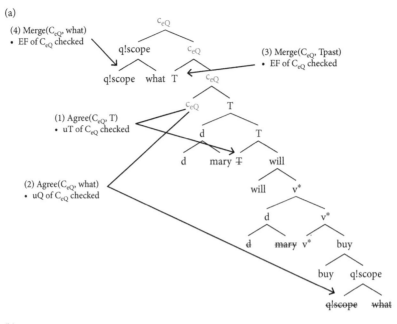

(b)

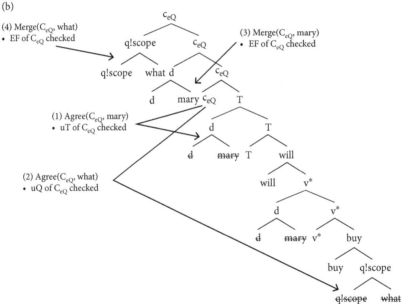

Figure 3.19 Derivation of (22a)

The relevant portion of the derivation of (23a) is shown in Figure 3.20. The relative C has uT and uRel features and each of these features has an EPP subfeature, thus meaning that anything that Agrees with uT or uRel must also remerge with C. When C Agrees with *who man*, the uT feature is checked by the Nominative Case of *who man* and the uRel feature is also checked, assuming that *who man* has an iRel feature. The EPP (which actually refers to a subfeature of uT and another subfeature of uRel) is then checked via remerge of *who man*. Then there is a higher c head, which has uPhi. The

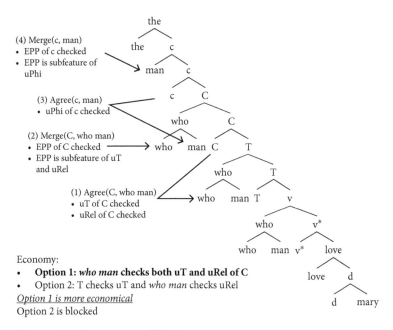

Figure 3.20 Derivation of (23a)

c head Agrees with the phi-feature bearing *man*. The Phi of *man* checks the uPhi of c, and an EPP subfeature of uPhi forces *man* to remerge with c. Then the determiner *the* is externally Merged. Note that this derivation involves a single Agree relation between the relative C and *who man*. The other option would be for the uT feature of C to be checked by T and then the uRel feature to be checked by *who man*, which would involve two Agree relations, and would also result in pronunciation of *that*, due to T appearing in C. But economy rules out this option, given that a single Agree relation is possible. Thus, economy accounts for the impossibility of *that* in subject relatives with a relative D *who*, thus blocking (23b).

Gallego also accounts for the fact that *that* is required and a zero relative is banned, in a subject relative clause such as (24a,b).

(24) a. the boy that called Mary (Gallego 2006: 158)
      b. *the boy called Mary

In this case, Gallego assumes that a DP with a null D cannot move, following Chomsky's (2001) view that an empty category cannot be pied-piped. In the derivation of (24a), as shown in Figure 3.21, the relative DP does not move. As a result, the relative DP does not remerge with C. Note also that because the relative DP has a null D, it cannot even move to Spec, T. The uT of C forms an Agree relation with T and an EPP subfeature of uT forces T to remerge. Note that T in C results in pronunciation of *that*. The uRel of C forms an Agree relation with the relative DP. But the uRel, conveniently, lacks an EPP subfeature, so the relative DP does not move. Then, the uPhi feature of c Agrees with *boy* and an EPP subfeature of uPhi forces *boy* to remerge with c. Crucially, because the relative DP cannot move, the uT of C must be checked by T, which forces pronunciation of *that*.

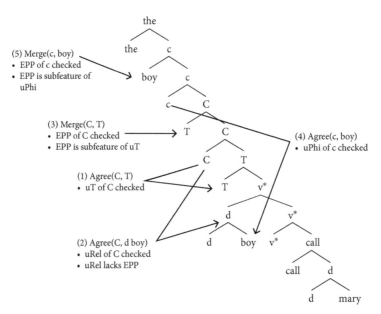

Figure 3.21 Derivation of (24b)

Gallego's analysis is not without problems. First of all, it isn't clear why a DP that has a null D cannot move, but a DP with an overt D can move. Also, it isn't clear why a uRel feature of C has an EPP subfeature when there is an overt D, as in (23a), but lacks an EPP subfeature when there is a null D, as in (24a). The uRel lacks an EPP subfeature only when convenient—i.e. in cases in which the relative DP cannot move. Another consequence of this analysis is that a subject with a null D cannot move to Spec of T, but subjects are generally considered to be in Spec of T. Also, Gallego's analysis requires a c head, as shown in Figures 3.20 and 3.21, but the question arises of why c Agrees with the relative noun to the exclusion of the relative D. Also, it isn't entirely clear why c is necessary.

We implemented a modified and improved version of Gallego's analysis. We adopt Gallego's proposal that a relative C has uT and uRel features. But, crucially, we do away with the c head, and we also do away with the stipulation that a null d can't move. There is also no Agree relation that targets the relative N to the exclusion of the D head. Our core assumptions about relative clauses are as follows.

(25)   Relative C (C_{rel}): [uRel,uT,EF]

(26)   N: [uD]

(27)   Relative Ds:
    a. d_{rel}: [Rel]
    b. who_{rel}: [Rel,T]

We assume that a relative C, our C_{rel}, has uRel and uT features, as well as an EF, as shown in (25). Our EF serves the purpose of remerging anything that an Agree relation is established with. So if a relative DP Agrees with the uRel of C_{rel}, then the EF of C_{rel} forces remerge of the relative DP. We propose that N, shown in (26), has a uD feature that requires checking via a D element. Therefore, if D and N Merge, the uD feature on N is typically checked by a D feature of D. A relative D, shown in (27), however, is defective in that it is unable to check a uD feature, as it lacks a D feature. This has the important consequence of leaving the N complement of a relative D unlicensed. We also assume that the null relative D, indicated as d_{rel}, (27a), has a Rel feature that can check a uRel, but it lacks what we refer to as a T feature. This T is akin to nominative Case that can check a uT. As a result of lacking a T feature, d_{rel} is unable to check a uT feature. Note that we assume that even if a relative DP headed by d_{rel} has Nominative Case, it cannot check a uT feature, due to a lack of a T feature. The other relative head who_{rel}, (27b), has both Rel and T features. Thus, it can check both uRel and uT. We also assume that there is an operation of Last Resort, (28), whereby an unlicensed argument remerges with the root of an SO. This serves the purpose of bringing an unlicensed argument into the appropriate position for forming a relative clause.

(28)   *Last Resort*
    At a phase boundary, remerge an unlicensed element with the root.

The derivation of (23a), as produced by our model, is shown in Figure 3.22. The relative DP has the form who_{rel} *man*, with the relative head who_{rel}, which has both Rel and T features. Thus, when C_{rel} Agrees with the relative DP, both the uRel and uT features of C_{rel} are checked. An EF on C_{rel} forces the relative DP to remerge. Note that the EF feature is not a subfeature of uRel or uT, *contra* Gallego. Rather, any element that Agrees with C_{rel} is forced to remerge due to C_{rel}'s EF. The other option would be to check the uRel feature by the relative DP and the uT feature by T, but this would involve two Agree relations, which is blocked by economy (16). This analysis accounts for why *that* is not possible, as in (23b). The uT feature cannot be checked by T, so *that*, which is T in C, is not permitted. When C_{rel} is complete, the relative N *man* is still unlicensed, assuming that it has a uD feature. At this point, the operation of Last Resort (28) applies and *man* remerges with the root node. Since *man* is a head, and the C_{rel} projection is an XP, the head *man* labels.[9] Then, when the external D *the* is Merged, the uD feature on *man* is checked and *the* labels. The D *the* has an unvalued uCase feature (indicated as !case), which is eventually checked when the DP obtains Case, for example as a subject or object of a larger syntactic structure.

The derivation of (24a) is shown in Figure 3.23. In this example, the relative DP is headed by d_{rel}, which crucially lacks a T feature, so it cannot check uT on C_{rel}. Therefore, there is no option of the relative DP checking both the uT and uRel features of C_{rel}. As a result, C_{rel} forms an Agree relation with d_{rel} *boy*, which checks the uRel feature, and C_{rel} must form a separate Agree relation with T to check the uT feature. An EF feature forces both T and d_{rel} *boy* to remerge. Remerge of T in C results in pronunciation of *that*. Then when the C_{rel} projection is complete, Last Resort applies to force the unlicensed relative noun *boy* to remerge, due to its uD feature. Being a head,

---

[9] See Cecchetto and Donati (2015) for a similar head-raising account of relativization. In Cecchetto and Donati's account, only heads (not phrases) may raise to relabel a clause. Furthermore, head raising is constrained by Gross Minimality considerations. We leave comparison of our account with that of Ceccehetto and Donati for future work.

(a)

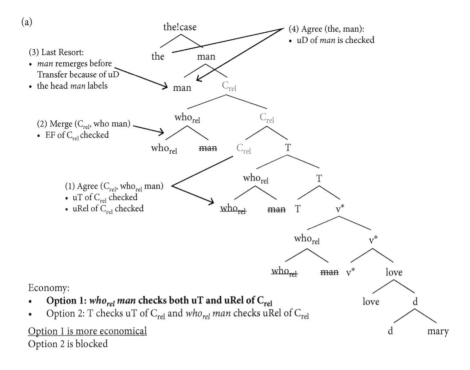

Economy:
- **Option 1: who_rel man checks both uT and uRel of C_rel**
- Option 2: T checks uT of C_rel and who_rel man checks uRel of C_rel

Option 1 is more economical
Option 2 is blocked

(b)

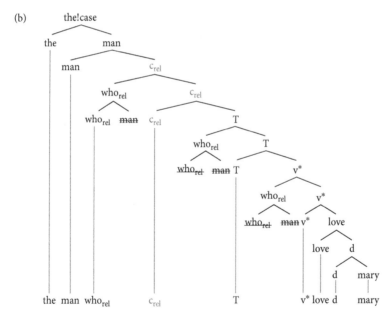

Spell-out:
the man who -s love -acc mary (after morpheme realization)
the man who love -s mary -acc (after affix-hop)
the man who loves mary

Figure 3.22 Derivation of (23a) (implementation)

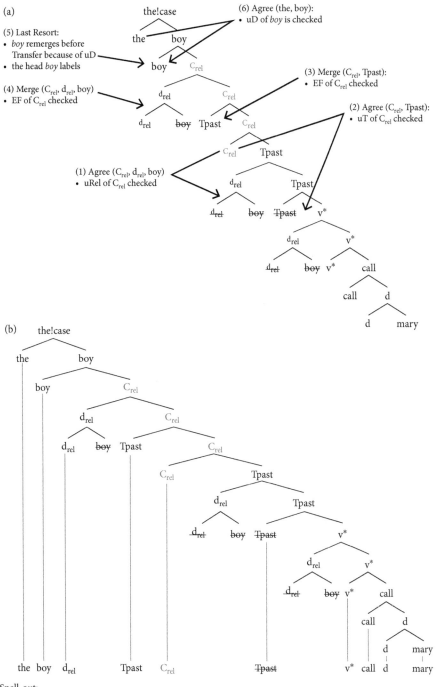

Spell-out:
the boy that -ed(sg) call -acc mary (after morpheme realization)
the boy that call -ed(sg) mary -acc (after affix-hop)
the boy that called mary

Figure 3.23 Derivation of (24a) (implementation)

boy labels. Then when the external D *the* is Merged, the uD feature of *boy* is checked and the relative clause is successfully completed as shown in Figure 3.23b.

Following the insights of P&T and Gallego, we have implemented relative clauses without an extra projection in the left periphery of the clause, and without recourse to optional EPP subfeatures. Rather, we simply use the idea that a relative C head, C_{rel}, has uT and uRel features, and a relative D differs in whether or not it can check the uT feature of C_{rel}. When the relative D can check uT, then economy requires this operation, thus blocking pronunciation of *that*. When the relative D cannot check uT, then T must check uT, thus requiring the presence of *that*.

3.7 Conclusion

We have highlighted important details of our implementation of expletives and multiple agreement (Chomsky 2001), thematization/extraction (Sobin 2014), *that*-trace effects and subject vs. object *wh*-movement (P&T 2001), and relative clauses (P&T 2001; Gallego 2006). We explained how we dealt with particular problems that arose in the theories that we implemented and how these problems can be resolved. Problems arising with respect to multiple agreement in Chomsky (2001) were dealt with via feature unification. Problems arising with respect to feature checking and the position of the expletive *there* were also resolved with feature unification, as well as with the notion that an expletive is Merged low in a position below T. Problems from Sobin (2014) regarding locality of affixes and Spell-Out were resolved via the use of EFs (prt has an EF) and distinguishing v~ into two separate types that differ in pronunciation (v~unacc and v~). We implemented P&T's account of *wh*-movement and *that*-trace effects, and in the process clarified how the fine details work; we utilized an EF instead of an EPP subfeature and we implemented movement of the highest verbal element to T in a matrix clause. Lastly, we resolved problems with Gallego's (2006) account of relative clauses. We utilized relative Ds that differ with respect to whether or not they can check a uT feature. We also incorporated a notion of Last Resort whereby an unlicensed relative N can undergo movement, thus doing away with the notion that an extra projection is needed in the left periphery. Crucially, all of these modifications and improvements of work from Chomsky (2001), P&T (2001), and Gallego (2006) were implemented via a single unified model, thus demonstrating that a wide variety of constructions can be accounted for with a single theory.

In conclusion, we have integrated core components of different linguistic theories to create a single unified theory that accounts for a wide variety of data. Our theory provides possible explanations for target phenomena, and this theory has been successfully tested.

Acknowledgements

We are grateful the participants of the Workshop on Minimalist Parsing for their useful comments.

4

Parsing with Minimalist Grammars and prosodic trees

Kristine M. Yu

4.1 Introduction

Advances in the syntactic parsing of written language have proceeded apace in the last few decades, but much less progress has been made in the syntactic parsing of *spoken* language. This chapter addresses one question important for such progress: *how can we bring prosody in to inform syntactic parsing of spoken language*? It has long been thought that prosody ought to be informative in syntactic parsing, for the simple reason that syntax determines certain aspects of prosody (Chomsky 1955: II-2fn). Yet how to bring prosody in to inform syntactic parsing has remained unclear. Why is this?

First, it is not enough to know that syntax conditions certain aspects of prosody; we must also understand how this conditioning works in a clear enough way to characterize and implement the interface between syntax and prosody. Here the computational parsing literature is almost silent: the norm is to refrain from stating how syntactic structure conditions prosody, e.g. "We avoid the pitfall . . . of specifying an explicit relationship between prosody and syntax; rather, the model infers the relationships from the data" (Dreyer and Shafran 2007). In contrast, the linguistic literature has enjoyed an abundance of theories. Over a decade ago, Harper et al. (2005: 58) wrote on parsing: "The lack of authoritative theories on syntax-phonology interface makes it difficult to develop a generative model for utilizing prosodic structure . . . ".

Proposals about the syntax–phonology interface have since continued to proliferate (see e.g. Elordieta 2008; Selkirk 2011; Féry 2017 for reviews). And while there are some theories that are treated as authorative, it is not obvious that the details of some proposal might be much closer to the truth than those of another. As such, a first step is to model general properties that a number of syntax–phonology interface proposals share as a class (see §4.1.2). One such general property is that linguists model prosodic structures with trees, while computational (syntactic) parsing models have not. If we admit prosodic trees as representations, then we must also consider how prosodic trees might be parsed. The question becomes not only how prosody can inform syntactic parsing, but also *how syntax can inform prosodic parsing*.

Another obstacle to the pursuit of prosodically informed syntactic parsing is that it is not just syntax that conditions prosody, of course—a multitude of interacting factors

Minimalist Parsing. First edition. Robert C. Berwick and Edward P. Stabler (eds.) This chapter © Kristine M. Yu 2019. First published 2019 by Oxford University Press.

conditions the appearance and realization of prosodic events in spoken language, beyond just syntax (see e.g. Ladd 2008; Yu 2014: 777). These factors range from linguistic ones like phonology (e.g. the rising pitch accent associated with predictable primary stress in Egyptian Arabic (Hellmuth 2009; 2006)) and pragmatics (e.g. the English contrastive topic rise–fall–rise contour (e.g Jackendoff 1972; Büring 2003; Constant 2014)); to socio-affective factors such as modulating interlocutor attention (Stern et al. 1982; Thorson and Morgan 2014); to individual differences in cognition (e.g. Clifton Jr. et al. (2002); Ferreira and Karimi 2015; Speer and Foltz 2015). The sensitivity of prosody to these diverse factors can obscure the informativity of prosody for syntactic analysis. As a first step around this, we can focus on modeling syntax–prosody interface phenomena in natural language where non-syntactic factors seem to play a minimal role, if any.

In computational work on parsing that has used prosodic information, the emphasis has been on prosodic edges coming in as (noisy) signals for sentences and syntactic constituent edges (see Shriberg et al. 2000; Kahn et al. 2005; Huang and Harper 2010, among many others). But relations between syntactic and prosodic domains are not the whole of the syntax–phonology interface. As pointed out by Selkirk (2011: 435), this is only one aspect of the interface; two "further core aspects" are "the phono-logical realization (spell-out) of the morphosyntactic feature bundles of morphemes and lexical items that form part of syntactic representation and the linearization of syntactic representation which produces the surface word order of the sentence as actually pronounced" (Selkirk 2011: 435). Prosodically informed computational parsing work has missed studying the distinct contributions of these other core aspects to conditioning prosody. And it may be precisely these other core aspects that provide interface phenomena where syntax plays (virtually) the only role in conditioning the prosody.

In summary, we've highlighted two[1] key challenges for understanding how to bring prosody in to inform syntactic parsing: (i) explicitly defining aspects of the syntax–prosody interface, including prosodic trees, and (ii) modeling distinct contributions of syntax to conditioning prosodic events, including aspects other than relations between

---

[1] There's another related and daunting challenge to introducing prosody into parsing that we'll abstract away from in this chapter. This is our poor understanding of the mapping from the speech signal to prosodic structure (see e.g. see Cole and Shattuck-Hufnagel 2016). Ultimately, to take advantage of prosodic information, we need to know how to recognize it. One aspect of this mapping that has received some attention in the computational parsing literature is the acoustics of prosodic concepts: "a challenge of using prosodic features is that multiple acoustic cues interact to signal prosodic structure, including pauses, duration lengthening, fundamental fre-quency modulation, and even spectral shape" (Tran et al. 2017). But another aspect of this mapping that has received scant attention is the definition of the range of the mapping: what are the atoms of prosodic structure, anyway; what should we be mapping from the speech signal to? The parsing literature has sometimes assumed that human expert-annotated intonational/break labels have ground truth status (e.g. Steedman 1991a; Kahn et al. 2005; Hale et al. 2006; Dreyer and Shafran 2007; Huang and Harper 2010). However, the particular intonational transcription system for English (MAE_ToBI) that has been used in the parsing literature, as well as intonational transcription more generally, has been under active scrutiny and development to the current day (see e.g. Gussenhoven 2016; Hualde and Prieto 2016, and other articles in a special issue of *Laboratory Phonology* on "Advancing Prosodic Transcription," D'Imperio et al. 2016). One interesting avenue for tackling the prosodic mapping has been pursued by Tran et al. (2017); this work used neural networks to learn word-level feature vectors from fundamental frequency and energy time-series, rather than using pre-determined hand-annotated prosodic category labels.

syntactic and prosodic domain edges. This chapter takes on these tasks. We present a proof-of-concept, detailed case study of parsing a single sentence in Samoan, a Polynesian language, and ask: *How might prosodic information come in to help in syntactic parsing? How might syntactic information help in prosodic parsing?* Our contribution to tackling the first challenge is to implement a model of the syntax–prosody interface following key properties of current theoretical proposals on the syntax–prosody interface. Unlike other work on prosodically informed syntactic parsing, we accordingly assume the existence of prosodic trees separate from syntactic trees, as well as an optimality-theoretic grammar with constraints penalizing misalignment of syntactic and prosodic constituents. Our implementation allows us to study the consequences of current theoretical proposals on the interface for parsing. Our contribution to grappling with the second challenge is to model both prosodic reflexes (spellout) of morphosyntactic structures and relations between prosodic and syntactic domains in the parser. In particular, we show how studying prosodically informed parsing in a language like Samoan—with clearly syntactically controlled prosodic events in addition to more variably occurring prosodic events—can be a fruitful first step to understanding the diverse ways that prosody (syntax) might inform syntactic (prosodic) parsing more generally. The spotlight on Samoan puts our work in contrast with previous work, which has been done almost entirely on English, with also a little work on German, French, and Mandarin. These are languages in which the relation between syntax and prosody is quite obscured by interactions with non-syntactic factors, and in which the different ways in which prosody can inform syntactic analysis are difficult to articulate and factor out.

The rest of this chapter is structured as follows; the remainder of this introductory section (§4.1) consists of background information on: previous work on prosodically informed syntactic parsing (§4.1.1), theoretical proposals about the syntax–prosody interface (§4.1.2), and Samoan syntax and prosody (§4.2). The introductory section is followed by a section that defines the syntactic grammar fragment (§4.3.2), a section that describes the generation of licit prosodic parses (§4.3.1), and a section that describes the implementation of the syntax–prosody interface (§§4.3.3,4.3.4). We close with a discussion and conclusion (§4.4).

4.1.1 Previous work on prosodically informed syntactic parsers

A representative selection of computational work on prosodically informed syntactic parsing is summarized in Table 4.1. This summary shows that much work has used broad-coverage probabilistic context-free grammars for syntactic analysis and been based on a single corpus of spoken language (the English Switchboard corpus). In contrast—and closer to the work presented here—the older case studies of Steedman (1991a), Blache (1995), and Batliner et al. (1996) targeted particular syntactic phenomena using hand-crafted Combinatory Categorial Grammar (CCG) and Head-driven Phrase Structure Grammar (HPSG) fragments. One challenge introduced

Table 4.1 Summary of a representative sample of relatively recent work on prosodically informed syntactic parsing

	Batliner et al. (1996)	Gregory (2004)	Kahn et al. (2005)	Hale (2006)	Dreyer and Shafran (2007)	Huang and Harper (2010)	Pate (2013)	Tran et al. (2017)
Language	German	English	English	English	English	English	English	English
Data/corpus	Verbmobil	Switchboard	Switchboard	Switchboard, Fisher	Switchboard	Switchboard, Fisher	WSJ, Brent, Switchboard	Switchboard-NXT
Special topic	V2 verbal traces	None	Disfluencies	Speech repair	None	None	Infant-directed speech	Disambiguation
Syntactic grammar/parser	HPSG hand-crafted BU parser	PCFG broad-coverage	PCFG N-best	PCFG CYK N-best, N = 1	PCFG N-best, N = 1	PCFG, PCFG-LA N-best	Unsupervised Bayesian dependency parser	Linearized PCFG trees represented as word embeddings, LSTM-RNNs
Acoustic features	Duration, f0 regression coeff	Energy, f0, f0' pause/phone duration	Mentioned but not given	F0, energy, duration	F0, energy, duration	Used for automatic break detection	Word duration	Word-level features. Pauses, duration; f0, energy input into CNN
Phonological features	None	Quantization of extreme values in acoustic distributions	Posterior probabilities of ToBI break indices	Decision trees for ToBI break indices	Decision trees for ToBI break indices	Previously detected ToBI break indices	Classification by word durations	None (output of CNN)
Syntactic features	presence of syntactic boundary	None	Non-local dependencies	"-UNF" unfinished tags daughter annotation	Category splits, EM	Category splits into latent tags	Word identity, POS tags, direction of dependency arc	Word embeddings
Interface	Acoustic features directly to syntactic boundaries	PCFG enriched with prosodic features	Weighted co-occurrence with syntactic features for re-ranking parses	Enriched PCFG	Prosodic breaks used in category refinement	PCFG enriched with break indices	Dependency learning conditioned on quantized duration	Prosodic and word embeddings in bag of features
Effect of prosody	Reduces runtime	Degrades performance	Improves rank order and F-score	Better accuracy in finding disfluencies	Better parse performance	Lack of performance gains unless further restrictions	Better constituency scores, dependency accuracy	Improves parse accuracy

by spoken language that has been the focus of some attention is parsing in the presence of disfluencies and speech repairs (e.g. Charniak and Johnson 2001; Spilker et al. 2001; Harper et al. 2005; Kahn et al. 2005; Hale et al. 2006; Lin and Lee 2009; Miller 2009; Wu et al. 2011; Zwarts and Johnson 2011); less work has focused on fluent speech. A number of parsers have included acoustic features such as fundamental frequency, energy, and duration measures to train classifiers for ToBI break index categories, especially a category for disfluencies. Tones and Break Indices (ToBI) is a widely used set of conventions for the intonational transcription of English (Pierrehumbert 1980; Beckman and Pierrehumbert 1986; Beckman and Elam 1997; Wightman et al. 1992). Also, prosody has generally entered into parsing either via a syntactic grammar enriched with prosodic tags, or in a bag of features used in (re-)ranking generated parses. A main result of the work has been to show that prosodic features such as changes in fundamental frequency (the acoustic correlate of pitch) and human-annotated prosodic break strength indices can sometimes be informative in the detection of points of disfluency, and introduce modest gains in parsing accuracy and efficiently in their presence.

4.1.2 The syntax–prosody interface

We've briefly reviewed the body of computational work on prosodically informed syntactic parsing and seen that prosody has entered into parsing either via a syntactic grammar enriched with prosodic tags or in a bag of features used in (re-)ranking generated parses. This work does not assume that prosody might have its own structure—independent from syntax—which itself may need to be parsed in the course of syntactic parsing. Yet this is exactly what has long been assumed about prosody in the linguistic literature (Selkirk 1978/1981; Pierrehumbert and Beckman 1988; Beckman 1996; Féry 2017), e.g. "Thinking now in terms of speech production and perception, we would hypothesize that the units for prosodic structure we have discussed here in linguistic terms are indeed the appropriate units in production and perception models, that the effect of syntactic phrasing in production, or access to that phrasing in perception, are crucially mediated by these units of the prosodic hierarchy" (Selkirk 1978/1981). In this chapter, we assume that this is one of the ways that prosody comes into parsing: via prosodic trees that are independent structures from syntactic trees.

   As the idea of trees as data structures in (prosodic) phonology is quite alien to the parsing literature,[2] we spend some time introducing it here. Two common assumptions about prosodic structure have endured in linguistics since its early formulations in the mid-1970s: (i) prosodic structure is *hierarchical*, and (ii) while prosodic structure reflects syntactic structure in systematic ways, prosodic and syntactic structure are distinct and independent. Below, we first explicate what is meant by 'hierarchical'

---

[2] And strikingly, mathematical/computational descriptions of phonological patterns have revealed strong structural universals without referring to constituents at all; see Heinz (2018) for a overview and review.

structure (§4.1.2.1), and then we sketch the working model of the syntax–prosody interface that we assume in our implementation here (§4.1.2.2).

4.1.2.1 "Hierarchical" structure in prosody

One of the earliest invocations of the term "prosodic structure" in theories of the syntax–phonology interface came in Selkirk (1978/1981), which defined prosodic structure as "a suprasegmental, hierarchically arranged organization to the utterance," in contrast to the "simple linear arrangement of segments and boundaries" assumed as the phonological data structure in Chomsky and Halle (1968)'s *The Sound Pattern of English* (SPE). The assumption (or definition) that prosodic structure is "hierarchical" has persisted (e.g. Selkirk 1984; Nespor and Vogel 1986; Selkirk 1986; Pierrehumbert and Beckman 1988; Ladd 1996; Ito and Mester 2003; Jun 2005a; Ladd 2014; Selkirk and Lee 2015; Cheng and Downing 2016; Féry 2017. But what does "hierarchical" mean, and how does that property distinguish a data structure from the data structures in SPE? If "hierarchical" is an informal way of referring to recursive data structures—data structures which can be defined in terms of themselves—then the "linear" segment sequences of SPE, i.e. strings, are also hierarchical, since strings are composed of substrings. What is really meant by "hierarchical" in this context is that prosodic data structures are ordered, rooted trees rather than strings, following Liberman (1975a: 49–51).[3] *And unlike strings, trees are data structures that can pick out substring chunks—in particular, a set of nodes that are exhaustively dominated by a common node in the tree forms a constituent.*

The motivation for introducing trees in prosody has been the same as that in syntax: positing constituents has been one alternative amongst the arsenal of theoretical machinery that has helped phonologists capture generalizations in the observed patterns of natural language, (see e.g. Nespor and Vogel 1986: 58–9). Phonological analyses suggest that constellations of phonological processes (Selkirk 1978/1981; McCarthy and Prince 1986/1996; Nespor and Vogel 1986; Pierrehumbert and Beckman 1988; Hayes 1995; Jun 1996; 1998; Selkirk 2011; Myrberg and Riad 2015), as well as phonotactic restrictions (Flack 2007) and syntagmatic prominence relations (Liberman 1975a; Liberman and Prince 1977), consistently target or refer to particular chunks of phonological material; it is these chunks that have then been posited to be categories in the derivation of prosodic trees (Selkirk 1978/1981; Nespor and Vogel 1986).[4]

---

[3] Other phonological data structures besides trees have been considered to be "hierarchical" or "non-linear" in contrast to the strings of SPE (McCarthy 1982; Hayes 1988). Most notably, these include the tiered representations of autosegmental theory (Goldsmith 1976; 1990) and the grids and bracketed grids of metrical theory (Liberman 1975a; Liberman and Prince 1977; Hammond 1984; Halle and Vergnaud 1987). Here, we set aside the question of how these different structures relate to one another and whether different structures are relevant for different aspects of prosody (see e.g. Liberman and Prince 1977; Selkirk 1984 §4.2; Pierrehumbert and Beckman 1988: ch. 6), and focus on trees—the kind of data structure most actively discussed in recent work on the syntax–prosody interface.

[4] Alternate analyses have also been proposed that do not assume prosodic constituents, (Kiparsky 1983; Kenstowicz 1995). See also a comparison of alternative analyses for Samoan word-level prosody in Zuraw et al. (2014).

While the motivation for introducing trees as data structures in prosody and syntax is shared, prosodic trees have been thought to be different from syntactic trees: "the reason for assuming the existence of an independent prosodic structure...is that the constituent structure with respect to which structure-sensitive phenomena of phonology and phonetics are defined may diverge in significant respects from the syntactic structure of the sentence" (Selkirk and Lee 2015: 5). A classic example of this divergence or (bracketing) "mismatch" introduced in Chomsky and Halle (1968: 372) is given in (1).[5] The prosodic tree has only one level of embedding—it's flat—while the syntactic tree exhibits five levels of embedding, as well as recursion $.

(1)   Classic example of mismatch between syntactic and prosodic domains (Chomsky and Halle 1968: 372)
       a. Syntactic constituency: This is [$_{NP}$ the cat [$_{S'}$ that caught [$_{NP}$ the rat [$_{S'}$ that stole [$_{NP}$ the cheese]]]]]
       b. Prosodic constituency: (This is the cat) (that caught the rat) (that stole the cheese)

Much work on the syntax–phonology interface in the 1980s and 1990s centered on finding evidence that: (i) there are "mismatches" between syntactic and prosodic domains, and (ii) that there exist phonological processes that are defined—and can *only* be defined/understood—with respect to prosodic rather than syntactic domains (Nespor and Vogel 1986; Selkirk 1986; Hayes 1989; Price et al. 1991; Jun 1996; 1998; Shattuck-Hufnagel and Turk 1996; Truckenbrodt 1999). To fit with the accumulating evidence of mismatches, interface theories assumed that prosodic constituents were aligned or related to syntactic constituents only at *one* edge, see Féry (2017: §§4.2–4.4) for a brief review. At the same time, some work defended the claim that there were some phonological processes that could be better understood in terms of syntactic domains (e.g. Kaisse 1985; Odden 1987). And some work pointed out that so-called "mismatches" might not in fact be mismatches; rather, apparent mismatches are actually cases where the prosodic structure reveals alternate syntactic structures, and syntax is much more flexible than we have thought (e.g. Liberman 1975a; 1975b; Steedman 1991b; Taglicht 1994; 1998; Wagner 2005; 2010; Steedman 2014; Hirsch and Wagner 2015). A strong version of this hypothesis has been articulated by Wagner (2010: 231–2):

> The original motivation in favor of edge-alignment came from certain apparent brack-
> eting mismatches. However, a closer look at the syntax in representative examples
> suggests the prosody does not mismatch syntax after all. If this conclusion is correct,
> then we can take prosodic evidence seriously as a source of syntactic evidence. In cases
> where syntactic and prosodic evidence seem in contradiction, we may have to rethink
> our syntactic analysis.   (Wagner 2010: 231–2)

---

[5] But see Wagner (2010: 224–6) for a discussion of whether this is really an example of a mismatch.

A weaker version of this hypothesis has become a kind of consensus view in at least some communities of theoretical work on the syntax–prosody interface in recent years: the default is that there is a grammatical correspondence relation between syntactic and prosodic domains—not that there are mismatches. If mismatches occur, they are "the consequence of properly phonological pressures on the hierarchical structure of phonological representation," i.e. what phonologists call "phonological markedness" (Selkirk and Lee 2015: 4), see §4.1.2.4. Another aspect of the consensus view seems to be that constraint-based grammars are well suited to define this correspondence. In such grammars, a mismatch can occur, e.g. if a phonological markedness constraint is ranked higher than a constraint demanding the faithful correspondence of prosodic domains to syntactic domains. What has remained a continuing source of debate is which syntactic objects are relevant for the correspondence relation (or relevant for phonological processes, under theories where phonological processes directly refer to syntactic objects). While some work has defined these objects to be syntactic constituents, other work has defined them to be phases (e.g. Dobashi 2004; Kratzer and Selkirk 2007; Downing 2010; Cheng and Downing 2016; Ahn 2016; McPherson and Heath 2016). However, the various phase-based theories that have been proposed have quite disparate assumptions about what phases are, so we set them aside for this first case study, and assume syntactic constituents to be the relevant object for the correspondence relation for now.

4.1.2.2 A working model for the relation between prosodic and syntactic trees

The definition and implementation of the syntax–prosody interface in this chapter is based on work in the Match Theory framework (Selkirk 2009; 2011), which uses (violable) MATCH constraints to enforce correspondence between syntactic and prosodic constituents. In recent years, Match Theory has been widely used to analyze a range of interface phenomena across different languages; see e.g. the special issue of *Phonology* on constituency in sentence phonology (Selkirk and Lee 2015), Ito and Mester (2013) on Japanese, Myrberg (2013) on Swedish, Kandybowicz (2015) on Asante Twi, and Ito and Mester (2015) on Danish, as well as work on verb-initial languages like Samoan: Elfner (2012; 2015); Bennett et al. (2016) on Irish, Clemens (2014) on Niuean, Sabbagh (2014) on Tagalog.

The statement of syntax–prosody MATCH constraints is intended to encode the core assumption of Match Theory that there is "a strong tendency for phonological domains to mirror syntactic constituents" (Selkirk 2011). The other core assumption about the interface treated in Match Theory is that syntax–prosody mismatches are due to the satisfaction of phonological markedness constraints at the expense of violating MATCH constraints. Thus, while Match Theory is one among many theories of the syntax–prosody interface, it is commonly used by linguists and exhibits the properties we described in §4.1.2.1 as characteristic of a kind of consensus view of the interface at the present.[6] Match Theory is therefore a suitable choice for the definition of the

---

[6] For comparative overviews that describe other theories, too, see Elordieta (2008), Selkirk (2011), and Féry (2017: ch. 4).

interface in this first case study. In the remainder of this section, we introduce MATCH constraints in §4.1.2.3 and phonological markedness constraints relevant to our case study in §4.1.2.4.

4.1.2.3 Match Theory: interface constraints

Suppose we are given a finite, ordered set of categories in a prosodic grammar such as (2) (Selkirk, 2011: (1)), and that prosodic trees are derived using these categories.

(2) Enumeration of prosodic categories
     a. Intonational phrase (ι)
     b. Phonological phrase (ϕ)
     c. Prosodic word (ω)
     d. Foot (Ft)
     e. Syllable (σ)

Given such an enumeration from highest to lowest in a "prosodic hierarchy," Match Theory assumes the existence of syntactic and prosodic trees for an utterance and a set of optimality-theoretic faithfulness constraints (Prince and Smolensky 1993; 2004) that enforce "matching" between the constituents in these trees, as stated in (3), quoted from Bennett et al. (2016). The interface constraints are defined as relations over syntax–prosodic tree pairs, and each of them is defined in such a way that it is multiply violated if there are multiple loci in the prosodic tree that don't satisfy the constraint.

(3) Definition of syntax–prosody MATCH constraints (Bennett et al. 2016: 187, (34))
     a. MATCHWORD: Prosodic words correspond to the heads from which phrases are projected in the syntax (heads that will often have a complex internal structure determined by head movement).
     b. MATCHPHRASE: Phonological phrases correspond to maximal projections in the syntax.
     c. MATCHCLAUSE: Intonational phrases correspond to those clausal projections that have the potential to express illocutionary force (assertoric or interrogative force, for instance).

More precisely, a prosodic constituent is defined as "corresponding" to a syntactic constituent when both the left and right edges of the prosodic constituent are aligned to the left and right edges of the syntactic constituent, respectively (Selkirk 2011: §2.2.1). For example, Selkirk (2011: (20)) defines MATCHPHRASE as in (4). Another set of prosody–syntax MATCH constraints enforce the correspondence of syntactic constituents to prosodic constituents, under the same edge-based definition of correspondence. We abstract away from these prosody–syntax constraints in our case study; one could say we consider them too low-ranked to be active in filtering out prosodic parses.

(4) Definition of MATCHPHRASE (MATCH(XP, ϕ)): The left and right edges of a constituent of type XP in the input syntactic representation must correspond to the left and right edges of a constituent of type ϕ in the output phonological representation.

Elfner (2012) developed a revised definition of MATCHPHRASE motivated by generalizations she discovered in her analysis of the syntax–prosody interface in Irish. This is given in (5) and is the one we use in our implementation.

(5)   Definition of MATCHPHRASE (Bennett et al. 2016: 188, (35); Elfner 2012: 28, (19)):

Given a maximal projection XP in a syntactic representation S, where XP dominates all and only the set of terminal elements $\{a, b, c, \ldots, n\}$, there must be in the phonological representation P corresponding to S a ϕ-phrase that includes all and only the phonological exponents of $a, b, c, \ldots, n$.

Assign one violation mark if there is no ϕ-phrase in the phonological representation that exhaustively dominates all and only the phonological exponents of the terminal nodes in $\{a, b, c, \ldots, n\}$.

The effect of the statement about phonological exponents in (5) is to redefine MATCHPHRASE over syntactic–prosodic tree pairs where the syntactic tree has been "flattened." The result of "flattening" is just the tree structure that is visible to the phonological constraints. By definition, phonological exponents must be phonologically overt, and the prosodic tree has only phonologically overt terminals. The definition in (5) says that the MATCHPHRASE relation for a tree pair $\langle S, P \rangle$ is computed over a flattened syntactic tree S' transduced from S, where any phonologically empty terminals are deleted, and then any two syntactic nodes in S are merged if they both exhaustively dominate the same set of remaining terminals.

Consider the discussion in Elfner (2012: 32–3, (24)), revisited here: suppose we are evaluating MATCHPHRASE (5) for the syntactic–prosodic tree pair $\langle S, P \rangle$ given in (6), where t is a trace or unpronounced copy left by a movement operation.

(6)   Syntactic–prosodic tree pair

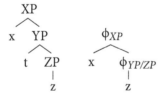

In this example, there are three maximal projections in the syntactic tree, which dominate all and only the terminals given in (7).

(7)   Terminals dominated by maximal projections in the syntactic tree in (6)
   a. XP: $\{x, t, z\}$
   b. YP: $\{t, z\}$
   c. ZP: $\{z\}$

But since t is phonologically null, it does not enter into the MATCHPHRASE relation. Thus, we can think of MATCHPHRASE as operating on a flattened syntactic tree where t is deleted and YP and ZP are merged, as shown in (8). YP and ZP are merged because they exhaustively dominate the same set of phonological (non-null) exponents, $\{z\}$.

(8)   Syntactic–prosodic tree pair, with flattened syntactic tree

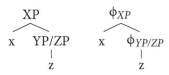

The syntactic–prosodic tree pair in (6,8) incurs no violation of MATCHPHRASE—
either definition, (4) or (5). For each unique set of terminals exhaustively dominated
by a node in the syntactic tree, there is a node in the prosodic tree that exhaustively
dominates the same set, as shown in (9).

(9)   Terminals dominated by maximal projections and phonological phrases in the
       tree pair in (8)
       a. XP: $\{x, z\} \mapsto \phi_{XP}$: $\{x, z\}$
       b. YP/ZP: $\{z\} \mapsto \phi_{YP/ZP}$: $\{z\}$

Now consider a different syntactic–prosodic tree pair, given in (10). This tree pair
has the same syntactic tree as (6), and thus the same set of terminals dominated by
each syntactic maximal projetion, (7).

(10)   Syntactic–prosodic tree pair (Elfner 2012: 32, (24))

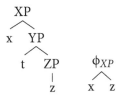

However, this tree pair incurs one violation of MATCHPHRASE as defined in (5), since
no ϕ exhaustively dominates the set of terminals exhaustively dominated by YP/ZP: $\{z\}$.
(Under the definition of MATCHPHRASE in (4), it incurs two violations, one for YP and
one for ZP.)

4.1.2.4 Match Theory: constraints on prosodic trees

Besides the assumption of a default correspondence between syntactic and prosodic
constituents, the other core assumption about the interface treated in Match Theory is
that while prosodic structure reflects syntactic structure in systematic ways, prosodic
and syntactic structure are distinct and independent. The way Match Theory encodes
this assumption is by positing the existence of phonological "markedness" constraints
that penalize "marked" properties of prosodic structure. If these outrank MATCH
constraints, then an optimal syntactic–prosodic tree pair under the constraint-based
interface grammar might be one that incurs violations of the MATCH constraints. Thus,
the phonological markedness constraints constitute the part of the interface grammar
that drives prosodic trees to diverge in structure from syntactic ones. Depending on the
relative rankings of the prosodic markedness constraints and the MATCH constraints,
from language to language, prosodic trees may not diverge from syntactic trees at

all, or might diverge in many ways. There is no consensus on what the "right" set of phonological markedness constraints is, but there are some constraints that are widely used and we define these here.

One class of these constraints regulates dominance relations and is defined following Selkirk (1996: 189–90) in (11).[7]

(11)   Definition of constraints on prosodic domination (Selkirk 1996: 189–90)
      (where C^n = some prosodic category)
      a. LAYEREDNESS: No C^i dominates a C^j, $j > i$, e.g., No σ dominates a Ft.
      b. HEADEDNESS: Any C^i must dominate a C^{i-1} (except if $C_i = σ$), e.g., A PWd must dominate a Ft.
      c. EXHAUSTIVITY: No C^i immediately dominates a constituent C^j, $j < i - 1$, e.g., No PWd immediately dominates a σ.
      d. NONRECURSIVITY: No C^i dominates C^j, $j = i$, e.g., No Ft dominates a Ft.

As summarized in Selkirk (1996: 190), a significant body of work has indicated cases where it appears that EXHAUSTIVITY and NONRECURSIVITY might be violated in prosodic forms, but there isn't a similar body of work pointing out cases where LAYEREDNESS and HEADEDNESS appear to be violated (although see Seidl 2000). In the work here, we will assume that LAYEREDNESS and HEADEDNESS are inviolable. (This same assumption seems to be made in Bellik et al. (2015)'s Syntax–Prosody for OTWorkplace (SPOT), software for "automatic candidate generation and violation assessment for investigations on the syntax-prosody interface". Their current web interface includes options to add EXHAUSTIVITY and NONRECURSIVITY to the constraint set, but not LAYEREDNESS or HEADEDNESS.)

Let us consider for a moment how the constraints on prosodic trees in (11) compare to constraints on syntactic trees. Examples of constraints similar to LAYEREDNESS, HEADEDNESS, and EXHAUSTIVITY in syntax include the restrictive rule schema of X-bar theory (Chomsky 1970: 210–11) and the universal, fixed order of categories proposed in cartographic approaches (Cinque 1999). However, it is difficult to think of a constraint on syntactic trees that has been proposed like NONRECURSIVITY. Indeed, Selkirk (2011) states that an important motivation for proposing MATCH constraints is to account for the preponderance of phonological analyses that conclude that there is recursivity in prosodic trees: the idea is that recursion in prosodic trees is a result of faithfulness to recursion in syntactic trees. §4.3.1 discusses further details about recursion in prosodic trees and its implementation in this work. §4.4 also considers prosodic hierarchies that have been proposed in the literature which do not admit recursivity (see e.g. Shattuck-Hufnagel and Turk 1996: 206, fig. 2).

Besides the constraints defined in (11), there are two more classes of prosodic markedness constraints that we implement in this work: binarity constraints (12)

---

[7] This set of constraints was developed from an older idea termed the "Strict Layer Hypothesis", following work suggesting that that hypothesis should be decomposed (Inkelas 1989; Ito and Mester 1992; 2003). The Strict Layer Hypothesis is: "a category of level i in the hierarchy immediately dominates a (sequence of) categories of level $i - 1$ (Selkirk 1981a). (Assuming *syllable* to be level 1, the others will be levels 2, . . . ,n.) We will call this the *strict layer hypothesis*" (Selkirk 1984: 26).

and constraints computed over sisters (13). A binarity constraint can be decomposed into two separate ones, as in Elfner (2012: 153, (4), and refs. within) (12): Bin-Min enforces that a prosodic constituent be minimally binary, while Bin-Max enforces that a prosodic constituent be maximally binary.

(12) Definition of constraints on binary branching (Elfner 2012: 153, (4), and references therein)

    a. Bin-Min(κ): assign one violation mark for every prosodic constituent of type κ that immediately dominates less than two daughter constituents.

    b. Bin-Max(κ): assign one violation mark for every prosodic constituent of type κ that immediately dominates more than two daughter constituents.

Given that a binary branching constraint is a widely held hypothesis for syntactic trees (Kayne 1984: ch. 7), Match constraints favor binary branching in prosodic trees, too. But a unary branch in a syntactic tree might not survive transduction to the prosodic tree if Bin-Min constraints are ranked above Match constraints. In the work here, we'll assume a single Binarity(κ) constraint that is a conjunction of Bin-Min(κ) and Bin-Max(κ).

A constraint computed over sisters[8] that we implement here is StrongStart (Selkirk 2011: 470, (38)), see (13).[9] The constraint is motivated by the typological tendency for "strengthening" to occur at the left edges of prosodic domains. Prosodically weak elements get strengthened at the left edge. Strong, stressed forms of function words occur here, e.g. pronouns that are otherwise appear as unstressed clitics appear in their strong, stressed form in initial position (Halpern and Zwicky 1996); weak pronouns are postposed rightward (Elfner 2012; Bennett et al. 2016).

(13) Definition of StrongStart (Elfner 2012: 157, (11)), also (Selkirk 2011; 470, (38))

    Assign one violation mark for every prosodic constituent whose leftmost daughter constituent is lower in the Prosodic Hierarchy than its sister constituent immediately to its right: $^{*}(\kappa_n \; \kappa_{n+1} \dots$.

The phonological pressure of StrongStart has been used to motivate "bracketing paradoxes," e.g. where a prosodically weak element cliticizes to the left (right), although it syntactically phrases to the right (left) (see e.g. Kiparsky 1983; Pesetsky 1985; Sproat 1985; Himmelmann 2014). For example, Bennett et al. (2016: 200, (62)) describes one repair for weak pronouns in contemporary Irish at the left edge of a φ-phrase as "Option B: Leave the pronoun in its syntactically expected position, but cliticize it to a preceding word or phrase, thereby removing it from the left edge of the φ-phrase

---

[8] Constraints computed over sisters are a fundamental part of syntactic theory via head–complement relations, e.g. between participles and auxiliaries.

[9] This definition makes the computation over sisters clear; computation over sisters is not needed by Bennett et al.'s (2016: 198, (55)) definition (2016: 198, (55)): "Prosodic constituents above the level of the word should not have at their left edge an immediate subconstituent that is prosodically dependent. For our purposes here, a 'prosodically dependent' constituent is any prosodic unit smaller than the word", although they point out that StrongStart can be thought of as a special case of EqualSisters (Myrberg 2013: 75, (4)): "Sister nodes in prosodic structure are instantiations of the same prosodic category."

and avoiding a violation of STRONG START." An instance of such a repair for Samoan is shown in (14) for the prosodic parse of the ergative case marker *e*. Here, the parse of *e le malini* 'ERG DET.SG marine' in (14a) violates STRONGSTART. The case marker *e*, which we assume is an unstressed light syllable (L), is phrased *rightward*. It is at the left edge of a ϕ-phrase and sister to a ϕ-phrase—a prosodic constituent higher than a syllable in the prosodic hierarchy (2). The repaired structure (14b) instead phrases the case marker *leftward* to be dominated by the preceding ϕ and sister to a ω (*lalaŋa* 'weave'). This results in a 'bracketing paradox' since *e* is syntactically phrased to the right, as the head of the DP$_{erg}$ *e le malini* 'the marine'.

(14)   A repair of a STRONGSTART violation by prosodically phrasing a weak element to the left

   a. ϕ-initial ergative case marker *e*:   b. ϕ-final ergative case marker *e*:
      STRONGSTART violated   STRONGSTART satisfied

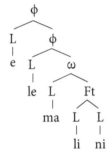
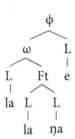

Summing up, in this section, we have introduced the idea of prosodic trees and the particular theory of the interface between syntactic and prosodic trees that we will adopt for our implementation here: Match Theory. Defining the interface means defining a map from syntactic to prosodic phonological grammar, so of course the definition of the mapping depends on the definition of syntactic grammar and the definition of prosodic phonological grammar. Our choice of implementing Match Theory doesn't commit us to some particular syntactic theory; here we follow Elfner (2012), Bennett et al. (2016), Féry 2017) in assuming aspects of bare phrase structure (Chomsky 1955), implemented with Minimalist Grammar (MG) (Stabler 1997, 2011b). As Match Theory has been stated in terms of optimality-theoretic constraint-based grammar, here we also assume such a grammar for the phonological grammar, as well as the interface so that we can interleave phonological and interface constraints. We implement the constraint-based phonological grammar using the finite state tools of xfst (Beesley and Karttunen 2003; Karttunen 1998).

4.2 Samoan syntax, spellout, prosody, and interfaces: background

Having introduced the theory of the interface assumed, in this section we introduce the particular linguistic aspects of the syntax–prosody interface in Samoan to be formalized and implemented. §4.2.1 introduces aspects of Samoan syntax and spellout relevant for the case study, based on Yu and Stabler (2017); §4.2.2 discusses current, tentative empirical evidence for aspects of Samoan prosodic constituency. §4.2.3 defines the syntax–prosody interface to be modeled for the parsing problem. Throughout, we discuss consequences of the linguistic analyses at hand for parsing.

4.2.1 Samoan syntax and spellout

Samoan is a Polynesian language with an ergative/absolutive case system (see Deal 2015 for an overview of ergativity). The two sentences in (15) show how this case system manifests: the subject of a transitive clause, e.g. *le malini* 'the marine' in (15a), is marked with a distinct case—the "ergative." The subject of an intransitive clause, e.g. *le malini* in (15b), and the object of a transitive clause, e.g. *le mamanu* 'the design' in (15a), both appear unmarked and receive "absolutive" case (Chung 1978: 54–6; Ochs 1982: 649). Samoan primarily has VSO word order in transitive clauses, as exemplified in (15a), which also shows that the transitive subject is marked by the ergative case marker *e*. The intransitive clause (15b) demonstrates that the prepositional element [i] is a marker of oblique case.

(15)   Ergative-absolutive patterns in transitive and intransitive clauses[10]
   a. Transitive clause

na	lalaŋa	*(e)	le	malini	le	mamanu.
PAST	weave	ERG	DET.SG	marine	DET.SG	design

   'The marine wove the design.'

   b. Intransitive clause

na	ŋalue	le	malini	(i	le	mamanu).
PAST	work	DET.SG	marine	OBL	DET.SG	design

   'The marine worked (on the design).'

Throughout this chapter, we use "absolutive" as an descriptive term. Under the analysis of Samoan syntax we assume—Collins (2016; 2015; 2014), following Legate (2008)—"absolutive" is in fact a default, syncretic marking of nominative and accusative case. While Massam (2001) and others have assumed that Samoan has absolutive case marking, Collins (2014) argues that Samoan is actually a language of the type Legate (2008) classifies as ABS=DEF, that is, a language where the marking that has been called "absolutive" is actually the default case marking for nominative and accusative.[11] While Collins and others originally assumed the default case marking in Samoan was null, Yu (2011; to appear) and Yu and Stabler (2017) showed that Samoan reliably presents a high edge tone (notated as H-) in these positions, immediately

---

[10] The following abbreviations are used in morphosyntactic glosses in this chapter: ABS absolutive; DET determiner; ERG ergative; GEN genitive; OBL oblique; SG singular; TOP topic marker.

[11] We follow Collins' analysis here because because it is relatively well worked out and defended, but there are various alternative views about case in Samoan and related languages (e.g Chung 1978; Bittner and Hale 1996; Massam 2006; 2012; Koopman 2012; Tollan 2015). We leave consideration of how adopting these alternative perspectives might affect the implementation of the interface and parsing to future work.

preceding the absolutive argument, as shown in (16). The specific challenge we take on here is: *How might we simultaneously parse the syntactic and prosodic structure of (16a), and how might the two different parsing tasks inform each other?* (We assume that (16a) is uttered out-of-the-blue, so that no elements are under contrastive focus, and all elements are new information to the discourse.)

(16)   Revision of (15): a high edge tone (H-) precedes absolutive arguments

  a. Transitive clause

na	lalaŋa	*(e)	le	malini	H-	le	mamanu.
PAST	weave	ERG	DET.SG	marine	ABS	DET.SG	design

  'The marine wove the design.'

  b. Intransitive clause

na	ŋalue	H-	le	malini	(i	le	mamanu).
PAST	work	ABS	DET.SG	marine	OBL	DET.SG	design

  'The marine worked (on the design).'

Yu and Stabler (2017) formalizes case marking in Samoan (whether ergative or absolutive) as a 'post-syntactic' operation (Marantz 1991; Bobaljik 2008). Under this proposal, ergative *e* and absolutive H- are inserted as pronounced reflexes of particular structural configurations. For example, DPs taken as an argument by a transitive verb are marked with ergative *e*.

We assume that (16a) has the derived post-syntactic structure (after case marking) given in (17). The tree in (17a) assumes X-bar theory (as in Yu and Stabler 2017: (11)). The tree in (17b) assumes aspects of Bare Phrase Structure (Chomsky 1995a), which is what we assume for implementation, as discussed in §4.1.2.2. We describe (17b) as "X-bar like" because it depicts aspects of both the derivational steps and the results of these derivational steps in one tree, like X-bar trees; cf. the derivational and derived trees depicted in (36), which separate the depiction of the derivational steps and the results of those steps. The structure given in (17) is almost the same structure as Yu and Stabler (2017: (11)); the difference is that the structure here abstracts away from head movement. In Yu and Stabler (2017: (11)) and Collins (2016, (66)), head movement moves T *na* to C. Here, we abstract away from head movement and focus on syntax–prosody interface issues, so the root of the tree is of category TP, not CP.[12] Following Collins (2016: (66)), verb-initial ordering is derived by fronting the VP to a functional head F below T after the arguments have been raised out of it. Phrasal movements are shown coindexed. The case markers inserted in spellout are shown as as adjoined to their arguments.

---

[12] We can handle head movement as well, as described in Yu and Stabler (2017: appendix B).

(17)

a. X-bar tree structure for (16a)   b. "X-bar like" bare phrase tree structure for (16a)

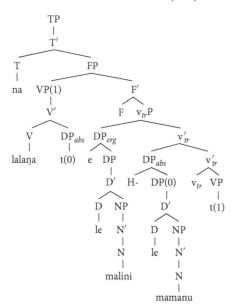

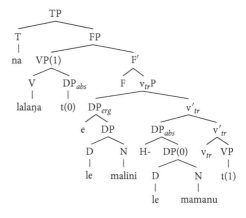

Yu and Stabler (2017: §7.1) shows that a range of syntactic structures in Samoan including those in (15)—prior to "post-syntactic" case marking—are finite-state definable on trees and can be computed with MGs. This result guarantees a range of provably correct and efficient parsing algorithms for these structures (Harkema 2000; 2001; Stabler 2013b; Fowlie and Koller 2017)—including the bottom-up MG parser we implement here. Furthermore, Yu and Stabler (2017: §7.2, appendix B) shows that the post-syntactic computation of case-marker insertion is also finite-state definable on trees and can be composed with the syntactic computations, following closure properties of MGs. Thus, the syntactic derivation and the spellout can be correctly and efficiently parsed.

Because the case marking in spellout is composable with the syntactic derivation of (16a), we can define a MG grammar for (16a) that "folds in" the spellout with the syntax, see §4.3.2. So this is the first place that prosody comes in to inform parsing: the H- is the spellout of absolutive case. Accordingly, we treat the H- not as a local cue for a prosodic domain edge, but as a (post-syntactic) lexical item in the "folded in" syntactic/post-syntactic MG grammar. Yu and Stabler (2017: fn. 28) notes that whether case marking is treated as "post-syntactic" reflex of case marking or syntactic, e.g. as a (syntactic) lexical item, is not in fact important for the point that a range of syntactic structures in Samoan and case marking can be computed with MGs and therefore correctly and efficiently parsed. We'll see that the assumption that case marking happens in spellout *does* have important and interesting implications for the computation of MATCHPHRASE in this case study: see §4.2.3.

4.2.2 Samoan prosodic constituency

Besides the tonal spellout of case, the other phonological component of our implementation of the interface is a transducer that generates a candidate set of derived prosodic trees for the sentence in (16a) that then gets passed to the MG parser for the computation of the interface. We assume that the prosodic tree for a typical production of utterance (16a) is something like the structure shown in (18): this is the prosodic tree that we would like our implementation of the interface to compute as being optimal, given the syntactic/post-syntactic analysis (17). The node labels in (18) follow the naming conventions given in (2), with the exception of node labels at the syllable level. Samoan has quantity-sensitive stress (see §4.2.2.1), so we have a finer-grained set of categories at the syllable level than just σ, and make a distinction between light (L) and heavy (H) syllables.

Empirical evidence to support the claim that this particular prosodic tree is definitely the "right" one, i.e. the prosodic structure of a typical production of (16a), is unfortunately not yet available. Moreover, there might be multiple ways to prosodically phrase the sentence in (16a)—of which this is one—while the syntactic structure remains constant. What matters for us is simply the following: (i) the structure exemplifies properties that makes this case study on Samoan interesting and relevant for work at the syntax–prosody interface, and (ii) the prosodic structure is a reasonable one given what we currently know about Samoan prosody. In (19), we highlight properties of (16a) that make it interesting and relevant as a case study. In the sections following, §4.2.2.1 and §4.2.2.2, we defend the claim that the prosodic structure (18) fits with the currently available empirical evidence. In (18), primary stress is indicated with the IPA diacritic ˈ.

(18)   A prosodic structure for (16a) on page 84 that fits the current empirical evidence

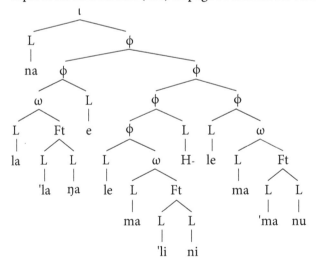

(19)   Properties of interest in the prosodic tree (18) for our case study
   a. The tonal case marker *H-* is treated as an element alongside segmental material in the input string. (See discussion of case marking and H- tones in §4.2.1).

b. The case markers, ergative *e* and absolute *H-*, are phrased to the left. Syntactically, they are phrased to the right in (17). (See discussion of STRONGSTART and "bracketing paradoxes" in §4.1.2.4).[13]

c. Each of the case markers is a (light) syllable immediately dominated by a category two levels higher in the prosodic hierarchy, a φ-phrase. (See discussion of EXHAUSTIVITY in §4.1.2.4.)

d. *na*, the tense marker initiating the sentence, is a (light) syllable immediately dominated by a category much higher in the prosodic hierarchy, an intonational phrase (ι). (See discussion of EXHAUSTIVITY in §4.1.2.4.)

e. There is recursivity in the tree in §4.1.2.4: φ-phrases dominate other φ-phrases. (See discussion of NONRECURSIVITY in §4.1.2.4.)

The inclusion of *H-* as material to be prosodically parsed allows us to model one way to factor out how diverse prosodic information is used for syntactic analysis. As a "post-syntactic" lexical item, H- provides information that guides the syntactic parse—it comes into the computation of MATCHPHRASE only through its role in the composed syntactic derivation and spellout. However, the prosodic parse (18) into φ-phrases, ω's, etc. is a candidate prosodic parse which enters in the computation of MATCHPHRASE, a computation that checks the alignment of a prosodic parse to the (post-)syntactic parse. The encliticization of the case markers, despite their being being syntactically phrased rightward, exemplifies a typologically common instantiation of "bracketing paradoxes". The violations of EXHAUSTIVITY and NONRECURSIVITY are also typical in current interface analyses, as described in §4.1.2.4. Thus, the assumed prosodic tree (18) clearly factors aspects of the syntax–prosody interface and exemplifies a number of properties that are typical in the analyses of a number of prosodic systems.

In the work here, we implement a phonological transducer that chunks an utterance into prosodic constituents using the categories of the prosodic hierarchy defined in (2). As a consequence—since stress assignment is defined over the prosodic domain of the prosodic word—the transducer also assigns stress to the individual content words, following Zuraw et al. (2014); Yu (2018) (primary stress is shown in (18)). Thus, where stress is observed gives us some clues about what the prosodic structure of an uttered sentence might be at the lower levels of the prosodic hierarchy. §4.2.2.1 describes how stress tells us about prosodic constituency up to the level of the prosodic word. In addition, we use preliminary evidence from studying phonological phrasing in a spoken corpus of Samoan fable retellings (Moyle 1981) to help support hypotheses about the prosodic structure at higher levels of the prosodic hierarchy in §4.2.2.2.

---

[13] The promotion of *lalaŋa* to a φ-phrase upon encliticization of the ergative *e* contravenes the Function Word Adjunction Principle hypothesized for Irish in Elfner (2012: 145). This states that when a function word (that isn't a prosodic word) is adjoined to a prosodic category of type β, the node at the adjunction has the same category β. But the current empirical evidence suggests that in Samoan, weak function words like *e* don't fall inside prosodic words (see §4.2.2.1). We leave further consideration of "prosodic adjunction" to future work.

4.2.2.1 Samoan word-level prosody: stress assignment

The basic primary stress pattern in Samoan is moraic trochees at the right edge, exemplified in (20), adapted from Zuraw et al. (2014: (4)). Footing is indicated with parentheses, and periods indicate syllable boundaries. If the final syllable is light (one mora), primary stress falls on the penult; if the final syllable is heavy (two moras), primary stress falls on the final syllable. So feet may be formed from a single heavy syllable ('H) or as two light syllables, with the first receiving primary stress: ('LL). In both cases, the foot is bimoraic, i.e., it has two moras.

(20)   Basic primary stress pattern: moraic trochees at the right edge
        . . . L('H)#   la.('vaː)   'energized'
        . . . ('LL)#   ('ma.nu)   'bird'
        . . . L('LL)#   i.('ŋo.a)   'name'

The phonological analysis we assume for stress assignment in Samoan is adapted from the optimality-theoretic analysis in Zuraw et al. (2014). For this case study, we leave aside some of the complexities treated there. Specifically, we abstract away from secondary stress assignment, effects of segmental features on stress assignment (like the complexities of vowel–vowel and vowel–vowel–vowel sequences, and epenthetic vowels), and morphologically complex words. However, we also tentatively expand beyond the phonological analysis in Zuraw et al. (2014) since it doesn't treat prosodic constituency above the level of the prosodic word: see the immediately following section, §4.2.2.2.

The constraint set for stress assignment in this chapter is a a subset of the constraints used in Yu's (2018) implementation of Zuraw et al. (2014)'s analysis, up to an additional inviolable constraint, HEADEDNESS. Besides removing constraints that are only relevant for segments, morphologically complex words and multiple prosodic words as in Yu (2018: §2.4), we also remove constraints relevant only for secondary stress assignment. The remaining constraints are given in (21); see Yu (2018) for more details on some slight differences between the definitions of these constraints in (21) vs. the definitions in Zuraw et al. (2014). For the purposes of our case study, since we consider only primary stress in monomorphs, we can treat all these constraints as "undominated" (no constraints are ranked above any of these constraints) and thus inviolable. This means that surviving prosodic parse candidates must satisfy each one of these constraints. We include the additional inviolable HEADEDNESS constraint instead of dominated PARSE-σ for simplicity of implementation. This way, all phonological constraints ranked above the interface constraint MATCHPARSE are inviolable.[14]

---

[14] For simplicity, we keep all (purely) phonological constraints except STRONGSTART undominated in the work here, since the focus is on the interaction of the interface constraint MATCHPHRASE with the purely phonological constraints. What's of interest here is simply whether a phonological constraint is ranked above or below MATCHPHRASE—not whether it is violable. We can, however, straightforwardly handle a series of ranked constraints, using an operation called "lenient composition" (Karttunen 1998), as illustrated in Yu (2018).

(21)   Constraints for primary stress assignment, all inviolable
   • FOOTBINARITY (FOOTBIN) A foot must contain exactly two moras.
   • RHYTHMTYPE=TROCHEE (RHTYPE=TROCHEE) A foot must have stress on its
     initial mora, and its initial mora only.
   • ALIGN(PWD,R; 'FT,R) (EDGEMOST-R) The end of the prosodic word must
     coincide with the end of a primary-stressed foot.
   • ALIGN(PWD;L,FT,L) The beginning of the prosodic word must coincide with
     the beginning of a foot.
   • HEADEDNESS(Ft) Any prosodic word must dominate a foot.

The definition of the constraints for stress assignment in (21) make it clear how
stress assignment is dependent on prosodic constituency: every constraint definition
refers to the foot, or the prosodic word, or both. Constraints on the position of stress
are defined in terms of the foot and the prosodic word (RHYTHMTYPE=TROCHEE and
ALIGN(PWD,R; 'FT,R)). The other constraints regulate how an utterance is chunked
into prosodic words and feet.

What does stress assignment—which is observable in elicitations with language
consultants[15]—tell us about prosodic constituency in the sentence to be parsed (16a)?
In elicitations with language consultants, the content words in the sentence *na lalaŋa
e le malini H- le mamanu* all receive penultimate stress when uttered in isolation or
when uttered as part of the sentence. Under the inviolable constraints in (21), we can
therefore infer the prosodic subtree for [ma.'li.ni] 'marine' and the other content words
([la.'la.ŋa] 'weave', [ma.'ma.nu] 'design') to be that shown in (22).

(22)   Prosodic constituency for [ma.'li.ni] and other content words in (16a)

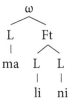

What about stress assignment for the functional elements in the sentence—the case
markers *e*, the determiner *le*, and for that matter, also the H-? First, we'll consider
e and *le*. These segmental function words do not show evidence of being stressed
when they are uttered in (16a): they never receive pitch accents, as far as we can
tell.[16] This means they cannot form a prosodic word alone. Moreover, there's no
positive evidence that they get incorporated into a prosodic word, if they are adjacent
to one: having these monomoraic functional elements uttered alongside the content

---

[15] See Zuraw et al. (2014) for a discussion of the phonetic realization of stress in Samoan.

[16] Perhaps the specific determiner *le* could receive a pitch accent under contrastive focus, with an alternative set
of non-specific determiners; we haven't tested this. Additionally, Yu and Stabler (2017: fig. 9, §6) shows examples
where case markers immediately after a pause are uttered with a "pitch reset." It could be that these are instances
when monomoraic functional elements are promoted to full prosodic words and receive stress. In any case, *e* and
le do not appear after pauses in the utterance parsed in this chapter, and so aren't in a context where they might
receive stress.

words does not affect stress assignment in the content words. Contrast this with the rightward primary stress shift that occurs with suffixation of the nominalizing, monomoraic -ŋa: [ŋa.'lu.e] 'work (V)' + -[ŋa] → [ˌŋa.lu.'e-ŋa] 'work (N)' (Zuraw et al. 2014: 309, (57)). We observe no such stress shift with [la.'la.ŋa] 'weave' + [e] 'erg' → [la.'la.ŋa e], *[''la.la.'ŋa.e]. Similarly, in a monomorphemic sequence of five light syllables, the observed stress pattern has an initial dactyl—with secondary stress on the first syllable: ((ˌte.mo)_{Ft}ka('la.si)_{Ft})_ω 'democracy' (Zuraw et al. 2014: 281, (8)). But we've never observed *[ˌe.le.ma.'li.ni], which is also a string of five lights, nor do we observe *[ˌla.la.ŋa.'e.le].[17] In sum, we tentatively conclude that the determiner and segmental case markers in Samoan are neither individual prosodic words nor are they chunked together in a prosodic word with neighboring content words in utterances of (16a). (An alternative would be to assume that the function words form recursive prosodic words with neighboring content words, and say that the only the deepest prosodic word is the domain of stress.) Rather, a reasonable structure for *e le malini* in the utterance of (16a) might be something like the right-branching prosodic subtree in (23), with *e* and *le* outside the ω. This leads us into prosodic constituency above the level of the prosodic word, where we'll also consider the prosodic phrasing of the H-.

(23)   A possible prosodic subtree for *e le malini* in the utterance of (16a)

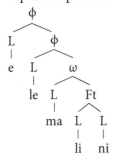

4.2.2.2 Samoan prosodic constituency above the prosodic word

There is some evidence that suggests that (23) is not, in fact, the most plausible prosodic structure for *e le malini*. Rather, there is reason to support the hypothesis that both ergative *e* and absolute H- are prosodically phrased to the left in a bracketing paradox, as in the STRONGSTART repair in (14); see e.g. see prosodic structures below in (24). We'll refer to case markers phrased like this descriptively as being "encliticized." In (24), ergative *e* is encliticized to preceding VP *lalaŋa* and absolutive H- is encliticized to preceding agent DP *le malini*. These prosodic trees satisfy STRONGSTART, but violate MATCHPHRASE.

---

[17] Zuraw et al. (2014) shows that five-mora loanwords can also surface with the stress pattern LˌLL'LL in the presence of epenthetic vowels, but we don't observe that stress pattern either.

(24)   Prosodic structures with case markers phrased to the left
        a. Encliticized φ-initial ergative *e*   b. Encliticized φ-initial absolute H-

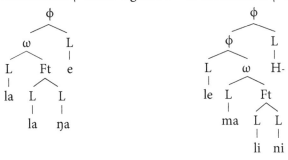

While the idea of an encliticized high tone may seem bizarre, we'll build up the case for it by first turning to evidence for encliticization of segmental monomoraic function words like ergative *e*. Unfortunately, we haven't yet found phonological processes besides stress shift that can potentially reveal prosodic constituency. But there has been work that has made connections between speech planning and prosodic chunking (e.g. Wagner 2012; Himmelmann 2014; Krivokapić 2014). In particular, in studies of corpora of unscripted English, German, and Tagalog retellings of a silent film called the *Pear Story* (Chafe 1980), Himmelmann (2014) found that articles and prepositions in English and German and Tagalog "phrase markers" were "frequently separated from their lexical hosts by disfluencies." That is, pauses and other disfluencies often occur between a function word phrased to the left and its following lexical (morphosyntactic) host. For example, *And that's the end of the … story* (Himmelmann 2014: 935, (5)). Moreover, there's an asymmetry in the distribution of disfluencies: they tended to occur after function words breaking them off from their following host, rather than occur before function words. Himmelmann (2014) places this asymmetry at the center of a speech planning/production account for the strong typological asymmetry that syntactic proclitics are often prosodically enclitic, while syntactic enclitics are rarely prosodically proclitic.

Following the methods in Himmelmann (2014), we've found some very preliminary evidence for encliticization of function words from studying phonological phrasing in a spoken corpus of unscripted Samoan fable retellings (Moyle 1981) (ongoing, joint work with Matthew Frelinger). While we haven't yet completed a quantitative study, we've certainly found a number of cases where case markers and even determiners are followed by disfluencies (e.g. in (25) below, recording available at http://www.fagogo.auckland.ac.nz/content.html?id=1). In (25), there are hesitations (which we indicate informally with …) between the determiner *le* and its following host noun, and between the topic marker *o* and its following proper name.

(25)   Example of disfluencies after function words in unscripted Samoan fable
        retellings collected in Moyle (1981)
        a. ʔo   le…   ulugaːliʔi.   ʔo   le   iŋoa   o   le   tama
           TOP   DET.SG couple   TOP   DET.SG name   GEN   DET.SG boy
           ʔo…   ʔulafala-Manoŋi-Sasala-ʔi-Tausala
           TOP   Ulafala-Manogi-Sasala-Tausala
           'There was once a couple; the young man's name was Ulafa-Manogi-Sasala-
           Tausala.'

What about the case for the encliticization of the absolute H-? A puzzling fact about the phonetic realization of the H- is that the associated peak in fundamental frequency (the acoustic correlate of pitch) occurs on the phonological material *pre-ceding* the absolutive argument, not on the absolutive argument (Yu to appear). As described in Yu and Özyıldız (2016) and Yu (to appear), one explanation for this tonal "encliticization" is that diachronically, the absolutive H- may be the remnant of a segmental absolutive particle *ia*. The particle *ia* is bimoraic and also seems to be stressed, while the other case markers and many other function words are monomoraic and unstressed. In contemporary Samoan, the usage of *ia* seems very much in flux and deprecated, but speakers do have systematic intuitions about its distribution and produce it sometimes reduced to monomoraic [jɛ]. If, like other function words (including case markers), this (possibly reduced) *ia* was also encliticized, then as the segmental material may have been reduced and elided, the associated pitch accent may have been left behind and also realized leftward.

In sum, there is some (admittedly speculative, preliminary) evidence for the encliticization of case markers. We therefore tentatively assume that the optimal prosodic trees computed in this case study should have prosodic structures like (24) that satisfy STRONGSTART but result in violations of MATCHPHRASE. Accordingly, we include STRONGSTART as a prosodic markedness constraint at the level above the prosodic word. Following the mainstream trend in interface work, we also assume HEADEDNESS (Any C^i must dominate a C^{i-1} (except if $C_i = \sigma$), e.g., a PWd must dominate a Ft) and LAYEREDNESS (No C^i dominates a C^j, $j > i$, e.g., no σ dominates a Ft) to be inviolable (see 11). We also assume BINARITY at all levels of the prosodic hierarchy (12). As we'll see in §4.2.3, a high-ranking BINARITY constraint can prune out prosodic parses with unary branches early on. While it may be the case that BINARITY constraints don't (all) need to be inviolable for the desired prosodic parse to be computed as optimal, we implemented them as such to prune the candidate set and reduce the processing load (otherwise, xfst ran out of memory). Finally, we restrict the prosodic parses to ones where a single intonational phrase exhaustively dominates the entire input. Sentences like (16a) can be uttered as multiple intonational phrases, but not usually in typical conversational speech.

4.2.3 The Samoan syntax–prosody interface

So far, we've enumerated phonological constraints for stress assignment and prosodic chunking up to the level of the prosodic word (21), as well as phonological markedness constraints active at higher levels in the prosodic hierarchy (§4.2.2.2). We've also introduced MATCHPHRASE as an interface constraint. Here, we'll discuss how we're ranking the interface constraint MATCHPHRASE relative to the various phonological constraints (§4.2.3.1). We'll also explain how we'll apply MATCHPHRASE to the composed syntactic/spellout tree (§4.2.3.2).

4.2.3.1 Constraint ranking: an interface constraint interleaved between phonological constraints

In constraint-based analyses of the interface in the literature, interface constraints often are ranked to be interleaved between higher-ranked and lower-ranked (purely) phonological constraints, so this is a property that we'd like to model in our case study. We already mentioned in §4.2.2.1 that all the phonological constraints relevant for stress assignment and prosodic parsing up to the level of the prosodic word are undominated. In §4.2.2.2, we also explained why HEADEDNESS and BINARITY constraints above the level of the prosodic word are treated as undominated. However, we rank STRONGSTART below MATCHPHRASE. This means that all phonological constraints except STRONGSTART are used to winnow down the candidate set of prosodic parses to be submitted to the MG parser. The MG parser is then used to compute MATCHPHRASE, given the syntactic analysis in (17b). Finally, the remaining prosodic candidates—those with the fewest violations of MATCHPHRASE—are passed to STRONGSTART for the final winnowing step to compute the optimal candidate.

The two prosodic parse candidates in (26) help provide an argument for ranking STRONGSTART below MATCHPHRASE. These two candidates are submitted to the MG parser because they satisfy all the inviolable phonological constraints. Moreover, each candidate has only a single violation of STRONGSTART, due to the stray syllable [na] at the left edge of the intonational phrase. However, as we'll show in the next section, §4.2.3.2, the optimal prosodic parse Candidate 9 (18) has 3 STRONGSTART violations. We'll also see in §4.2.3.2, that Candidate 9 incurs no MATCHPHRASE violations, while the prosodic trees in (26) each incur 3 (under our extension of the definition of MATCHPHRASE to post-syntactic material in (27)). Therefore, under our constraint set, STRONGSTART must be ranked below MATCHPHRASE to keep Candidate 9 from being pruned out before being submitted to the MG parser.

(26) Prosodic candidates with only 1 STRONGSTART violation submitted to MG parser

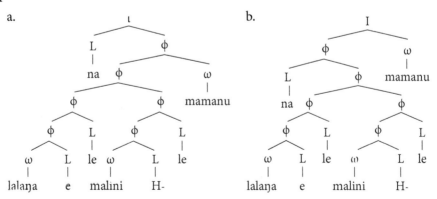

4.2.3.2 Extending the definition of MATCHPHRASE to spellout

The definition of MATCHPHRASE given in (5) and explicated in §4.1.2.3 doesn't extend to post-syntactic material; but the insertion of case markers e and H- and derivation steps involving the phrases they project, DP_{erg} and DP_{abs}, are post-syntactic and composed with the syntactic lexical item insertion and derivation in this case study. Therefore, we need to extend the definition of MATCHPHRASE. We extend it as stated in (27). The motivation for defining the extension this way will become clear by the end of this section.

(27)   Extension of MATCHPHRASE to spellout
    a. Maximal projections derived post-syntactically, e.g. DP_{erg} and DP_{abs}, are not in the domain of MATCHPHRASE. Only maximal projections derived *syntactically* are. Thus, MATCHPHRASE is not assessed for either DP_{erg} or DP_{abs}.

    b. Phonological material inserted post-syntactically, e.g. ergative *e* and absolutive H-, is visible to prosodic parsing, but not to MATCHPHRASE. That is, the case markers are parsed prosodically like any other morpheme, and the resulting prosodic parse is entirely visible to MATCHPHRASE, but the case markers aren't visible as phonological exponents for MATCHPHRASE.

      For instance, since [lalaŋa] 'weave' projects to a VP in (17b), it incurs a MATCHPHRASE violation unless it also projects to a φ-phrase. But the prosodic subtree (24a) does not incur a MATCHPHRASE violation even though [lalaŋa] projects to a prosodic word, because the encliticization of *e* to the prosodic word forms a φ-phrase. Even though the φ-phrase dominates both [lalaŋa] and *e*, since the phonological exponent *e* is invisible to MATCHPHRASE, there is a φ-phrase that dominates only [lalaŋa].

With the syntactic analysis in (28a) (repeated from (17b) above), the constraint ranking defined in §4.2.3.1, and the extension of the definition of MATCHPHRASE given in (27), we compute (28d) to be an optimal prosodic parse (repeated from (18) above), and filter out the prosodic parse (28c), which is isomorphic to the flattened bare syntactic tree (28b). The prosodic tree (28d) abstracts over prosodic structure below the word level that is shown in (18), e.g. it doesn't show the footing of [malini]. This abstraction makes the comparison to the (post-)syntactic trees more transparent. We call this prosodic tree Candidate 9 in our implementation.

(28)
a. bare syntactic tree for (16a)

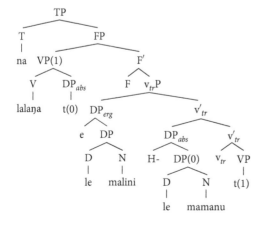

b. flattened bare syntactic tree for (16a)

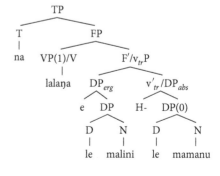

c. prosodic tree isomorphic to (b)   d. "actual" prosodic tree (Candidate 9)

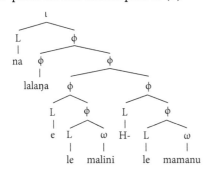 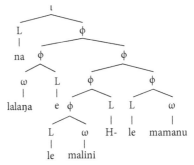

Both (28c) and (28d) incur no violations of MATCHPHRASE. (28c) is isomorphic to the flattened bare tree (28b), and (28d) incurs no violations because of the definition (27) of the extension of MATCHPHRASE to post-syntactic material: the encliticization of post-syntactic e to [lalaŋa] forms a φ-phrase that corresponds to the VP dominating [lalaŋa], and the encliticization of the case markers results in no MATCHPHRASE violations for DP_{erg} or DP_{abs} because those are post-syntactic maximal projections—not syntactic ones. Both these prosodic parses violate phonological constraints, though. Candidate (28c) has 5 STRONGSTART violations, due to the prosodification of the light syllables [na], [e], [H-], [le], and [le]; candidate (28d) has only 3 STRONGSTART violations, due to the prosodification of [na], [le], and [le]. In addition, (28c) incurs a violation of BINARITY because of the unary branch to [lalaŋa]. Therefore, (28c) is actually never even passed to the MG parser at the interface, since BINARITY is ranked above MATCHPHRASE and undominated.

There are two other prosodic parse candidates passed to the MG parser besides Candidate 9 (28d) that incur no violations of our extended definition of MATCH-PHRASE: Candidate 10 (29a) and Candidate 7 (29b). Candidate 10 has 4 STRONGSTART violations due to the prosodification of [na], [H-], [le], and [le], while Candidate 7 has only 3—the same number as Candidate 9—due to the prosodification of [na], [le], and [le]. Thus, Candidate 7 is also computed to be an optimal candidate, alongside Candidate 9, while Candidate 10 is filtered out by STRONGSTART when the remaining parses are passed back from the MG parser. The survival of an additional candidate to Candidate 9 was a surprise to us during the implementation, demonstrating the importance of implementation to check our analyses. Generally, a constraint-based grammar is expected to compute a single optimal candidate among the input candidate set—if this isn't the case, then it's assumed that the analyst has missed some crucial constraint(s). The difference between the two winning candidates is whether the absolutive H- is encliticized to the prosodic word [malini] (Candidate 7), or if it is enclitized to the φ-phrase [le malini] (Candidate 9). In this case, we don't find the difference between Candidate 7 and 9 to be one that points clearly to some missed constraint, or one that might be empirically observable (at least given our current understanding of the Samoan syntax–prosody interface).

(29)   Other prosodic parses with no MATCHPHRASE violations

a. Candidate 10   b. Candidate 7: also a winning candidate

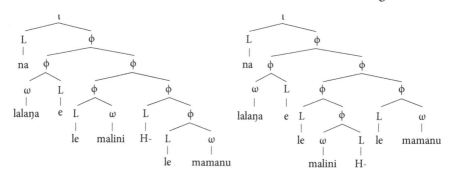

Now we are ready to motivate the extension of MATCHPHRASE to post-syntactic material (27). Suppose, *contra* (27a), that we included maximal projections derived post-syntactically in the domain of MATCHPHRASE. If we did, then the encliticization of the ergative case marker *e* and the absolutive case marker H- would result in a violation of MATCHPHRASE for DP_{erg} and DP_{abs}, respectively. Then, since our desired winning candidates, Candidates 7 (29b) and 9 (28d), enclitize both case markers, each would incur 2 violations of MATCHPHRASE—one for DP_{erg}, and one for DP_{abs}. However, Candidate 10 (29a), which encliticizes only the H-, would incur just 1 MATCHPHRASE violation. The desired winning candidates would therefore both be filtered out by this alternate extension of MATCHPHRASE.

Turning to the second part of the definition (27b), suppose, *contra* (27b), that phonological elements inserted post-syntactically, e.g. ergativ *e* and absolutive H-, were visible as phonological exponents for MATCHPHRASE. Then we could not repair the MATCHPHRASE violation incurred by mapping a VP to a prosodic word for *lalaŋa* by the encliticization of ergative *e*, as in (24a). The VP would dominate a singleton set of terminals {*lalaŋa*}, while the φ-phrase would dominate the set of terminals {*lalaŋa, e*}, still resulting in a MATCHPHRASE violation. We also would incur other MATCHPHRASE violations due to encliticization. For example, the FP in (28b) would dominate the terminals {*e, le, malini, H-, le, mamanu*}, but its correspondent φ-phrase in (28d) would dominate only {*le, malini, H-, le, mamanu*}. We'll discuss the extension of MATCHPHRASE to post-syntactic material further in §4.4.

This concludes the presentation of background and overview of the implementation of prosodically informed parsing of an utterance of (16a). The next section, §4.3, builds on this section to explicate the full implementation.

4.3 Samoan syntax, spellout, prosody, and interfaces: implementation

We present the implementation of the computation of the interface and parsing in three sections. First, in §4.3.1, we describe the implementation of the phonological transducer in xfst that generates and filters prosodic parses to arrive at a final candidate set to submit to the MG parser. Then, in §4.3.2, we define the MG syntactic/post-syntactic lexicon that derives the assumed (post)-syntactic tree (17b). Finally, in §4.3.3, we describe the implementation of the MG parser to simultaneously syntactically parse (16a) and compute MATCHPHRASE for the submitted prosodic parses, returning only the prosodic parses with the fewest violations of MATCHPHRASE to be evaluated by STRONGSTART. The final STRONGSTART transduction is described in §4.3.4. The code for the implementation is available at https://github.com/krismyu/smo-prosodic-parsing.

4.3.1 Generation of candidate prosodic parses with an xfst transducer

We generate the set of candidate prosodic parses to be submitted to the MG parser by defining a phonological transducer in xfst that adds prosodic markup to the input, an utterance of (16a), *na lalaŋa e le malini H- le mamanu*. It is based on the finite state optimality-theoretic foot-based grammar fragment for Samoan word-level prosody defined in Yu (2018: §2.4), but is simplified to abstract away from secondary stress, and also extended to parse the input into prosodic constituents higher than the prosodic word, as described in §4.2.2. The transduction results in a set of 36 prosodic parses to be passed to the MG parser.

We represent an utterance of *na lalaŋa e le malini hi le mamanu* as an input string of syllables marked for weight (light (L) or heavy (H)) and morphosyntactic word boundaries (+), as in (4.3.1). The [ŋ] is transcribed as 'g', following Samoan orthography, and the *H-* as 'hi'.

(30) Input to the xfst transducer that adds markup indicating prosodic constituency
      `+[L,na]+[L,la] [L,la] [L,ga]+[L,e]+[L,le]+[L,ma]`
      `[L,li] [L,ni]+[L,hi]+[L,le]+[L,ma] [L,ma] [L,nu]+`

For instance, `+[L,e]+` denotes that the syllable *e* is its own morphosyntactic word (as it is immediately preceded and succeeded by +), and that it is a light syllable (as indicated by L). The generated parses contain markup indicating left and right edges of following prosodic constituents, enumerated from highest to lowest level, see (31), cf. the prosodic hierarchy given in (2).

(31) Markup indicating left and right edges of prosodic constituents enumerated in (2)
      a. Intonational phrase (IP) - . . ._
      b. (Maximal) Phonological phrase (PhP$_{max}$) z . . . z
      c. (Non-minimal) Phonological phrase (PhP$_{nmin}$) Y . . . y
      d. (Functional) Phonological phrase (PhP$_{fxn}$) X . . . x
      e. (Minimal) Phonological phrase (PhP$_{min}$) < . . . >
      f. Prosodic word (PWd) { . . . }
      g. Foot (Ft) (. . .)
      h. Syllable [L, . . .] (Light), [H, . . .] (Heavy)

The definition of prosodic structure we gave in §4.1.2.1 and §4.1.2.2 allows for recursivity in prosodic trees, as exhibited in the recursive φ-phrases in (18). But our implementation is not truly recursive: *we allow recursion only up to finite bounds.* Different levels of embedding in φ-phrases—four in total—are indicated by different prosodic markup given in (31). Imposing finite bounds is a methodological abstraction, not a theoretical stance. Maintaining distinct markup for each level of φ-phrase allows us to have a simple implementation of MATCHPHRASE for this first case study. Namely, we can assess whether MATCHPHRASE is violated using just the prosodically marked-up string, as detailed in §4.3.3.2. If we allowed recursion to arbitrary depth, we'd have to compare non-isomorphic prosodic and syntactic trees. We discuss the implications of prosodic recursion to arbitrary depth for parsing further in §4.4.

A sketch of the algorithm defined for the xfst transduction is given in §4.3.1. The output from each step is the input to the following step. The basic structure of the algorithm is to loop over alternating steps of overgeneration of parses and pruning at each level in the prosodic hierarchy. HEADEDNESS is not used to prune parses for φ-phrases above the level of non-minimal φ-phrases in Step (i) in (32). As long as at least one φ-phrase has been introduced, i.e. at the level of PhP_{min}, then an intonational phrase will dominate a φ-phrase. Each step in the algorithm is implemented as a transducer, and the entire transduction is a cascade of these individual transduction composed together.

(32)   Sketch of xfst transduction to generate prosodic parses
   a. **define** input string (30)
   b. **overgenerate** candidates for stress assignment to input string
   c. **overgenerate** stress-marked, foot-parsed candidates
   d. **prune** using foot-based constraints in (21)
   e. **overgenerate** prosodic-word parsed candidates
   f. **prune** prosodic word parses using prosodic-word-based constraints in (21)[18]
   g. **overgenerate** candidates parsed into minimal phonological phrases (PhP_{min})
   h. **prune** with HEADEDNESS(PhP_{min}) and BINARITY
   i. **for** phonological phrases PhP in (PhP_{fxn}, PhP_{nmin}, PhP_{max}):
      i. **overgenerate** candidates parsed into PhP
      ii. **prune** with BINARITY
   j. **overgenerate** candidates parsed into intonational phrases (IPs)
   k. **prune** with HEADEDNESS(IP), BINARITY, and for input to be exhaustively parsed into a single IP

---

[18] In addition to those constraints, we also prune using NOFUNCTIONWDPWD: Don't parse function words as prosodic words. This is purely an implementational detail, to reduce the number of candidates remaining at this stage from 28 to 2. Whether it is included or not does not affect the resulting set of candidates passed to the MG parser. It is included only to reduce the amount of processing needed in the transduction.

4.3.2 Syntactic/post-syntactic grammar fragment: MG lexicon and derivation

Once the prosodic parses have been filtered by the phonological constraints ranked above MATCHPHRASE, they are submitted to the MG parser. For our case study, we assume that the sentence to be parsed, (16a), is not ambiguous. Therefore, we define the MG grammar to admit only the parse shown in the derived structure (17b). We will not give a detailed explication of MGs here. For a leisurely introduction to minimalist grammars, including a comparison to Minimalism, see Graf (2013: chs. 1 and 2). Graf (p. 8) informally summarizes the fundamental characteristics of MGs with five points, given in (33).

(33)   Graf (2013: 8)'s informal description of the feature calculus of MGs
   a. Lexical items (LIs) consist of a (possibly null) phonetic exponent and one or more features.
   b. Features come in two polarities, and both Merge and Move delete exactly two features that differ only in their polarity.
   c. Each LI's features are linearly ordered and must be checked in that order.
   d. Besides checking features, Merge and Move also build phrase structure trees in the familiar way.
   e. The Shortest Move Constraint blocks every configuration where more than one phrase can be moved in order to check a given feature.

Given that MGs are feature-driven as described in (33), an MG is specified by its lexicon, where each lexical item specifies some phonological content (here we use IPA transcription, except for the high edge tone) and a sequence of features. Below we define the lexicon we use to derive and parse (16a). It suffices for the derivation here, and is inspired by—but much simplified from—Collins (2016; 2014). The lexicon has an unusual property that makes it different from typical minimalist lexicons (e.g. the first lexicon given in appendix B in Yu and Stabler (2017), which is similar to the one here). It is a syntactic *and post-syntactic* lexicon rather than a purely syntactic lexicon, and the case-marking rules in spellout are folded into the transduction rules, as well. The lexicon thus includes the case markers *e* and H- (here, notated as *hi*), as case-marked DPs, too. As discussed and justified in §4.2.3 and §4.2.2.2, the (tonal) H- enters the MG no differently than segmental lexical items, i.e. the same way as the ergative [e].

The definition of the lexicon below follows standard MG notation. For instance, ε indicates an empty functional head, '::' indicates that the item is lexical and not derived, and the feature '=D' indicates that a DP is to be selected. The feature '+EPP:D' triggers the movement of a '-EPP:D' phrase to a specifier; and the feature +EPP:V triggers the movement of a '-EPP:V' phrase to a specifier.

(34)   MG lexicon for the syntactic derivation and spellout of (16a)

na::=F T	'past', selects FP to form T
ε::=v_{tr} +EPP:V F	selects v_{tr}p, moves -EPP:V, to form F
lalaŋa::=D_{abs} V -EPP:V	'weave', selects DP_{abs} to form VP, then moves to EPP
hi::=D D_{abs} -EPP:D	selects D to form DP_{abs}, then moves to EPP
e::=D D_{erg}	selects D to form DP_{erg}
le::=N D	selects NP to form DP
malini::N	'marine', noun
mamanu::N	'design', noun
ε::=V +EPP:D =D_{erg} v_{tr}	selects VP, moves EPP:D, selects DP_{erg} to form v

Given the lexicon in (34), (16a) can be derived using standard MG Merge and Move rules. This derivation—that is, the actual step-by-step process, not the result of the derivation—is depicted in the "augmented derivation tree" (see Graf 2013: 12–15) in (35). The tree displays the lexical items as leaves at the point in which they enter the derivation, and internal nodes are labeled with the operation taking place at that point and the feature being checked.[19]

(35)   An augmented derivation tree showing the composed derivation and spellout of (16a) given the MG lexicon in (34)

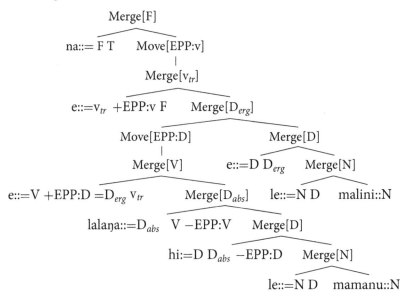

A simplified derivation tree is given in (36a) below. This is the same depiction as the augmented derivation tree (35), but with node labels for Merge and Move operations abbreviated to reduce notational clutter. Following standard practice for MG derivation trees, • indicates a Merge step, while ∘ indicates a Move step. We can

---

[19] As pointed out in Graf (2013: 13), an augmented derivation tree can be described as a "strictly binary branching multi-dominance tree", since a subtree could be involved in both Merge and Move operations. For completeness, we could indicate movement dependencies in (35) with lines between the dependents in the pairs (Move[EPP:v], lalaŋa::=V -EPP:V) and (Move[EPP:D], hi::=D D_{abs} -EPP:D), but doing so is redundant since the dependency is already specified in the lexicon.

also straightforwardly transduce the derivation tree (35) into the derived bare tree (36b), similar to the Bare Phrase Structure trees in Chomsky (1955), as well as the X-bar-like bare tree (36c). The derived tree (36b) shows the result of the derivation (36a) at each step. The lexical items are stripped of their feature stacks because all their features have been consumed by the point they are shown in the tree. The interior nodes are labeled with arrows < and > that point to the projecting head after each derivational step—as noted in Graf (2013: 23), derived trees generated by MGs, e.g. (36b), are *ordered* trees. MGs are defined this way because ordered trees, compared to unordered ones, are well-behaved mathematically. The ordering is the same as that obtained by the c-command linearization algorithm of Kayne (1994).[20]

(36)

a. derivation tree for (16a)

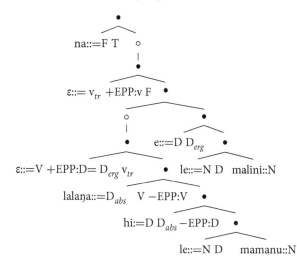

b. derived bare tree

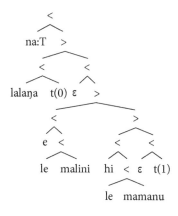

c. "X-bar-like" bare tree

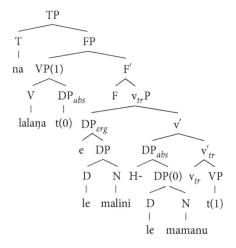

---

[20] Note that the property that MG derivations result in ordered trees sets aside issues about linearization that are of interest to linguists, including the role of prosodic information in linearization considered in Richards (2010) and Bennett et al. (2016). But MGs can also be used to model different linearization procedures by adding additional assumptions to the machinery of MGs (e.g. Graf 2012)—we leave these issues to further work.

Further details about the definitions of Merge and Move operations in MGs become important in the implementation of MATCHPHRASE. We introduce those in §4.3.3.

4.3.3 Simultaneous (post-)syntactic parsing and MATCHPHRASE computation

Harkema (2000; 2001); Stabler (2013b); and Fowlie and Koller (2017) have already defined a range of provably correct and efficient parsing algorithms for MG structures like the ones we've defined in the previous section. We implement one of these, a bottom-up parser for MGs without head movement (Harkema 2001: ch. 4), adapted from code in Stabler (2013a: 110–22). We use it to simultaneously (post-)syntactically parse (16a) and compute MATCHPHRASE. We first explain the implementation of the bottom-up parser for (post-)syntactic analysis in §4.3.3.1. Then we explain how MATCHPHRASE is computed during the (post-)syntactic parse in §4.3.3.2.

4.3.3.1 Bottom-up (post)-syntactic parsing of MGs

We repeat the derivation tree for (16a) in (38), first introduced in §4.3.2. It is annotated at each node with the alphabetic label of the individual derivation step being depicted, where the labels come from the 11-step derivation given in (40). The derivation steps in (40) are given in a reformulated, tuple notation (Harkema 2001: §4.1–4.3) that is used by the parser. The Merge and Move functions can also be reformulated in this notation into several different functions and are exemplified in (41) using steps from (40). We'll discuss these functions in more detail when we describe the implementation of MATCHPARSE in §4.3.3.2. The numbers in parentheses in the reformulated notation define the span of an expression generated by the grammar and refer to the string yield of (16a), represented as a finite state acceptor in (39). For instance, (6,8) in Step $\boxed{\text{A}}$ in (40b) can be read off of (39) as *le mamanu*. The reformulation also replaces each tree by a tuple of categorized strings where commas are used to separate moving phrases, as can be seen by comparing the examples in (41) with their reformulated versions in (40b). These reformulated rules are further discussed in the context of the computation of MATCHPHRASE in §4.3.3.2.

The algorithm for the bottom-up parser is similar to the CKY algorithm for context-free languages (see e.g. Younger 1967). The initial steps are schematized in the matrix in Table 4.2, where each cell (i, j) corresponds to the span (i, j) in (39). The feature stacks of lexical items and empties are inserted in the matrix in the appropriate cell. For instance, feature stacks from empties ε go in all cells (i, j) where $i = j$, since empties have an empty span. Each inserted item is added to an agenda stack. After initialization, the parser scans down the stack and checks to see if any of the different Merge and Move functions can be applied. If a successful derivational step is taken, it is recorded in the matrix. So each step given in (40) would be recorded in cells (i, j) according to the spans of the resulting expressions, as illustrated in (37).

(37)   Recording the results of the derivational steps shown in (41) in the chart shown in Table 4.2

    a. Merge-1, $\boxed{\text{A}}$ in (40b)
       • The feature D is recorded in cell (6,8), i.e., the cell in row 6, column 8.

    b. Merge-2, $\boxed{\text{H}}$ in (40b)
       • The expression v_{tr}, (1,2) −EPP:V is recorded in cell (2,8). The comma in the expression separates out the moving phrase from the feature v_{tr}.

    c. Merge-3, $\boxed{\text{C}}$ in (40b)
       • The expression V −EPP:V, (5,8) −EPP:D is recorded in cell (1,2).

    d. Move-1, $\boxed{\text{E}}$ in (40b)
       • The expression $=D_{erg}$ v_{tr}, (1,2) −EPP:V is recorded in cell (5,8).

(38)
  a. derivation tree for (16a)   b. derived bare tree

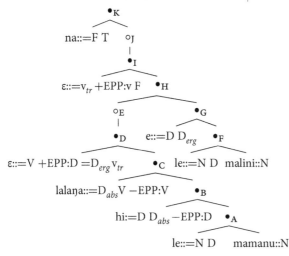
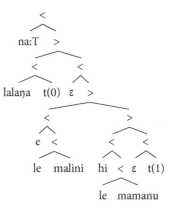

  c. 'X-bar like' bare tree

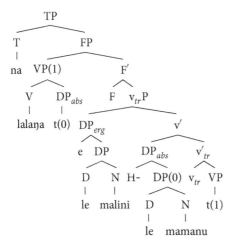

(39)   Finite state acceptor for the string yield of (16a)

(40)   Derivation of sentence in tuple notation

a. Lexicon:

$\boxed{1}$	na::=F T	malini::N	$\boxed{6}$
$\boxed{2}$	lalaŋa::=D_{abs} V -EPP:V	hi::=D D_{abs} -EPP:D	$\boxed{7}$
$\boxed{3}$	ε::=v_{tr} +EPP:V F	mamanu::N	$\boxed{8}$
$\boxed{4}$	e::=D D_{erg}	ε::=V +EPP:D =D_{erg} v_{tr}	$\boxed{9}$
$\boxed{5}$	le::=N D		

b. Derivation, 11 steps:

Merge-1($\boxed{5}$,$\boxed{8}$)	= (6,8):D		$\boxed{A}$
Merge-1($\boxed{7}$,$\boxed{A}$)	= (5,8):D_{abs} −EPP:D		$\boxed{B}$
Merge-3($\boxed{2}$,$\boxed{B}$)	= (1,2):V −EPP:V, (5,8): −EPP:D		$\boxed{C}$
Merge-3($\boxed{9}$,$\boxed{C}$)	= (8,8):+EPP:D=D_{erg} v_{tr}, (1,2):V −EPP:V, (5,8): −EPP:D		$\boxed{D}$
Move-1($\boxed{D}$)	= (5,8):=D_{erg} v_{tr}, (1,2):−EPP:V		$\boxed{E}$
Merge-1($\boxed{5}$,$\boxed{6}$)	= (3,5):D		$\boxed{F}$
Merge-1($\boxed{4}$,$\boxed{F}$)	= (2,5):D_{erg}		$\boxed{G}$
Merge-2($\boxed{E}$,$\boxed{G}$)	= (2,8):v_{tr}, (1,2):−EPP:V		$\boxed{H}$
Merge-1($\boxed{3}$,$\boxed{H}$)	= (2,8):+EPP:V F, (1,2):−EPP:V		$\boxed{I}$
Move-1($\boxed{I}$)	= (1,8):F		$\boxed{J}$
Merge-1($\boxed{1}$,$\boxed{I}$)	= (0,8):T		$\boxed{K}$

(41)   Examples of reformulated Merge and Move operations from the derivation (40), annotated with spans and illustrated with derived trees

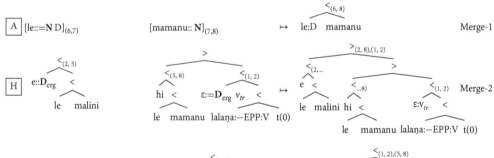

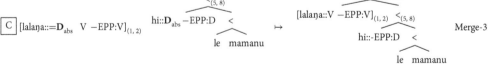

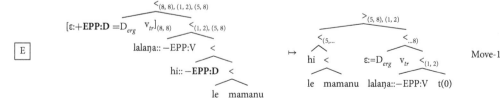

Table 4.2 Matrix after initialization of empties and lexical items. The features for empty categories down the diagonal are abbreviated for space as ε_F (9) for ::=v_{tr} +EPP:V F and $\varepsilon_{v_{tr}}$ (3) for ::=V +EPP:D =D_{erg} v_{tr}.

	0	1	2	3	4	5	6	7	8
0	ε_F $\varepsilon_{V_{tr}}$	①:: =F T							
1		ε_F $\varepsilon_{V_{tr}}$	②:: = D_{abs} V −EPP:V						
2			ε_F $\varepsilon_{V_{tr}}$	④:: = D D_{erg}					
3				ε_F $\varepsilon_{V_{tr}}$	⑤:: = N D				
4					ε_F $\varepsilon_{V_{tr}}$	⑥::N			
5						ε_F $\varepsilon_{V_{tr}}$	⑦:: = D D_{abs} −EPP:D		
6							ε_F $\varepsilon_{V_{tr}}$	⑤:: = N D	
7								ε_F $\varepsilon_{V_{tr}}$	⑧:: N
8									ε_F $\varepsilon_{V_{tr}}$

4.3.3.2 Computing MATCHPHRASE

In the description of the MG parsing algorithm so far, we left out the modifications needed for the computation of MATCHPHRASE. To also compute MATCHPHRASE, we must parse 36 candidates with the same phonetic content but different prosodic markup. For efficiency, we can compress the representation of these candidates into a prefix tree acceptor, rather than represent each prosodically marked-up candidate as a separate acceptor like (16a). Then we don't need to compute derivational steps shared among candidates multiple times.

For each of the 36 parses, we keep a running count of how many MATCHPHRASE violations there are. Any time we compute MATCHPHRASE, this count might increase. At each step in the parsing algorithm where a syntactic constituent could be formed— any derivational step where two expressions land or merge to be adjacent to one another—we check if the result of the Merge or Move step is a syntactic maximal projection. (If the result is DP_{erg} or DP_{abs}, it is not a syntactic maximal projection, but a post-syntactic one.) If the result is a syntactic maximal projection, then we compute MATCHPHRASE and increment the violation count if there is a violation.

Each derivational step illustrated in (41) is one where two expressions land or merge to be adjacent to one another. In Merge-1, a lexical head selects a complement. For example, in A , head *le* selects complement *mamanu* to form the syntactic DP *le mamanu*. The feature D is then recorded in the chart (Table 4.2) in cell (6,8) (see (37)), and a MATCHPHRASE computation is triggered. In Merge-2, a head merges with a specifier, e.g. in H , a D_{erg} head merges with specifier DP_{erg} *e le malini* to form a v_{tr}P, triggering a MATCHPHRASE computation. (For details of what is recorded in the chart in this and the following examples, see (37).) Merge-3 "launches" a moving element and thus doesn't place two expressions next to each other, but can result in the formation of a temporary merged complex that is a syntactic XP in the derived tree. For instance, in $\boxed{\text{c}}$, *lalaŋa* forms a VP with complement DP_{abs} *hi le mamanu*, before the DP_{abs} later moves out to leave a trace; this triggers a MATCHPHRASE computation. In Move-1, a constituent lands next to something else, which could result in the formation of an XP. In $\boxed{\text{E}}$, the EPP:D feature is checked as an empty ($\boxed{9}$) lands next to *hi le mamanu*. In this case, no constituent is formed because the result is not an XP.

Even if the MATCHPHRASE algorithm is called, the computation doesn't proceed in two cases: (i) if it is passed an empty span, or (ii) if it is passed a span from an initial to final state. In the first case, the expression is an empty category with no phonetic exponence. In the latter, the expression is the entire string, and thus maps to an intonational phrase, not a φ-phrase, so it is in the domain of MATCHCLAUSE (3), not the domain of MATCHPHRASE. If the computation proceeds, then MATCHPHRASE, as defined in (5) and extended to post-syntactic material in (27), assesses violations only for φ-phrases. Thus, in our implementation, the only phonological constituents relevant for computation—as indicated by particular open–close bracket pairs— are listed in (42):

(42)   Phonological phrase open–close bracket pairs
    a. Phonological phrase (PhP_{max}) Z . . . z
    b. Phonological phrase (PhP_{nmin}) Y . . . y
    c. Phonological phrase (PhP_{fxn}) X . . . x
    d. Phonological phrase (PhP_{min}) < . . . >

Abstracting away from dealing with post-syntactic material, we can state MATCHPHRASE as in (43):

(43)   Definition of MATCHPHRASE in implementation, abstracting away from post-syntactic material
    a. If XP is a syntactic phrase that is not unary branching down to a terminal element, and if the yield of XP is exactly enclosed in one of the following open–close bracket pairs:
        i. < . . . > (PhP_{min})
        ii. X . . . x (PhP_{fxn})
        iii. Y . . . y (PhP_{nmin})
        iv. Z . . . z (PhP_{max})
        then assess no violations.
    b. If the yield of XP is not exactly enclosed in one of those bracket pairs, assess a violation.

This case-by-case implementation of MATCHPHRASE is possible because we place a finite bound on recursion in prosodic trees and label each level of recursion in φ-phrases with distinct open–close bracket pairs.

The complication added by treating post-syntactic material according to (27b) is that it is not enough to consider the yield of XP contained in span (i, j). On the one hand, we have to extend the span to be prefixed by the predecessor state of i and suffixed by the successor state of j, and then consider the yield of this extended span. If the two phonetic exponents at the edges in (i, j) are not post-syntactic, i.e. a case marker, but a case marker is adjacent to an edge, then MATCHPHRASE could be satisfied if we also include the case marker in the span. For instance, the enclitization of *e* to prosodic word *lalaŋa* forms a φ-phrase to repair a potential violation of MATCHPHRASE, see (24a).

On the other hand, we also have to shrink the span to range from the successor state of i to the predecessor state of j, and then consider the yield of this shrunken span. This is because the extension of MATCHPHRASE to post-syntactic material in (27) states that phonetic exponents that are post-syntactic are invisible to MATCHPHRASE. Thus, if a phonetic exponent at the edges of (i, j) is a case marker, then the open–close bracket pairs in the domain of the MATCHPHRASE computation enclose the span shrunken to exclude the case marker. For example, step $\boxed{\text{H}}$ in (40) results in the formation of a v_{tr}P with the span (2,8), spanning *e le malini hi le mamanu*. This is a syntactic XP, even though it is initiated by the the case marker *e*, so it triggers a MATCHPHRASE computation. Consider the prosodic parse Candidate 9, (28d). If we checked the alignment of the v_{tr}P edges to the open–close bracket pair around *e le malini hi le mamanu*, then there would be a MATCHPHRASE violation. The case marker *e* has been encliticized to *lalaŋa* to the left. However, if we shrink the span to be included in the open–close bracket pair to only *le malini hi le mamanu*, then we have a v_{tr}P mapping to a φ-phrase, and no MATCHPHRASE violation is assessed.

After computing the number of MATCHPHRASE violations for each of the 36 prosodic parses, we keep just the parses with the least number of violations—in this case, none, leaving just three candidates.

4.3.4 Final phonological transduction after MG parse: STRONGSTART

The remaining three prosodic parses, Candidate 7 (29b), Candidate 9 (28d), and Candidate 10 (29a)—all with no MATCHPHRASE violations—are passed back for a final xfst transduction implementing STRONGSTART. Unlike the other (purely) phonological constraints implemented (taking MATCHPHRASE to be an interface constraint), STRONGSTART is a multiply violable constraint and dominated by other constraints. It must be implemented in such a way that we can count the total number of violations in a candidate. The other phonological constraints are inviolable, and so it is not necessary to assess how many times they are each violated (for constraints that can be multiply violated): as long there is at least one violation in a candidate, that candidate will be filtered out. Following Karttunen (1998)'s implementation of multiply violated PARSE-SYLLABLE (see also Yu 2018), we define STRONGSTART as a "leniently composed" family of STRONGSTARTn constraints, each of which allow candidates only up to n violations. Note that this finite-state implementation can only handle counting up to a finite number of violations—or, put another way, it can only make a finite number of distinctions in well-formedness. Here we only need to count up to four, since the winning candidates have three violations and the losing candidate has four.

4.4 Discussion and conclusion

In this chapter, we demonstrated a proof-of-concept implementation of simultaneous (post-)syntactic and prosodic parsing, with syntactic parsing informed by prosody, and prosodic parsing informed by syntax. We showed how syntactic and post-syntactic structures could be derived by a composed Minimalist Grammar and parsed simultaneously bottom-up for a string of Samoan. We modeled the inclusion of a high-tone absolutive case marker as a post-syntactic item in the MG lexicon that entered the (post)-syntactic derivation like the segmental ergative case marker, alongside lexical items. In this way, a prosodic reflex of syntactic structure informed the syntactic parser. We also incorporated the computation of a syntax–phonology interface constraint into the (post-)syntactic parsing. The bottom-up MG parser computed the number of violations of MATCHPHRASE, a constraint penalizing the misalignment of prosodic and syntactic constituent edges for a set of candidate prosodic parses of the string. Thus, the (post-)syntactic analysis of the string was used to rank and filter the prosodic parses. For this first case study, we abstracted away from ambiguity in syntactic parsing, and thus did not model how prosodic parses could help disambiguate between a set of syntactic parses. However, the present model provides the scaffolding for such an extension—we leave this to future work.

For computational models of syntactic parsing, our work contributes to showing how prosodic information can be brought into syntactic parsing in other ways than as a local, noisy signal of syntactic domain edges. We showed how prosodic information could come in from spellout and via prosodic trees, and hope to inspire more work along these lines and more connections between the computational parsing and linguistic literature. We hope that consideration of how syntax might inform prosodic parsing can lead to a fresh and fruitful perspective on how prosody might inform syntactic parsing. If Wagner (2005; 2010), Steedman (2014), Hirsch and Wagner (2015), and others are (even only partly) right about the flexibility of syntax and the re-analysis of syntax–prosody mismatches as only apparent mismatches, then prosodic structure could be very informative indeed.

For linguistic theories of the syntax–phonology interface, our case study shows that constraint-based grammars of the interface defined on prosodic trees—and possibly with interface constraints interleaved between phonological constraints—can, in principle, be implemented. However, there's a caveat—the imposition of finite bounds. We were able to compose spellout and syntax in the MG grammar because all syntactic and post-syntactic structures were finite state definable over trees. Additionally, we assumed a finite depth of recursion in prosodic trees, and we assumed a finite bound on the number of violations of a constraint. The cap on the number of violations allowed us to define the constraint-based grammar using a finite-state implementation of optimality theory (Karttunen 1998). Without that cap, it's not clear how we would have been able to implement the grammar. The question of whether phonology needs unbounded recursion and whether optimality-theoretic phonology needs unbounded counting has been extensively discussed in the literature (see e.g. Frank and Satta 1998;

Karttunen 1998; Wagner 2005; 2010; Hao 2017). We leave to future work the question of how the finite bounds might be relaxed.

Carefully exploring the consequences of recursion in prosodic trees for computing the interface and parsing could also inform phonological perspectives on the role of recursion in prosodic structure. In §4.1.2.4, we set up a perspective where prosodic trees are recursive, following Selkirk (2011), among many others (e.g. Ladd 1986; Ito and Mester 1992; 2003; Féry and Truckenbrodt 2005; Wagner 2005; Krivokapić and Byrd 2012; Elfner 2012; Ito and Mester 2013; Kentner and Féry 2013; Myrberg 2013; Elfner 2015; Kügler 2015; Truckenbrodt and Féry 2015). However, there are other phonological perspectives where it is assumed that prosodic trees are not recursive— rather, they have a small, finite number of categories (e.g. Pierrehumbert 1980; Beckman and Pierrehumbert 1986; Nespor and Vogel 1986; Hayes 1989; Beckman 1996; Jun 2005ab; 2014). While the debate on recursion in prosodic structure has been informed by fieldwork, experiments, and theoretical analyses in a wide range of languages, mathematical and computational perspectives have not yet come into play.

More generally, extensions of the work here could help characterize the complexity of computing different kinds of syntax–phonology interface relations and how these relations might accordingly be restricted. Formalizing different proposals precisely enough to implement them would allow us to analyze them in ways that could be prohibitive with pen-and-paper analyses (Karttunen 2006b; 2006a; Bellik et al. (2015); Hulden (2017)). Further work could continue to probe the interaction of factored components of the syntax–phonology interface—not only spellout and relations between prosodic and syntactic trees, but also linearization, e.g. building on work by Richards (2010), Bennett et al. (2016), and Kusmer (2019). Our proposed extension of MATCHPHRASE to spellout in (27) could be examined further. The case study has shown how special treatment of spellout in the interface computation is necessary (under the defined constraint set) to compute optimal prosodic parses with bracketing mismatches like the enclitized case markers here. We could explore how the special treatment of post-syntactically derived and inserted material defined here would fare in characterizing other interface phenomenon defined with post-syntactic operations.

Finally, we can build on the work here to connect with empirical work on real-time prosodic/syntactic parsing (e.g. Beckman 1996; Brown et al. 2012). While the chart parser used here is not psychologically compatible, we can extend our model to incremental parsing models. And we can also eventually extend the model to include the computation of the map from the speech signal to the phonological parse.

5

Parsing ellipsis efficiently

Gregory M. Kobele

5.1 Introduction

The problem of recovering a meaning from a linguistic expression is one that we solve by and large effortlessly every day of our lives. A main way to approach this problem formally has been to identify the relevant linguistic expressions with sentences, and to develop algorithms which recover parse trees for sentences.

For many interesting linguistic grammar formalisms, this problem turns out to be efficiently exactly solvable: the set of *all* possible parses of a sentence can be computed in time polynomial in the length of the sentence.

Focussing on recovering parses is in general a reasonable approximation to recovering meanings; a parse tree typically uniquely identifies a meaning representation (via a compositional semantics). However, this is not always the case. In particular, in anaphoric constructions typically more information is required to map the parse tree into a meaning representation than is represented in the parse tree itself. Thus the problem of identifying a parse tree for a sentence with anaphoric expressions is only a proper subpart of the problem of recovering a meaning for the sentence.

In addition to making the complexity of recovering a meaning potentially more complex than that of recovering a parse tree, anaphoric constructions also disrupt the simplifying assumption that discourses are "bags of sentences." This assumption guarantees that the cost of parsing a discourse is simply the sum of the costs of parsing each of its sentences. The problem posed by anaphoric dependencies is that whether a sentence has a fully fleshed out meaning can depend on whether there is available in the surrounding discourse a legitimate antecedent.[1]

---

[1] A similar problem arises with discourse relations, which impose more structure on discourses than is present in the bag-of-sentences model. One possible difference between these two cases is that it does not seem that different discourse structurings can render sentences *meaningless* in the same way that lack of an antecedent can. Still, especially under theories which treat discourse structure as an extension of syntactic structure, the number of parses of the discourse grows as a polynomial function of the number of words in the discourse.

Minimalist Parsing. First edition. Robert C. Berwick and Edward P. Stabler (eds.) This chapter © Gregory M. Kobele 2019. First published 2019 by Oxford University Press.

In this chapter I focus on ellipsis[2] in the framework of minimalist grammars (Stabler, 1997), in particular the theory of Kobele (2015). I show that the problem of parsing sentences with ellipsis sites (i.e. the problem of recovering all parse trees for a given sentence) is efficiently solvable, and that, given a parse tree, and a set of possible antecedents, determining a legitimate resolution of its ellipsis sites, if one exists, can be done in constant time. Thus in the system of Kobele (2015), the problem of recovering a meaning for a string in a particular discourse context can be solved in polynomial time, even in the presence of ellipsis. I then show that the problem of updating a discourse context with the newly available antecedents of a freshly parsed sentence is also solvable in polynomial time, given standard linguistic assumptions about the licensing of ellipsis sites (Lobeck 1995), and features of the grammar formalism particular to linguistic grammar formalisms. From this, it follows that the cost of parsing discourses with ellipsis reduces to the sum of the costs of parsing their component sentences.

While couched in terms of minimalist grammars, the approach to ellipsis developed in Kobele (2015) can be extended to any grammar formalism characterizable in terms of second-order ACGs (de Groote 2001; de Groote and Pogodalla 2004). However, the linguistic applications touted in Kobele (2015) depend crucially on particularities of the analysis therein, which seem difficult to replicate outside of the minimalist grammar formalism.

5.2 Ellipsis in minimalist grammars

The formal framework of minimalist grammars was developed by Stabler (1997) as a formalization of the core aspects of Chomsky's then nascent Minimalist Program (Chomsky 1995a). It was proven shortly thereafter (Michaelis 1998) that there is a constructive procedure to transform a minimalist grammar into a strongly equivalent[3] multiple context-free grammar (Seki et al. 1991), and thus that minimalist grammars enjoy an efficiently solvable parsing problem (Harkema 2001).

Minimalist grammars have proven to be a good formalization of the Minimalist Program, in that virtually all extensions thereof and amendments thereto either already have been or at least appear to be directly and faithfully implemented in this framework.[4]

---

[2] The status of ellipsis as an anaphoric construction is not uncontroversial, at least in the sense here of its structure not uniquely determining its meaning. A long-standing proposal in the transformational community (going back to at least Lees (1960); Merchant (2001) is a more recent champion) has it that the ellipsis site has a fully articulated structure appropriate to its meaning. I believe that this controversy is irrelevant for two reasons. From a purely pragmatic standpoint, the anaphoric ("proform") treatment provides a clear divide between the cost of parsing (plus identifying ellipsis sites), which is known, and the cost of resolving the ellipses. Syntactic theories of ellipsis mix these two, seemingly leaving us with no clear way to investigate the problem, short of developing completely novel theories of parsing. From a more empirical perspective, Kobele (2015) argues that the standard arguments in favor of refined syntactic structures inside of ellipsis sites are in fact compatible with proform theories, given a slightly more sophisticated treatment of syntactic categories. Note that Kobele (2012a) argues that syntactic theories are simply alternative notations for proform theories.

[3] I use "strongly equivalent" in the sense that the *derivation trees* assigned by both grammars to strings are isomorphic.

[4] In some cases, the straightforward implementation increases the generative capacity of the framework, even to turing completeness (Kobele and Michaelis 2005).

I adopt in section 5.2.1 a particularly spare, "chain-based" version of minimalist grammars (Stabler and Keenan 2003). This version, viewed from the perspective of theoretical linguistics, commits to a strong version of "cyclic spellout" (Chomsky 2000), where spell-out is effected at each derivational step (i.e. compositionally). Other versions are admissible, so long as they do not affect the fact that the set of derivation trees is regular, as discussed in section 5.2.2. Relevant aspects of the theory of ellipsis in Kobele (2015) are given in section 5.2.3.

5.2.1 Minimalist grammars

A minimalist grammar (over some alphabet Σ) is determined by a finite set `AtFeat` of *atomic features*, and a finite set `Lex` of lexical items. A lexical item $\ell = \langle w, \delta \rangle$ is a pair consisting of a word w (over Σ) and a feature bundle δ. A feature bundle is a finite list $\delta = f_1, \ldots, f_n$ of features, which are elements of the finite set `Feat` defined below.[5]

$$\textsf{Feat} := \{\texttt{f}, \texttt{=f}, \texttt{+f}, \texttt{-f} : f \in \textsf{AtFeat}\}$$

A feature is either an *attractor* (`=f`, `+f`) or an *attractee* (`f`, `-f`) and is either a *selection* feature (`=f`, `f`) or a *licensing* feature (`+f`, `-f`). A feature bundle is a complex structured category, as in categorial grammar, although feature bundles are structured as unary trees (strings).

A minimalist grammar defines a set of minimalist expressions, which are finite sequences of *chains*. A chain $\phi = \langle w, \delta \rangle$ is a pair of a string (over Σ) and a feature bundle. The expressions E derivable by a minimalist grammar, written $\vdash E$, are neatly presented in terms of a set of inference rules. In the rules below, it is assumed that δ is non-empty.

$$\frac{\ell \in \textsf{Lex}}{\vdash \ell} \ \textrm{Select}_\ell$$

$$\frac{\vdash \langle u, \texttt{=x}\gamma \rangle, \phi_1, \ldots, \phi_i \qquad \vdash \langle v, \texttt{x} \rangle, \psi_1, \ldots, \psi_j}{\vdash \langle uv, \gamma \rangle, \phi_1, \ldots, \phi_i, \psi_1, \ldots, \psi_j} \ \textrm{Merge}_1$$

$$\frac{\vdash \langle u, \texttt{=x}\gamma \rangle, \phi_1, \ldots, \phi_i \qquad \vdash \langle v, \texttt{x}\delta \rangle, \psi_1, \ldots, \psi_j}{\vdash \langle u, \gamma \rangle, \phi_1, \ldots, \phi_i, \langle v, \delta \rangle, \psi_1, \ldots, \psi_j} \ \textrm{Merge}_2$$

$$\frac{\vdash \langle u, \texttt{+x}\gamma \rangle, \phi_1, \ldots, \phi_{i-1}, \langle v, \texttt{-x} \rangle, \phi_{i+1}, \ldots, \phi_j}{\vdash \langle vu, \gamma \rangle, \phi_1, \ldots, \phi_{i-1}, \phi_{i+1}, \ldots, \phi_j} \ \textrm{Move}_1$$

$$\frac{\vdash \langle u, \texttt{+x}\gamma \rangle, \phi_1, \ldots, \phi_{i-1}, \langle v, \texttt{-x}\delta \rangle, \phi_{i+1}, \ldots, \phi_j}{\vdash \langle vu, \gamma \rangle, \phi_1, \ldots, \phi_{i-1}, \langle v, \delta \rangle, \phi_{i+1}, \ldots, \phi_j} \ \textrm{Move}_2$$

[5] A list $a_1, \ldots, a_n$ has a head a_1 and a tail $a_2, \ldots, a_n$, and can be thought of as a unary branching tree. It can be implemented as a pair, whose first element is the head of the list, and whose second element is the tail of the list. A finite sequence is a (flat) tuple of elements. Despite being structurally distinct, I systematically confuse lists and sequences notationally throughout this chapter.

The language of a minimalist grammar G at a feature f is defined to be

$$L(G,f) := \{w : \vdash \langle w, f \rangle\}$$

This version of minimalist grammars was shown in Salvati (2011) to be extremely complex: its membership problem is reducible to provability in multiplicative exponential linear logic, which, though decidable (Bimbó 2015), is at least ExpSpace-hard (Lincoln 1995). A polynomial membership problem is obtained by imposing the following well-formedness constraint, called the **SMC** (Stabler 1997), on the inputs and outputs of the operations defined previously.[6]

$$\frac{f_1, \ldots, f_i \text{ are pairwise distinct}}{\textbf{SMC} \left(\langle w_1, f_1 \delta_1 \rangle, \ldots, \langle w_i, f_i \delta_i \rangle \right)}$$

The **SMC** holds of an expression if all of its chains have distinct first features. When the **SMC** is imposed, the operations defined previously become partial, as, even when restricted to inputs satisfying **SMC**, their outputs might not. From this point on, I will assume that all expressions satisfy **SMC**, and thus that the operations have been so restricted, without explicit mention.

5.2.2 Derivational structure

I define a *category* $c = \delta_1, \ldots, \delta_i$ to be a sequence of feature bundles. Given an expression $e = \phi_1, \ldots, \phi_i$, its category $\texttt{cat}(e) := \pi_2 \phi_1, \ldots, \pi_2 \phi_i$ is the sequence of the same length which has at each position the feature bundle of the chain at the same position in e. The symbol π_i denotes the ith projection function: the function which maps a tuple to its ith component.

Whether an operation may apply to a sequence of expressions $e_1, \ldots, e_i$ is completely determined by the sequence of their categories $\texttt{cat}(e_1), \ldots, \texttt{cat}(e_i)$, as is the category of the result. For **op**, an operation on minimalist expressions, I write $\texttt{cat}(\textbf{op})$ for the relation between categories obtained by extracting the categories of the expressions in the graph of **op**. The previous observation amounts to saying that $\texttt{cat}(\textbf{op})$ is functional (although partial), for each

$$\textbf{op} \in \{\textbf{Select}_\ell, \textbf{Merge}_i, \textbf{Move}_i : 1 \leq i \leq 2, \ell \in \textsf{Lex}\}.$$

One observes, by inspecting the definitions of the operations, that each feature bundle in an expression either remains the same or decreases in size (by losing its head) as it undergoes an operation. From this one derives the consequence that there are *only finitely many* categories which can be involved in any proof of a derivable expression (Michaelis 2001).

---

[6] Salvati (2011) shows that it is simply keeping track of unboundedly many unchecked features which is the source of the computational difficulty. The **SMC** relieves the computational system of this burden by imposing an upper bound on the number of unchecked features in any derivable expression. As there are finitely many features, any expression satisfying **SMC** has length of at most k, where $k = |\textsf{Feat}|$. As the length of a feature bundle never increases after any rule application, this places an upper bound of kn on the number of unchecked features in a derivable expression satisfying **SMC**, where k is as before, and $n = \max(\{|\delta| : \langle w, \delta \rangle \in \textsf{Lex}\})$. Any reasonable way of imposing a finite bound on the number of unchecked features in expressions leads to a similarly restricted system.

Given a lexicon Lex, the set of *derivation trees* over Lex is the smallest set Der(Lex) closed under the following operations.

$$\frac{\ell \in \mathtt{Lex}}{\mathbf{Select}_\ell \in \mathtt{Der(Lex)}}$$

$$\frac{t \in \mathtt{Der(Lex)} \qquad 1 \le i \le 2}{\mathbf{Move}_i(t) \in \mathtt{Der(Lex)}}$$

$$\frac{t_1 \in \mathtt{Der(Lex)} \qquad t_2 \in \mathtt{Der(Lex)} \qquad 1 \le i \le 2}{\mathbf{Merge}_i(t_1, t_2) \in \mathtt{Der(Lex)}}$$

A derivation tree is *well-formed* just in case it describes a derivation of an expression. Whether or not a derivation tree is well-formed can be determined by a simple bottom-up procedure: replace each subtree $t = \mathbf{op}(c_1, \dots, c_n)$ with the category $\mathrm{cat}(\mathbf{op})(c_1, \dots, c_n)$, beginning with the leaves (necessarily of the form $\mathbf{Select}_\ell$, where $\mathrm{cat}(\mathbf{Select}_\ell)() = \pi_2\ell$). A derivation tree t is well-formed iff it is replaced with a category c by this procedure.[7] As noted in Kobele et al. (2007), this coïncides with the definition of a *bottom-up tree automaton* (Comon et al. 2002), whence the set of well-formed derivation trees for a given minimalist grammar is *regular*. This is in stark contrast to the *non-regularity* of the string languages of minimalist grammars. As a derivation tree completely determines the expression it is the derivation of, the problem of parsing reduces to finding a derivation tree underlying an input string; being regular, the space of derivation trees has a simpler structure than the space of well-formed expressions.

5.2.3 Ellipsis

A common perspective on ellipsis is that elliptical sentences are derived with nothing in the "ellipsis site."[8] In analyses in the tradition of transformational grammar, there are many constructions in which expressions which appear in the surface string would normally be analyzed as having been moved out from inside of the ellipsis site. This tradition adopts a different perspective on ellipsis—elliptical sentences are derived with the full syntactic structure of a non-elided constituent in the ellipsis site. This of course allows expressions to move out from inside of the ellipsis site. The fact that ellipsis sites are not pronounced is dealt with by means of an operation which phonologically deletes the remaining material inside of the ellipsis site.[9] Kobele (2015) proposes to treat ellipsis as a family of grammatical operations; intuitively, one for each way of building up, and then deleting, an ellipsis site.

To define the behavior of these operations, I first extend the notion of derivation to allow for hypotheses. Intuitively, I will extend the derivational system to allow

---

[7] A tree t fails to be well-formed if it contains a subtree $t' = \mathbf{op}(c_1, \dots, c_n)$ for which $c_1, \dots, c_n$ is not in the domain of the operation $\mathrm{cat}(\mathbf{op})$.

[8] For a concise overview of ellipsis see Kobele (2012b).

[9] See Merchant (2001) for a modern exposition of this theory.

expressions to be constructed which are missing one or more constituents (represented by hypotheses). Building up an expression, and silencing all of it except for some moving pieces, is reconceptualized as building an expression which is missing some parts, and silencing all of it. The resulting expression can be thought of as specifying a way of changing the features, and rearranging the phonetic components, of its missing parts; i.e. an operation on expressions. Even though there are (in general) infinitely many ways to construct an expression which is missing a fixed array of parts, these boil down to only finitely many distinct operations. An ellipsis operation will be seen as realizing the effect of this construction and deletion process, without actually needing to construct or delete anything. The use of hypothetical derivations is solely at the meta-level, to define the behaviour of ellipsis operations; I am not here enriching (or proposing to enrich) minimalist grammars with hypothetical reasoning.

5.2.4 Hypothetical derivations

A hypothetical expression of category $c = \delta_1, \ldots, \delta_i$ is of the form $\mathsf{hyp}(c) = \langle \mathbf{x}_1, \delta_1 \rangle, \ldots, \langle \mathbf{x}_i, \delta_i \rangle$, where $\mathbf{x}_1, \ldots, \mathbf{x}_i$ are pairwise distinct *variables*. I will write $\mathbf{x} : \mathsf{hyp}(c)$ to indicate that the variables used in $\mathsf{hyp}(c)$ will be referred to as $\mathbf{x}_1, \ldots, \mathbf{x}_i$. Derivability is extended from a property of expressions ($\vdash e$) to a relation between hypothetical expressions and expressions ($\Gamma \vdash e$) in the following way.

$$\frac{\ell \in \mathsf{Lex}}{\vdash \ell} \; \text{Select}_\ell$$

$$\frac{}{\mathbf{x} : \mathsf{hyp}(c) \vdash \mathsf{hyp}(c)} \; \text{Axiom}_c$$

$$\frac{\Gamma \vdash \langle u, {=}x\gamma \rangle, \phi_1, \ldots, \phi_i \qquad \Delta \vdash \langle v, x \rangle, \psi_1, \ldots, \psi_j}{\Gamma, \Delta \vdash \langle uv, \gamma \rangle, \phi_1, \ldots, \phi_i, \psi_1, \ldots, \psi_j} \; \text{Merge}_1$$

$$\frac{\Gamma \vdash \langle u, {=}x\gamma \rangle, \phi_1, \ldots, \phi_i \qquad \Delta \vdash \langle v, x\delta \rangle, \psi_1, \ldots, \psi_j}{\Gamma, \Delta \vdash \langle u, \gamma \rangle, \phi_1, \ldots, \phi_i, \langle v, \delta \rangle, \psi_1, \ldots, \psi_j} \; \text{Merge}_2$$

$$\frac{\Gamma \vdash \langle u, {+}x\gamma \rangle, \phi_1, \ldots, \phi_{i-1}, \langle v, {-}x \rangle, \phi_{i+1}, \ldots, \phi_j}{\Gamma \vdash \langle vu, \gamma \rangle, \phi_1, \ldots, \phi_{i-1}, \phi_{i+1}, \ldots, \phi_j} \; \text{Move}_1$$

$$\frac{\Gamma \vdash \langle u, {+}x\gamma \rangle, \phi_1, \ldots, \phi_{i-1}, \langle v, {-}x\delta \rangle, \phi_{i+1}, \ldots, \phi_j}{\Gamma \vdash \langle vu, \gamma \rangle, \phi_1, \ldots, \phi_{i-1}, \langle v, \delta \rangle, \phi_{i+1}, \ldots, \phi_j} \; \text{Move}_2$$

The category of a hypothetical expression $E = \Gamma \vdash e$ is $\mathsf{cat}(E) := c_1 \times \ldots \times c_n \to \mathsf{cat}(e)$, for $\Gamma = \mathsf{hyp}(c_1), \ldots \mathsf{hyp}(c_n)$.[10] The notion of a derivation tree is extended so as to include leaves labeled with **Axiom**$_c$.

As is standard, we require that hypothetical contexts have at most one hypothesis associated with a particular variable. The use of variables in this system is intended

---

[10] When $\Gamma = \varnothing$ I write simply $\mathsf{cat}(e)$ instead of $1 \to \mathsf{cat}(e)$, where 1 is the unit for $\times$.

to be *linear*, which means that variables on the left of the turnstile occur exactly once on its right. (This is implicitly assumed in the **Merge** rules.) I am implicitly assuming that each use of the **Axiom** rule introduces a *globally fresh* variable; in particular, when speaking of multiple derivation trees $t_1, \ldots, t_n$, it is assumed that the expressions to which they evaluate have no variables in common.

Note that there is no rule of hypothesis discharge (i.e. no way of moving hypotheses across the turnstile); the role of hypotheses is simply to specify the behaviour of incomplete derivations (derivation *contexts* as opposed to derivation *trees*).

5.2.5 Ellipsis operations

Given two hypothetical expressions $E = \Gamma, \mathbf{x} : \mathsf{hyp}(c), \Gamma' \vdash e$ and $E' = \Delta \vdash e'$ such that $\mathsf{cat}(e') = c$, we define the *substitution* of E' for $\mathsf{hyp}(c)$ in E to be the expression $E[E'/\mathbf{x}] := \Gamma, \Delta, \Gamma' \vdash e[\mathbf{x}_1/\pi_1 e'_1 \ldots, \mathbf{x}_i/\pi_1 e'_i]$, where $[\mathbf{x}_1/w_1 \ldots, \mathbf{x}_i/w_i]$ is the *simultaneous substitution* of strings $w_1, \ldots, w_i$ for variables $\mathbf{x}_1, \ldots, \mathbf{x}_i$, extended over pairs $\langle w, \delta \rangle$, and sequences $\phi_1, \ldots, \phi_n$ in the obvious way. Let $t[\mathbf{Axiom}_c]$ be a derivation tree with a designated leaf labeled with $\mathbf{Axiom}_c$, and let t' be a derivation tree. Then $t[t']$ is the derivation tree obtained from $t[\mathbf{Axiom}_c]$ by replacing the designated leaf with t'. If $t[\mathbf{Axiom}_c]$ evaluates to $E = \Gamma, \mathbf{x} : \mathsf{hyp}(c), \Gamma' \vdash e$ and t' evaluates to $E' = \Delta \vdash e'$ such that $\mathsf{cat}(e') = c$, then $t[t']$ evaluates to $E[E'/\mathbf{x}]$.

Finally, the *phonological deletion* of a hypothetical expression $E = \Gamma \vdash e$ is the expression $\mathsf{delete}(E) = \Gamma \vdash \mathsf{delete}(e)$, where delete maps strings over Σ^* to the empty string, and variables to themselves, and is extended in the obvious way over chains and expressions. Note that for any hypothetical category C, the set $\mathsf{Delete}_C := \{\mathsf{delete}(E) : \mathsf{cat}(E) = C\}$ is finite modulo renaming of variables—there are just finitely many ways of assigning the variables in the hypotheses to chains. Elements of the set $\bigcup_C \mathsf{Delete}_C$ will be called *deletion profiles*; note that a deletion profile θ is an element of exactly one Delete_C.

I write $\Gamma \vdash e : c$ to mean that $\Gamma \vdash e$ and that $\mathsf{cat}(e) = c$. To the basic operations of minimalist grammars I now add the following, for any categories $c, c_1, \ldots, c_n$ and $\theta \in \mathsf{Delete}_{(c_1 \times \ldots \times c_n) \to c}$.

$$\frac{\vdash e_1 : c_1 \qquad \ldots \qquad \vdash e_n : c_n}{\vdash \theta[\mathbf{x}_1/e_1 \ldots, \mathbf{x}_n/e_n] : c} \; e_\theta$$

This family of operations faithfully implements the idea that ellipsis is a matter of deleting the phonological material in an expression previously derived. However, whereas phonological deletion must be conditioned on some often complex (even undecidable[11]) relation holding between an antcedent and an ellipsis site, there are no such conditions on the family e_θ; an operation e_θ may apply in a context-free way.

---

[11] Merchant (2001) proposes that *mutual entailment* must hold between (the existential closures of) the respective meanings of antecedent and ellipsis site.

The fact that the meaning of an elliptical sentence is somehow parasitic on some other linguistic expression in a discourse is accounted for by treating e_θ as semantically anaphoric; an ellipsis site e_θ requires a salient semantic antecedent *which is the meaning of a hypothetical derivation which has occurred in the surrounding discourse*. This property, described in more detail in section 5.2.6 and demonstrated in 5.3, can be efficiently tracked and updated during the processing of a discourse.

Kobele (2015) defines (in effect) a minimalist grammar with ellipsis to be given by a finite set Ellipsis $\subset \bigcup_{n\in\mathbb{N}} \bigcup_{c_1,\ldots c_n,c}$ Delete$((c_1 \times \ldots \times c_n \to c))$, in addition to At Feat and Lex, which determines the operations e_θ usable by the grammar. He motivates this empirically by noting the (currently) brute fact that different languages seem to have different elliptical processes at their disposal; for example, German has no verb phrase ellipsis.

5.2.6 Interpreting ellipsis

The approach to ellipsis presented in section 5.2.5 takes the syntax of ellipsis to be quite straightforward, which in turn forces the semantics of ellipsis to be non-trivial.[12] Kobele (2015) adopts a *pro-form* theory of ellipsis interpretation, whereby the meaning contribution of an ellipsis operation e_θ is to act as an anaphor, being resolved to a salient meaning in the discourse context. Not just any salient meaning is an appropriate antecedent, however; the meaning must in addition be the meaning of a hypothetical derivation occuring in the discourse context of appropriate type.[13] This is stated formally below, where, for convenience, I write $[\![e_\theta]\!]^D \mapsto M$ to indicate that M is a possible meaning for e_θ in the discourse context D. I take D to be a finite set of derivation trees; a derivation tree d is in D just in case d is the chosen parse of a sentence in the discourse context.

$$[\![e_\theta]\!]^D \mapsto M \text{ iff } \exists e, e', d_1, \ldots, d_n. \quad \begin{array}{l} 1.\ e[e'[d_1, \ldots, d_n]] \in D \\ 2.\ [\![e']\!] = M \\ 3.\ \theta = \texttt{delete}(e') \end{array}$$

---

[12] This is in contrast to approaches, such as the PF-deletion approach, which make the syntactic distribution of ellipsis quite complicated (ellipsis may only obtain if the sentence in question stands in a computationally non-trivial relation with another sentence in the discourse context), while making the semantics of ellipsis trivial.

[13] Schachter (1977) points out, arguing against a claim made by Hankamer and Sag (1976), that there are perfectly well-formed elliptical constructions with no overt linguistic antecedent. Miller and Pullum (2014) provides a summary of the literature, as well as a corpus-informed study of so-called *exophoric* verb phrase ellipsis. In the context of the present theory, there is a straightforward, but not particularly compelling, way of treating cases of exophoric ellipsis. This is to allow that an always available default antecedent exists, something along the lines of *do it*. I would need to have some way of making this default antecedent dispreferred; perhaps the default can only be used in case nothing else is available. This strategy of allowing for certain always available antecedents, while not pretty, can also be used to describe other cases of mismatch between antecedent and ellipsis site, such as in the example below (from Hardt (1993)):

- Decorating for the holidays is easy, if you know how ~~to decorate for the holidays~~

5.2.7 An example

Consider the following simplified dialogue between two parties, **A** and **B**.

A   Oskar might sleep.

B   Carl will not.

I analyze sentences **A** and **B** in terms of the lexical items in Table 5.1. In this table, and elsewhere in this section, I separate features in feature bundles with a period to enhance legibility. Sentences **A** and **B** have derivations d_A and d_B in Figures 5.1 and 5.2 respectively. Note that in both sentences the subject of the clause moves to its surface position. In the derivation tree for sentence **B**, the ellipsis operation $\mathbf{e}_\theta$ is such that $\theta \in \text{Delete}_{d.-k \to v,-k}$. The exact identity of θ will be specified later in this example.

Now assume that the discourse context D contains the derivation d_A for sentence **A**. This can be broken up into the three parts e, e', and d, shown in Figure 5.3, such

Table 5.1 Lexical items

sleep :: =d.v	will :: =v.+k.t	might :: =v.+k.t
Oskar :: d.-k	Carl :: d.-k	not :: =v.v

$$\text{Move}_1$$
$$|$$
$$\text{Merge}_1$$
$$\diagup \quad \diagdown$$
$$\text{Select}_{\text{might}} \quad \text{Merge}_2$$
$$\diagup \quad \diagdown$$
$$\text{Select}_{\text{sleep}} \quad \text{Select}_{\text{Oskar}}$$

Figure 5.1 The derivation for **A**

$$\text{Move}_1$$
$$|$$
$$\text{Merge}_1$$
$$\diagup \quad \diagdown$$
$$\text{Select}_{\text{will}} \quad \text{Merge}_1$$
$$\diagup \quad \diagdown$$
$$\text{Select}_{\text{not}} \quad e_\theta$$
$$|$$
$$\text{Select}_{\text{Carl}}$$

Figure 5.2 The derivation for **B**

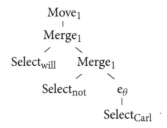

$$d = \text{Select}_{\text{Oskar}}$$

Figure 5.3 Breaking d_A into parts

that $e[e'[d]] = d_A$. The hypothetical expression E' corresponding to the derivation e' is given below. Observe that $\mathtt{cat}(E') = \mathtt{d.\text{-}k} \rightarrow \mathtt{v, \text{-}k}$ and that

$$\mathtt{delete}(E') = x : (\langle x_1, \mathtt{d.\text{-}k}\rangle) \vdash \langle \varepsilon, \mathtt{v}\rangle, \langle x_1, \mathtt{\text{-}k}\rangle.$$

$$\cfrac{\cfrac{\mathsf{sleep} :: \mathtt{=d.v}}{\vdash \langle \mathsf{sleep}, \mathtt{=d.v}\rangle} \text{Select} \quad \cfrac{}{x : (\langle x_1, \mathtt{d.\text{-}k}\rangle) \vdash \langle x_1, \mathtt{d.\text{-}k}\rangle} \text{Axiom}}{x : (\langle x_1, \mathtt{d.\text{-}k}\rangle) \vdash \langle \mathsf{sleep} : \mathtt{v}\rangle, \langle x_1, \mathtt{\text{-}k}\rangle} \text{Merge}_2$$

Returning to the issue of which $\mathbf{e}_\theta$ should be used in d_B, we choose $\theta = \mathtt{delete}(E')$. We can see that d_B corresponds to the derivation below.

$$\cfrac{\cfrac{\mathsf{will} :: \mathtt{=v.+k.t}}{\vdash \langle \mathsf{will}, \mathtt{=v.+k.t}\rangle} \text{Select} \quad \cfrac{\cfrac{\mathsf{not} :: \mathtt{=v.v}}{\vdash \langle \mathsf{not}, \mathtt{=v.v}\rangle} \text{Select} \quad \cfrac{\cfrac{\mathsf{Carl} :: \mathtt{d.\text{-}k}}{\vdash \langle \mathsf{Carl}, \mathtt{d.\text{-}k}\rangle} \text{Select}}{\vdash \langle \varepsilon, \mathtt{v}\rangle, \langle \mathsf{Carl}, \mathtt{\text{-}k}\rangle} \mathbf{e}_{\mathtt{Delete}(E')}}{\vdash \langle \mathsf{not} : \mathtt{v}\rangle, \langle \mathsf{Carl}, \mathtt{\text{-}k}\rangle} \text{Merge}_1}{\cfrac{\vdash \langle \mathsf{will\ not} : \mathtt{+k.t}\rangle, \langle \mathsf{Carl}, \mathtt{\text{-}k}\rangle}{\vdash \langle \mathsf{Carl\ will\ not} : \mathtt{t}\rangle} \text{Move}_1} \text{Merge}_1$$

5.3 The complexity of ellipsis resolution

The problem of comprehending sentences involving ellipsis can be usefully broken up into three independent problems. The first is how to parse sentences (to their underlying structures) when the spate of grammatical operations includes ellipsis (section 5.3.1). The second is how the meaning of ellipsis sites (once postulated) is to be determined (section 5.3.2). The final problem is how to extend the previous discourse context with the new antecedents made available after parsing an additional sentence (section 5.3.3). The main result is that, in the context of the theory developed above, all of these problems are solvable in polynomial time. Or rather, common linguistic assumptions restrict the problem space in a way which makes linguistically possible solutions efficiently obtainable.

5.3.1 Parsing in the presence of ellipsis

Parsing will be here viewed as the problem of mapping a string to the set of its possible derivations given a grammar. As this set can be infinite, we must work with a finite representation thereof, the size of which should be related to the size of the input string in a reasonable way. Since Bar-Hillel et al. (1961), it is standard to view parsing as intersecting the input string (or more generally, a regular grammar) with the original context-free grammar. The derivations of the intersection grammar faithfully represent the derivations in the original grammar of the input string, and the size of the intersection grammar is a polynomial function of the sizes of the original grammar and of the input string. This perspective can be generalized to richer formal systems in a natural way (Kanazawa 2007).

Sound and complete chart-parsing algorithms for minimalist grammars (Harkema 2001) essentially compute the intersection of the regular grammar of minimalist derivations with the input string. In the context of a finite number of ellipsis operations e_θ, the derivation tree language remains regular, whence the standard parsing techniques apply without change. Although the problem of sound and complete parsing in the presence of ellipsis is therefore a trivial extension of previous results, it depends on the *linguistic assumption* below.

Linguistic Assumption 1. There are a fixed, finite number of ellipsis operations available in a given language.

5.3.2 Resolving ellipsis

Ellipsis resolution will be viewed as the problem, given a *single* parse tree t, and a discourse context D, of coming up with *one* way of interpreting the ellipsis operations in t given D, if one exists, and of announcing failure, if none exist. A more realistic account of the resolution problem would take into account some metric of the *plausibility* of an antecedent.

I assume that a discourse context acts as a function mapping deletion profiles to lists of meanings of hypothetical expressions of that category.[14] As given Linguistic Assumption 1, there are finitely many ellipsis operations e_θ, a discourse context can be implemented as a finite map, and thus lookup can be done in time on the order of $\log n$, for n the number of ellipsis operations in the grammar.

To resolve an ellipsis site e_θ, simply take the head of the list returned at position $D(\theta)$, if it exists, and announce failure, otherwise.

There is a potential difficulty that I will now describe but not resolve (I return briefly to this in the conclusion). If the antecedent to an ellipsis site contains itself an unresolved ellipsis site, then there are pathological choices of resolutions which could lead to an infinite regress, thus dashing hopes of a polynomial time resolution strategy. I do not see a simple way of avoiding this problem, while permitting antecedents to contain unresolved ellipsis sites. Accordingly, I impose an *ad hoc* restriction on the number of resolution steps that may be undertaken in attempting to resolve a particular ellipsis site. A bound greater than 0 has the consequence that the entire list of possible antecedents for an ellipsis site may have to be explored to determine whether it can be resolved in the discourse context.

Linguistic Assumption 2. Antecedents may not contain unresolved ellipsis sites.

Linguistic Assumption 2 is, in contrast to the other lingusitic assumptions in this chapter, *not* widely accepted. Indeed, recursive ellipsis resolution figures prominently

---

[14] I show in section 5.3.3 how this assumption about the discourse context can be ensured during discourse processing.

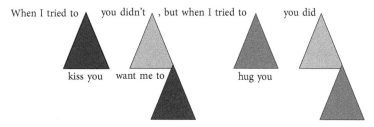

Figure 5.4 Sloppy VPE

in some analyses of sloppy VPE readings (Tomioka 2008), as exemplified in Figure 5.4, which is intended to be understood as meaning the same as "*when I tried to kiss you, you didn't want me to kiss you, but when I tried to hug you, you did want me to hug you.*"

Under Linguistic Assumption 2, the final *you did* of the sentence in the figure should be derived with two ellipsis operations, one (which should be resolved to *want me to*) taking the other (which should be resolved to *hug you*) as its argument.

5.3.3 Updating the discourse context

The main difficulty in parsing elliptical sentences to meanings in discourse revolves around updating the discourse context so as to ensure that ellipsis resolution can be done simply. In this section I show that this is possible to do efficiently, given certain otherwise motivated linguistic assumptions. The main result is the following:

Theorem 1. *We can enumerate* all possible antecedents *in a derivation of* w *in time* polynomial *in* $|w|$.

An antecedent is a hypothetical derivation E, and computing $\mathtt{delete}(E)$ and inserting $[\![E]\!]$ in the antecedent database at the appropriate position is also efficient. Thus, Theorem 1 guarantees that discourse context update is efficiently computable in the length of the input sentence.

It is easy to see that the number of n-ary contexts in a tree t is bounded by $|t|^{n+1}$.[15] Thus, given Linguistic Assumption 1, the number of possible antecedents in a derivation tree d is polynomial in *the size of d*. There is, however, no bound on the size of a tree given its yield.[16] To demonstrate Theorem 1, I reduce first the dependency on $|t|$ to a dependency on the number of *leaves* of t, and then reduce this further to the number of *pronounced* leaves.

---

[15] One chooses one node of t to be the top of the context, and then n additional nodes to be the holes (and then $\binom{m}{n} \leq m^n$) Although this is clearly a very loose bound, a tighter one is not necessary for the purposes of this chapter.

[16] This is due to the possibility both of unary branching and of silent leaves.

5.3.4 Eliding maximal projections

In a minimalist grammar *without* ellipsis, each leaf in the derivation tree (corresponding to a particular lexical item $\ell = \langle w, \delta \rangle$) uniquely determines the sequence of nodes dominating it, of which it is on a left-branching path.[17] The length of this path is bounded by the number of features in the lexical item, and thus the ratio between the number of nodes and number of leaves in the derivation tree is bounded by a constant $c \leq |\delta|$ where δ is the largest feature bundle in the lexicon.

That the lexical items in a derivation uniquely determine it (Hale and Stabler 2005) has been exploited (in (Graf 2011; Kobele 2011; Salvati 2011)) to give an alternative, tree-adjoining grammar-like, representation of minimalist derivations. Here, all nodes of the tree are labeled with lexical items ℓ (for various choices of ℓ). The *rank* of a lexical item $\ell = \langle w, \delta \rangle$ is the number of selector features ($=x$) in its feature bundle δ. This alternative representation equates the size of the tree with the number of lexical items it contains. Using this alternative representation for determining antecedents involves the following substantive (but uncontroversial) linguistic assumptions.

Linguistic Assumption 3. All ellipsis is lexicalized.

Linguistic Assumption 4. Only maximal projections can be elided.

Linguistic Assumption 3 means that each antecedent must contain at least one lexical item; concretely, Move(Assume$_C$) is not a legitimate antecedent. Although Linguistic Assumption 4 is incompatible with early transformational analyses of so-called N-bar deletion, it *is* compatible with current theories and analyses, and seems to be, at least implicitly, uniformly assumed.

5.3.5 Bounding ellipsis

The discussion in the previous section establishes that, without ellipsis, the size of derivation trees is a constant (depending on the grammar) factor of the number of lexical items used in the derivation. *With* ellipsis, however, there is no such bound; an ellipsis operation might map an expression of one category to another of the same (giving rise to a *cyclic* derivation). In analyses given by linguists, such a cyclic ellipsis configuration never arises. Lobeck (1995) claims that each ellipsis site must be *governed* by a particular head. This can be translated into the terminology of the chapter as per the below.

Linguistic Assumption 5. Each ellipsis operation must be associated with a (unique) lexical item.

---

[17] Speaking in terms of Gorn addresses, for any lexical item ℓ, there is some number n such that any leaf in a well-formed derivation labeled with Select$_\ell$ has Gorn address $u0^n$, where u is either empty or ends with a 1. Furthermore, the labels of all nodes with addresses $u0^m$, for $m \leq n$ are determined by ℓ.

As a corollary of Linguistic Assumption 5, the ratio of ellipsis operations to lexical items in a well-formed derivation tree is bounded by a constant $e = 2$, and the number of possible n-ary antecedents is bounded by $((e + 1) \times \|\text{leaves}(t)\|)^{n+1}$.

An alternative (stronger) way of formulating Linguistic Assumption 5 would be to require that every ellipsis operation be immediately dominated by some lexical item (in the tree-adjoining grammar-like representation of derivations).[18] Such a condition would appear to be incompatible with the analysis of sloppy VPE discussed in section 5.3.2, however.[19]

5.3.6 Stopping silence

The linguistic assumptions made thus far have brought the number of possible antecedents in a given derivation down to a polynomial of the number of leaves of that derivation. However, there is, given the possibility of silent lexical items, no connection between the number of words in a sentence and the number of lexical items used in its derivation.

While linguists in the transformational tradition postulate a great deal of silent lexical items, an analysis which allowed for structures of arbitrary size to be populated solely with silent lexical items would be considered bizarre. I instantiate this as a final linguistic assumption.

Linguistic Assumption 6. The ratio of silent lexical items to overt lexical items in a derivation is bounded by a constant k.

With this, there are at most $((e + 1) \times (k + 1) \times |w|)^{n+1}$ possible n-ary antecedents in a derivation tree for w, which is a polynomial function in w, as e, k, and n are constants fixed by the grammar.

Corollary 1. *There are $\mathcal{O}(|w|)$ possible antecedents in a derivation tree of w.*

5.4 Conclusion

I have shown that the theory of ellipsis in Kobele (2015) can be implemented efficiently in a parsing algorithm. In particular, maintaining and updating a discourse context sufficient to permit the resolution of ellipsis can be done efficiently during parsing *in the size of the to-be-parsed input string*.

Although much of the discussion in section 5.3.2 (culminating in Linguistic Assumption 2) revolved around blocking pathological resolution dependencies, further study is necessary. In particular, such pathological dependencies do not seem

---

[18] This stronger formulation is closer to what is intended by Lobeck (1995).

[19] It needn't be actually incompatible, so long as one were willing to posit an otherwise unmotivated silent lexical item in between the two ellipsis sites.

to arise if the discourse context is populated with antecedents obtained during parsing. (Although some care is needed to ensure that a terminating resolution sequence is found quickly.) A weaker alternative to Linguistic Assumption 2, which would admit Tomioka's analysis of sloppy VPE, is to disallow an antecedent from being used more than once in resolving ellipsis sites (stemming from a particular one). While I worried in that section about the unbounded number of potential ellipsis sites, it seems that not all potentially possible antecedents are actually possible for a given ellipsis site; if there were some fixed upper bound on the number of possible antecedents which could be used at any given time, the efficiency results would still hold. This is provided, of course, that the process of keeping track of the accessibility of antecedents could itself be done efficiently.

In order to use ellipsis resolution to influence the parser's online decisions, a natural idea is to include relevant information about antecedents in the discourse context. This information might include identities of lexical items (for topic modeling, or lexical priming effects), or the identites of the peripheral pronounced words (for bigram transition probabilities), etc. Of course, should this information become infinite, we would come into conflict with Linguistic Assumption 1, and with it could go the efficiency of parsing.

In this vein, it would be interesting to consider in more detail the actual implementation of a parser for minimalist grammars with ellipsis. In particular, various seemingly *ad hoc* properties of the formalism may appear different from the perspective of an on-line predictive parsing algorithm.

6

Left-corner parsing of minimalist grammars

Tim Hunter

Much recent research in the experimental psycholinguistics literature revolves around the resolution of long-distance dependencies, and the manner in which the human sentence processor "retrieves" elements from earlier in a sentence that must be related in some way to the material currently being processed. A canonical instance is the resolution of a wh-dependency, where a filler wh-phrase must be linked with an associated gap site; in this case it is now well established, for example, that humans actively predict gap sites in advance of definitive confirming bottom-up evidence. At present, however, there is no obvious way for discussion of these findings to be framed in terms of an MG parser. Stabler (2013b) presents a top-down MG parser that is incremental, but does not involve any corresponding notion of "retrieval": it requires that a phrase's position in the derivation tree be completely identified before the phrase can be scanned, which has the consequence that a filler cannot be scanned without committing to a particular location for its corresponding gap.

In this chapter I will attempt to develop a parsing algorithm that is inspired by Stabler (2013b), but which allows a sentence-initial filler (such as a wh-word) to be scanned immediately while delaying the choice of corresponding gap position. In addition to mixing bottom-up with top-down information in the familiar manner of left-corner parsers, the crucial innovation is in allowing the various features of a moving phrase to be checked at different points in the parser's progress: for example, allowing a filler's wh-feature to be checked without checking its theta-role feature (or equivalent) at the same time. This requires enriching the usual stack to allow categories that have only some of their features checked to "wait in the background," while normal processing in the manner of a context-free left-corner parser moves from the filler position, where the waiting phrase had its movement features checked, to the gap position, where the waiting phrase has its base-position features checked.

The resulting system, as it stands, naturally handles constructions involving movement of constituents that do not themselves contain traces. Movement of constituents containing traces (i.e. remnant movement) creates complications that I have not completely resolved, but I outline one approach to these puzzles that handles some cases and seems to have the potential to generalize.

Section 6.1 very briefly reviews some relevant experimental findings involving retrieval, as motivation. I describe the top-down MG parser from Stabler (2013b) in section 6.2, point out the difficulties in connecting this to questions about retrieval, and then present an initial attempt at a left-corner MG parser that avoids these difficulties

Minimalist Parsing. First edition. Robert C. Berwick and Edward P. Stabler (eds.) This chapter © Tim Hunter 2019. First published 2019 by Oxford University Press.

in section 6.3. Some extensions are required to deal with remnant movement, which I motivate and introduce in section 6.4; these extensions accommodate at least some remnant movement configurations, but their consequences are not yet fully understood. While still incomplete, the system presented here does already point towards some interesting new questions about the subtleties of the experimental findings, which I discuss in section 6.5.

6.1 Human processing of long-distance dependencies

6.1.1 Empirical background

A significant problem that confronts the human sentence-processor is the treatment of *filler-gap* dependencies. These are dependencies between a pronounced element, the *filler*, and a position in the sentence that is not indicated in any direct way by the pronunciation, the *gap*. A canonical example is the kind of dependency created by wh-movement, for example the one shown in (1).

(1)   What did John buy ____ yesterday?

The interesting puzzle posed by such dependencies is that a parser, of course, does not get to "see" the gap: it must somehow determine that there is a gap in the position indicated in (1) on the basis of the properties of the surrounding words, for example the fact that *what* must be associated with a corresponding gap, the fact that *buy* takes a direct object, etc.

Experimental psycholinguistic work has uncovered a number of robust generalizations about how the human parsing system decides where to posit gap sites in amongst the pronounced elements as it works through a sentence incrementally. In most standard cases humans follow the "active gap-filling" strategy (Fodor 1978; Stowe 1986): that is, hypothesize that there is a gap in any position where there might be one, and retract this hypothesis if the next word provides bottom-up evidence disconfirming it. (This is intuitively perhaps the "safe" strategy, erring on the side of the easily disconfirmed hypothesis to be sure that we leave no stone unturned.) Specifically, evidence suggests that the dependency in (1) is constructed before the parser encounters *yesterday*. This conclusion is based on the so-called "filled-gap effect": in a sentence like (2), we observe a reading slowdown at *a book* (Stowe 1986).

(2)   What did John buy a book about ____ yesterday?

This slowdown is what one might expect if a dependency between *what* and the object position of *buy* were constructed before the subject reads past *buy*, and then had to be retracted when *a book* is read. (What was hypothesized to be a gap position is in fact filled, hence "filled-gap effect.")

This basic generalization prompts a number of questions about the details of when and how this sort of hypothesizing of a gap takes place, and in particular the way this mechanism interacts with the intricate grammatical constraints upon the relevant long-distance dependencies; I mention just a few instances to illustrate. For example, it has been shown that active gap-filling is island-sensitive: readers do not pre-emptively posit a gap after *wrote* in (3), in keeping with the fact that complete sentences with an analogous gap in that position, such as (4), are unacceptable (Traxler and Pickering 1996).

(3)   What did [the author who wrote the book]_{island} see _____ yesterday?

(4)   *What did [the author who wrote _____]_{island} see a movie yesterday?

Interestingly, the active gap-filling strategy *does* extend to parasitic gaps that precede their licensing gap: readers pre-emptively create a link between *what* and the object position of *repair* in examples like (5), despite the fact that this would be ill-formed without the accompanying gap after *destroy* (Phillips 2006). This strategy does *not*, however extend to parasitic gaps that follow their licensing gap: there is no pre-emptive dependency creation at *researching* in (6) (Wagers and Phillips 2009).

(5)   What did the attempt to repair _____ ultimately destroy _____?

(6)   What did John attempt to repair _____ before researching _____?

More recent research has investigated analogous questions about different kinds of long-distance dependencies besides filler-gap dependencies, such as the dependency between a pronoun or reflexive and its antecedent (e.g. Dillon 2014), and the dependency between an NPI and its licensor (e.g. Parker and Phillips 2016). These other kinds of dependencies bring with them their own grammatical constraints on the structural locations that they can link, raising questions along the lines of the island-related questions for wh-movement. They also differ in the degree to which pronounced elements at each "end" of the dependency provide evidence that the dependency must be posited: in the classical filler-gap dependency, the filler *must* be connected to something further downstream, but the location of the something must be guessed; a pronoun, by contrast, may or may not require linking to an antecedent elsewhere in the sentence, either earlier or later; a reflexive (or NPI) does require such a link to an antecedent (or negative element) that generally comes earlier in the sentence, but unlike a wh-filler this earlier element doesn't trigger any such requirement.

The term "retrieval" has come to be used as a relatively general-purpose name for the mechanisms that create these kinds of long-distance dependencies[1] at the latter of the two positions being related, linking the current position in the sentence to some element from earlier that is said to be retrieved. The idea that there is something in common across all these different kinds of dependencies comes from the fact that their grammatical descriptions seem to have c-command as a common ingredient.

---

[1] The descriptor "long-distance" is generally understood to mean dependencies that are non-local relative to a surface-structure tree. For example, an agreement dependency between the head of a large NP subject and the verb that follows it would not typically be thought of as long-distance in this sense, even if there is a large linear

6.1.2 Retrieval decisions as ambiguity resolution

At present it is difficult for the generalizations emerging from the experimental work just discussed to be framed in terms of the workings of a comprehensive MG parser. Consider for comparison the earlier empirical work on attachment preferences and garden path theory (e.g. Frazier and Clifton 1996): since the focus was on grammatical relationships that were local in phrase-structural terms (e.g. the dependency between an adjunct PP and its host, or between a verb and its optional object), the strategies being discovered could be understood as strategies for searching through the hypothesis space induced by the operations of a context-free parser. For example, the garden-path effect in (7) can be interpreted as evidence that given the locally ambiguous prefix *When the dog scratched the vet*, readers pursue the analysis in (8a) rather than the one in (8b). This is an instance of the Late Closure preference.

(7)   When the dog scratched the vet and his new assistant removed the muzzle.

(8)   a. When [$_s$ the dog scratched the vet] [$_s$ ...]
      b. When [$_s$ the dog scratched] [$_s$ the vet ...]

Another way to put this is to say that after the word *scratched*, a bottom-up parser has the choice between performing a reduce step (to analyze this verb as a complete, intransitive VP) or performing a shift step (supposing that other remaining input will also be part of the VP), and it prefers the latter.

   In principle, it should be possible to give an analogous description of the active gap-filling generalization: we can imagine a description of the parser's search space that allows us to state preferences for one kind of transition (the kind that interrupts "local processing" and performs retrieval of a filler, roughly) over another (the kind that continues working with local material, roughly). This is difficult at present, however, because there are relatively few formal models of parsing that treat both long-distance dependencies and local dependencies in a cohesive, integrated manner. Aside from this technical hurdle, however, the active gap-filling generalization can be seen as one with the same form as the Late Closure preference: just as humans' first guess given the prefix *When the dog scratched the vet* is (8a) rather than (8b), their first guess given the prefix *What did John buy* is (9a) rather than (9b).

(9)   a. What did John buy _____ ...
      b. What did John buy ...   _____

   One incremental parser that does treat both long-distance dependencies and local dependencies is the top-down MG parser of (Stabler 2013b). It is difficult to connect the empirical generalizations about when retrieval occurs to the choices faced by this parser, however, because it doesn't involve any appropriate notion of retrieval: as I will discuss in section 6.2, before consuming a filler (e.g. a wh-phrase) it must commit

---

distance separating the head noun from the verb (in terms of number of words), because it is a realization of the local relationship between two sisters in a headed/endocentric phrase-structure tree. One of the questions that the work described here aims to bring into sharper focus is to what degree these two kinds of "linearly long-distance" dependencies need to be thought of separately.

to a particular location for its corresponding gap to appear.[2] This means that there is no choice point of the sort mentioned above, where the parser must decide between performing retrieval to create some long-distance dependency involving the current position and continuing on without doing so.

6.2 The top-down MG parser

I will assume familiarity with the MG formalism (Figure 6.1) (Stabler 1997; Stabler and Keenan 2003), and in particular with the close relationship between MGs and MCFGs (Michaelis 2001). I will use MCFG-style derivation trees, of the sort shown in Figure 6.2, throughout. Each node is labeled with a tuple of feature-sequences, and the size of this tuple corresponds to the arity of the MCFG nonterminal; I will call such a tuple a category, and if the length of the tuple is one I will call it a singleton category. Each leaf node must be labeled by a singleton category, and must be accompanied by a string; the lexicon is a list of allowed pairings of a singleton category with a string. The category labeling each unary-branching node must be derivable from the category labeling the single daughter node in accord with the MG operation MOVE. The category labeling each binary-branching node must be derived from the categories labeling the two daughter nodes in accord with the MG operation MERGE. (And there are no nodes with more than two daughters.)

Stabler's (2013b) top-down MG parser adapts the idea underlying the straightforward top-down CFG parser to this MCFG-like understanding of MGs. We begin with the start category—taking C to be the distinguished starting feature of the MG, this will be the singleton category (C)—and rewrite in a top-down manner, expanding the

Given an alphabet Σ and a set of basic types Ty, the set of features is $Feat = \bigcup\{\{x, =x, +x, -x\} \mid x \in Ty\}$, and the set of expressions is $Expr = (\Sigma^* \times Feat^*) \times (\Sigma^* \times Feat^*)^*$. Given a finite lexicon $Lex \subset \Sigma^* \times Feat^*$, merge is a binary partial function on $Expr$ and move is a partial unary function on $Expr$, defined as follows where $s, t \in \Sigma^*$, $\alpha, \beta \in Feat^*$, $\gamma \in Feat^+$, $f \in Ty$, $\phi, \psi \in (\Sigma^* \times Feat^*)^*$.

$$\text{MERGE} = \text{COMP-MERGE} \cup \text{SPEC-MERGE} \cup \text{NONFINAL-MERGE}$$

$$\frac{s :: = f\, \alpha \in Lex \quad t :: f, \psi}{st :: \alpha, \psi}\ \text{COMP-MERGE} \qquad \frac{s :: = f\, \alpha, \phi \notin Lex \quad t :: f, \psi}{ts :: \alpha, \phi\psi}\ \text{SPEC-MERGE}$$

$$\frac{s :: = f\, \alpha, \phi \quad t :: f\, \gamma, \psi}{s :: \alpha, \phi(t, \gamma)\psi}\ \text{NONFINAL-MERGE}$$

$$\text{MOVE} = \text{SPEC-MOVE} \cup \text{NONFINAL-MOVE}$$

$$\frac{s :: + f\alpha, \phi(t, -f)\psi}{ts :: \alpha, \phi\psi}\ \text{SPEC-MOVE} \qquad \frac{s :: + f\, \alpha, \phi(t, -f\gamma)\psi}{s :: \alpha, \phi(t, \gamma)\psi}\ \text{NONFINAL-MOVE}$$

where we require, in both cases, that there is no other $(t', -f)$ or $(t', -f\gamma')$ in ϕ or ψ

Figure 6.1

[2] In principle, multiple hypotheses might be pursued in parallel, of course, but each one will be committed to a particular gap location.

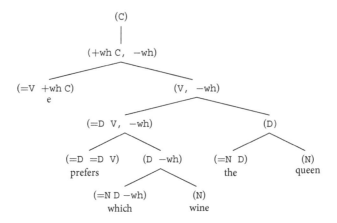

Figure 6.2

Table 6.1

$_0$ which $_1$ wine $_2$ the $_3$ queen $_4$ prefers $_5$

Step	Rule	Counter	Queue
0		0	(C)
1	spec-mv	0	$(+\text{wh C}, -\text{wh}_0)_1$
2	comp-merge	0	$(=\text{V} +\text{wh C})_{10}, (\text{V}, -\text{wh}_0)_{11}$
3	spec-merge	0	$(=\text{V} +\text{wh C})_{10}, (=\text{D V}, -\text{wh}_0)_{111}, (\text{D})_{110}$
4	nonfinal-merge	0	$(=\text{V} +\text{wh C})_{10}, (=\text{D} =\text{D V})_{111}, (\text{D} -\text{wh})_0, (\text{D})_{110}$
5	comp-merge	0	$(=\text{V} +\text{wh C})_{10}, (=\text{D} =\text{D V})_{111}, (=\text{N D} -\text{wh})_{00}, (\text{N})_{01}, (\text{D})_{110}$
6	scan	1	$(=\text{V} +\text{wh C})_{10}, (=\text{D} =\text{D V})_{111}, (\text{N})_{01}, (\text{D})_{110}$
7	scan	2	$(=\text{V} +\text{wh C})_{10}, (=\text{D} =\text{D V})_{111}, (\text{D})_{110}$
8	scan	2	$(=\text{D} =\text{D V})_{111}, (\text{D})_{110}$
9	comp-merge	2	$(=\text{D} =\text{D V})_{111}, (=\text{N D})_{1100}, (\text{N})_{1101}$
10	scan	3	$(=\text{D} =\text{D V})_{111}, (\text{N})_{1101}$
11	scan	4	$(=\text{D} =\text{D V})_{111}$
12	scan	5	ε

frontier of the tree by replacing one category at a time. Each such predictive rewriting step corresponds exactly either to one of the three subcases of MERGE (if it introduces two new categories) or to one of the two subcases of MOVE (if it introduces one new category). The first few steps shown in Table 6.1 (ignoring the subscripts for now) are examples of this, carrying out the first few top-down expansions starting from the root of the tree in Figure 6.2. When such predictive rewriting steps eventually introduce a category that the lexicon pairs with the first word waiting in the input buffer, that word will be scanned, and the category will be removed from the parser's record of the frontier of the tree—that prediction has been fulfilled. What remains is a record of that part of the frontier of the tree that is yet to be matched with input.

   In the context-free case, a top-down parser can perform what is in effect a leftmost derivation, always expanding the leftmost category in its store, since this is guaranteed to be the one category on the frontier that dominates the next word to be consumed. (The parser's store therefore operates as a stack, with the "top" of the stack corresponding to the "leftmost" symbol on the frontier.) What makes things more complicated in the MG top-down parser is that this simple relationship no longer holds between the order of the category symbols that make up the current frontier of the tree and the order of the incoming words: in the tree in Figure 6.2, the path from the root node down to the terminal node *which* is *not* simply the path obtained by stepping down to the leftmost daughter at each point. This is a direct consequence of the way MCFGs generalize beyond the simple situation that holds in a CFG, where the yield of a tree with two daughter subtrees is the yield of the left daughter concatenated with the yield of the right daughter.

Turning to the specifics of Table 6.1: notice that of the two categories in the store in Step 2—corresponding to the frontier of the tree as it stands after two expansions—it is the *rightmost* one, that is expanded next, according to the rule

$$(\text{V, -wh}) \quad \rightarrow \quad (\text{=D V, -wh}) \ (\text{D})$$

to reach the configuration shown in Step 3. Of the two categories thereby introduced, it is the leftmost one (the middle one of the three shown in Step 3) that is expanded next, according to the rule

$$(\text{=D V, -wh}) \quad \rightarrow \quad (\text{=D =D V}) \ (\text{D -wh})$$

to reach Step 4. Next the rightmost of these is expanded, to result in a situation where the tree has been expanded down to the frontier

$$(\text{=V +wh C}) \quad (\text{=D =D V}) \quad (\text{=N D -wh}) \quad (\text{N}) \quad (\text{D})$$

in Step 5, and the next step can now scan the first word of the input, *which*, to fulfill the prediction represented by the third category in this frontier, which is then removed in Step 6.

Since the tree-based order in which the categories are shown in Table 6.1 does not suffice to answer the question of "where to look next" in the way it does for a simple context-free parser, the MG parser must track some more information about the relationships amongst the various derivational subconstituents that are in its store. Specifically, it must track the relative ordering of the *derived positions* of those various subconstituents. This extra information is in the subscripts that we have ignored until now. The subscripts are Gorn addresses into the derived tree. Notice that in Step 5, (=N D -wh) has the leftmost Gorn address of the five categories present (namely 00); it is for this reason that it (and not any other category in the store) is a candidate for matching a word from the input buffer. Having the leftmost Gorn address corresponds to being on the top of the stack in the context-free case: that is where the parser looks to work next, whether that work is scanning a word from the input buffer or rewriting a category according to some other rule. To take an example of the latter, the fact that (D -wh) has the leftmost Gorn address (namely 0) of the four categories present in Step 4 is what dictates that this, rather than any other category, should be expanded at the next step. Notice that when (D -wh) is expanded, the address of the new left daughter is obtained by appending 0 to the parent address (producing 00), and the address of the new right daughter is obtained by appending 1 (producing 01).

In general, however, the notion of the "derived position" of a particular derivational subconstituent is not so straightforward. It is relatively simple in the cases just discussed (Steps 4 and 5), because all the categories involved there are singleton categories: they have no moving subparts, and therefore correspond directly to subtrees of the derived tree (even if their order in the derivation tree differs from the order of the corresponding subtrees of the derived tree). With complex, multi-component categories the situation is different: notice that the two-component categories in Steps 2–4 have an additional address for their moving -wh components. For example, in Step 2 we have $(V, \text{-wh}_0)_{11}$, indicating a completed V projection out of which a -wh phrase will move, where the V projection's address in the derived tree is 11 and the -wh phrase's address is 0. This address was given to the -wh component when it was first introduced in Step 1, as part of the rewriting of the start symbol (C): in derivation-tree terms this is a unary rewriting step that replaces (C) with the category (+wh C, -wh), but the consequence of this in derived-tree terms is that the completed C projection that we have predicted will appear at address ε (i.e. the root node) will have a phrase that has moved to check a -wh feature as its left daughter (address 0), and will have all the other, non-moving parts of the (+wh C, -wh) expression somewhere within its right daughter (address 1). The moving subcomponent with address 0 stands by as the non-moving parts are expanded in Steps 2 and 3, and then in Step 4 the 0 becomes the full-fledged address of a singleton category: this is the crucial step where we decide to expand (=D V, -wh) as an instance of the nonfinal-MERGE rule, meaning that one of the daughters of this node *is* the moving -wh subcomponent.

The crucial point to notice for present purposes is that a word can only be scanned once the full root-to-leaf path to that word in the derivation tree has been expanded. Committing to such a sequence of expansions commits the parser to particular choices about where *each* of that word's features are checked. In Table 6.1, expansions that precede the first scan step involve the checking of a -wh movement feature at (in derived-tree terms) the specifier of the root CP *and* the checking of a D selectional feature at the object position of the matrix clause. Therefore when *which* is scanned at Step 6, it is being scanned *as* (the head of) a wh-phrase that moves from the matrix object position to the matrix SpecCP position; the steps taken down to and including Step 6 are not compatible with any other base (pre-movement) position for the phrase headed by *which*.

To illustrate the point, consider Table 6.2, where we have a fronted wh-phrase that has moved from the matrix subject position instead. Only an initial portion of the parser's behavior is shown, but we can see that the expansion steps that lead up to the scanning of *which* (and also the scanning of *book* at the very next step) are different from those that lead up to this first scan step in Table 6.1. Only the first two steps are shared, which correspond to breaking down the sentence into the wh-attracting complementizer (category (=V +wh C)) and a V projection out of which a wh-phrase will move (category (V, -wh)). Beyond this, the parser must choose between expanding

Table 6.2

$_0$ which $_1$ wine $_2$ prefers $_3$ the $_4$ queen $_5$

Rule	Counter	Queue
	0	(C)
spec-mv	0	$(\text{+wh C}, \text{-wh}_0)_1$
comp-merge	0	$(\text{=V +wh C})_{10}, (\text{V}, \text{-wh}_0)_{11}$
nonfinal-merge	0	$(\text{=V +wh C})_{10}, (\text{=D V})_{110}, (\text{D -wh})_0$
comp-merge	0	$(\text{=V +wh C})_{10}, (\text{=D V})_{110}, (\text{=N D -wh})_{00}, (\text{N})_{01}$
scan	1	$(\text{=V +wh C})_{10}, (\text{=D V})_{110}, (\text{N})_{01}$
scan	2	$(\text{=V +wh C})_{10}, (\text{=D V})_{110}$
$\vdots$	$\vdots$	$\vdots$

the latter in a way that takes the moving wh-phrase the subject (as in Table 6.2) and doing so in a way that takes the moving wh-phrase to be somewhere further embedded. So the parser must make a choice between these two analyses even before scanning the word *which*.

The underlying assumption running through discussions of the experimental results reviewed above, however, is that it is possible to scan a filler (here, *which wine*) while remaining uncomitted to any particular corresponding gap site. Having scanned a filler at the left edge of a clause, interesting questions arise about how a parser can subsequently—as it reads through the rest of the sentence—decide where to posit the corresponding gap, and these questions are the target of investigation in those experimental studies. This top-down MG parser, however, does not make available any corresponding notion of deciding where to discharge a pending obligation to posit a gap site, because the decision has already had to be made before the filler which creates this obligation could be scanned. The identification of filler sites is inseparable from the identification of gap sites. This is the issue that motivates the search for a left-corner-based parsing strategy described in the next section.

6.3 Towards a left-corner MG parser

In order to improve upon the top-down MG parser in the sense just discussed, I take inspiration from the left-corner parsing strategy for context-free grammars. I provide a quick review of context-free left-corner parsing, largely to fix some notation and terminology, before turning to the left-corner MG parser that I propose.

6.3.1 CFG left-corner parsing

Assume a context-free grammar with nonterminal alphabet N and terminal alphabet V, with start symbol $S \in N$. Then the left-corner parsing schema defines a transition relation on *configurations*, where a configuration is an ordered pair: the first component of a configuration, the *stack*, is a sequence of elements of $\{X : X \in N\} \cup \{\bar{X} : X \in N\}$, and the second component, the *buffer*, is a sequence of elements of V. For a given

$w_1 w_2 \ldots w_n \in V^*$ to be parsed, the starting configuration is $(\bar{S}, w_1 w_2 \ldots w_n)$, and the goal configuration is $(\varepsilon, \varepsilon)$. The transition relation is the union of the four relations defined in (10).[3] (I make the simplifying assumption that each production rule has on its right hand side either a single terminal symbol or a sequence of nonterminal symbols, not a mixture of the two.)

(10)   For $w_i \in V$, X, $Y_i \in N$, $\alpha \in (\{X : X \in N\} \cup \{\bar{X} : X \in N\})^*$

a. $(\alpha, w_i \ldots w_n) \xrightarrow{\text{shift}} (X\alpha, w_{i+1} \ldots w_n)$
   where $X \to w_i$ is a rule of the grammar

b. $(\bar{X}\alpha, w_i \ldots w_n) \xrightarrow{\text{scan}} (\alpha, w_{i+1} \ldots w_n)$
   where $X \to w_i$ is a rule of the grammar

c. $(Y_1\alpha, w_i \ldots w_n) \xrightarrow{\text{predict}} (\bar{Y_2} \ldots \bar{Y_m}X\alpha, w_i \ldots w_n)$
   where $X \to Y_1 \ldots Y_m$ is a rule of the grammar

d. $(Y_1\bar{X}\alpha, w_i \ldots w_n) \xrightarrow{\text{connect}} (\bar{Y_2} \ldots \bar{Y_m}\alpha, w_i \ldots w_n)$
   where $X \to Y_1 \ldots Y_m$ is a rule of the grammar

Table 6.3 shows how these rules operate on the sentence whose derivation is shown in (11). (The grammar is left implicit.)

(11)

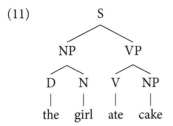

Nonterminal symbols with a bar over them correspond to unfulfilled predictions; hence the start configuration containing the symbol $\bar{S}$. The shift rule consumes a word from the input, and adds a symbol to the stack indicating the appropriate bottom-up, already-recognized nonterminal (i.e. the symbol has no bar over it). The scan rule also consumes a word from the input, but uses it to remove a symbol from the stack, specifically a predicted instance of a nonterminal that the word can satisfy. The predict rule and the connect rule both "trade in" a bottom-up recognized nonterminal (no bar) for some number of predictions (with bars) corresponding to that nonterminal's hypothesized sisters, according to some chosen rule. When predict applies in Step 2 of Table 6.3, for example, the already-recognized D is hypothesized to be the left corner of an NP constituent expanded according to the rule "NP → D N"; it is therefore traded in for a predicted N, accompanied by a bottom-up NP symbol that will be available to work with if that prediction of an N is fulfilled. When connect applies in Step 4, the recognized NP (left corner of the rule "S → NP VP") is similarly traded in for a predicted VP; what makes the connect rule different is that we put this recognized

---

[3] This presentation is closely based on that of Kanazawa (2016).

Table 6.3

Step	Rule		Remaining input	Stack
0			the girl ate cake	$\overline{S}$
1	shift	D → the	girl ate cake	D $\overline{S}$
2	predict	NP → D N	girl ate cake	$\overline{N}$ NP $\overline{S}$
3	scan	N → girl	ate cake	NP $\overline{S}$
4	connect	S → NP VP	ate cake	$\overline{VP}$
5	shift	V → ate	cake	V $\overline{VP}$
6	connect	VP → V NP	cake	$\overline{NP}$
7	scan	NP → cake	ε	ε

NP towards the satisfaction of an *already predicted* instance of the parent nonterminal (here, $\overline{S}$), so we remove this symbol from the stack rather than adding a bottom-up instance of this parent nonterminal.

The guiding intuition behind the MG parser proposed below is that it should consume a filler (e.g. a wh-phrase), and update its predictions accordingly in something like the way a context-free left-corner parser would when working with a GPSG-style rule like S → WH S$_{[/wh]}$. An illustrative example is shown in (12).

(12)

Step	Rule		Remaining input	Stack
0			what did the girl eat	$\overline{S}$
1	shift	WH → what	did the girl eat	WH $\overline{S}$
2	connect	S → WH S$_{[/wh]}$	did the girl eat	$\overline{S_{[/wh]}}$

The crucial point here is that the parser consumes the filler, and updates its state accordingly to reflect the fact that it is now expecting a "gapped sentence" to follow, without yet committing to any particular structural position for the gap. Recall that this contrasts with the way the top-down MG parser discussed above must decide on *all* the positions in which a filler phrase checks features before that phrase can be scanned.

6.3.2 Basic cases

We can carry over to the MG setting the distinction between bottom-up recognized elements (e.g. the wh-phrase in (12), represented by symbols without bars) and top-down predicted elements. In addition, we will need to separate out the different feature-checking steps that a particular constituent is involved in in the course of a derivation: for example, given a phrase of category (D -wh), we wish to be able to talk about the D-position of the -wh-position of this phrase, in either a bottom-up or top-down manner. This second step crucially differs from the workings on the top-down MG parser.

Table 6.4 Parsing the derivation with no movement shown in Figure 6.3

Step	Rule	Input	
0		e the queen prefers the wine	$\overline{(C⌊)}$
1	shift	the queen prefers the wine	$(=V\ C])_1$ $\overline{(C⌊)}$
2	comp-mrg-connect	the queen prefers the wine	$\overline{(V⌊)}$
3	shift	queen prefers the wine	$(=N\ D])_1$ $\overline{(V⌊)}$
4	comp-mrg-predict	queen prefers the wine	$\overline{(N⌊)}$ $(D])_0$ $\overline{(V⌊)}$
5	scan	prefers the wine	$(D])_0$ $\overline{(V⌊)}$
6	spec-mrg-connect	prefers the wine	$\overline{(=D\ V⌊)}_0$
7	shift	the wine	$\overline{(=D\ =D\ V])}_1$ $\overline{(=D\ V⌊)}_0$
8	comp-mrg-connect	the wine	$\overline{(D⌊)}$
9	shift	wine	$(=N\ D])_1$ $\overline{(D⌊)}$
10	comp-mrg-connect	wine	$\overline{(N⌊)}$
11	scan	ε	ε

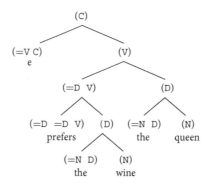

Figure 6.3 A derivation with no movement yet. The parse is shown in Table 6.4.

To begin, Table 6.4 shows a left-corner parse of the simple derivation shown in Figure 6.3. Since there is no movement yet, we do not yet need to make use of the separation of the feature-checking steps for moving elements. For clarity of exposition I take lexical items that are usually phonologically null to have overt pronunciations (usually 'e'). In addition to shift and scan rules that are analogous to the rules of the same name in the CFG case, the left-corner MG parser has a connect transition rule and a predict transition rule for each of the five MG rules (the three cases of merge and two cases of move as shown in Figure 6.1). The full array of these ten transition rules is shown below in Figure 6.6. For now, the only two MG rules relevant to the simple movement-free derivation in Figure 6.3 are comp-mrg and spec-mrg; the parse in Table 6.4 makes use of the comp-merge-connect, comp-merge-predict, and spec-merge-connect transition rules.

The first two steps in Table 6.4 mimic the way a CFG left-corner parser would work with the rules

$$(\textsc{c}) \quad \rightarrow \quad (\textsc{=v c}) \quad (\textsc{v}) \qquad\qquad (\text{comp-merge})$$
$$(\textsc{=v c}) \quad \rightarrow \quad e$$

namely shifting on the bottom-up recognized (=V C), and then connecting it to the predicted start category (C) to create a predicted (V). The 1 subscript on the shifted category indicates that the corresponding constituent is known to be lexical: this is tracked in case it becomes relevant to distinguishing between whether comp-mrg or spec-mrg can apply. A 0 subscript indicates that a constituent is known to be non-lexical; the absence of a subcript leaves the lexicality undetermined. (The unusual "hook" marks that appear inside the closing parenthesis of each category can be ignored for now; these are relevant to the separation between the checking of selectee features and licensee features, which will be illustrated below.)

Steps 3 and 4 in Table 6.4 mimic the way a CFG left-corner parser would work with the rules

$$(\textsc{d}) \quad \rightarrow \quad (\textsc{=n d}) \quad (\textsc{n}) \qquad\qquad (\text{comp-merge})$$
$$(\textsc{=n d}) \quad \rightarrow \quad \text{the}$$

again shifting on the lexical category (=N D), but this time positing a new parent category (D) to follow the predicted sister (N), rather than connecting to an existing prediction as above. After the next input word *queen* is scanned (Step 5) to fulfill this prediction, the now-established bottom-up (D) is connected (Step 6) to the subsequent top-down prediction according to the rule

$$(\textsc{v}) \quad \rightarrow \quad (\textsc{=d v}) \quad (\textsc{d}) \qquad\qquad (\text{spec-merge})$$

to leave a predicted (=D V). Notice that although (D) appears as the right daughter in the tree (and in the rule above), because I am adopting the convention that the expression whose selector feature is being checked is always the left daughter of a merge step, we are taking it to be the linearly left daughter of the (V) (i.e. a specifier); therefore the resulting prediction has a 0 subscript marking it as non-lexical, with the effect that, unlike other top-down predictions, it *cannot* be satisfied with a scan step.

The remaining steps are similar to what has come before them.

We can now turn to a case involving one simple movement step. For comparison, I will use the derivation for which a top-down parse was discussed above. The derivation tree is repeated in Figure 6.4, this time with an additional dashed line: from now on I will include lines like this indicating the implicit dependency between the movement step at the top of the tree and the subtree rooted at the node labeled (D -wh). I will say that the (D -wh) node is a *quasi-daughter* of the root (C) node, and is a *quasi-sister* of the (+wh C, -wh) node. Notice that these relationships mirror the fact that the wh-phrase *which wine* is a daughter of the root CP node, and sister to a C′ node, in the relevant derived tree. Making these relationships more salient is one step towards implementing the idea gestured at in (12).

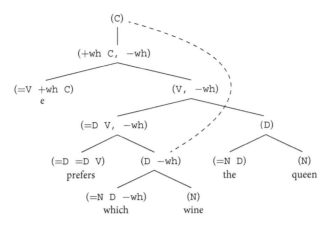

Figure 6.4 A derivation with one movement, from object position. The parse is shown in Table 6.5.

Table 6.5 Parsing the object-movement derivation in Figure 6.4

$_0$ which $_1$ wine $_2$ e $_3$ the $_4$ queen $_5$ prefers $_6$

Step	Rule	Counter	
0		0	$\overline{(\text{C}\lceil)}$
1	shift	1	$(=\!\text{N D -wh}\rceil)_1$ $\overline{(\text{C}\lceil)}$
2	comp-merge-predict	1	$\overline{(\text{N}\lceil)}$ $(\text{D -wh}\rceil)_0$ $\overline{(\text{C}\lceil)}$
3	scan	2	$(\text{D -wh}\rceil)_0$ $\overline{(\text{C}\lceil)}$
4	spec-move-connect	2	$(\text{D}\rceil\text{-wh})_0$ $\overline{(+\text{wh C}\lceil, -\text{wh})}$
5	shift	3	$(=\!\text{V +wh C}\rceil)_1$ $(\text{D}\rceil\text{-wh})_0$ $\overline{(+\text{wh C}\lceil, -\text{wh})}$
6	comp-merge-connect	3	$(\text{D}\rceil\text{-wh})_0$ $\overline{(\text{V}\lceil, -\text{wh})}$
7	shift	4	$(=\!\text{N D}\rceil)_1$ $(\text{D}\rceil\text{-wh})_0$ $\overline{(\text{V}\lceil, -\text{wh})}$
8	comp-merge-predict	4	$\overline{(\text{N}\lceil)}$ $(\text{D}\rceil)_0$ $(\text{D}\rceil\text{-wh})_0$ $\overline{(\text{V}\lceil, -\text{wh})}$
9	scan	5	$(\text{D}\rceil)_0$ $(\text{D}\rceil\text{-wh})_0$ $\overline{(\text{V}\lceil, -\text{wh})}$
10	spec-merge-connect	5	$(\text{D}\rceil\text{-wh})_0$ $\overline{(=\!\text{D V}\lceil, -\text{wh})_0}$
11	nonfinal-merge-connect	5	$\overline{(=\!\text{D} =\!\text{D V}\lceil)}$
12	scan	6	ε

A trace of the MG left-corner parser's construction of this derivation is shown in Table 6.5. The first three steps involve transitions we have seen before: specifically, they correspond to shifting a determiner, analyzing it as the left corner of a DP, and then scanning the predicted N, just as in Steps 3–5 in Table 6.4. The additional -wh feature is irrelevant so far. As the "stack" in Step 3 indicates, we end up with a bottom-up recognized (D -wh) which we hope to put towards fulfilling a predicted (C).

Step 4 is a connect step: we connect this bottom-up constituent to the predicted (C). The connection being made is not one between a node and its mother in the tree in

Figure 6.4, but rather—since this transition is based on an application of the spec-move rule—one between the (D -wh) node and its *quasi-mother*. Just as the connect step in Step 2 of Table 6.4 can be thought of as drawing the two lines that branch down from the (C) node in Figure 6.3, this instance of spec-mv-connect can be thought of as drawing the dashed line in Figure 6.4 and also the single solid line from the root (C) node down to its daughter. It is our version of the connect step in (12). It amounts to "deciding that" the predicted (C) constituent will be formed by a movement step which checks the -wh feature on the bottom-up recognized (D -wh) phrase. (Using spec-mv-connect at this point would not be an option if the bottom-up recognized category were simply (D).) The predicted (C) is therefore replaced with a prediction of category (+wh C, -wh), as we might expect: this is our prediction of a "sentence with a gap."

Of course we are not yet finished with the wh-phrase *which wine*. It has two requirements: it must be moved into a position where its -wh feature can be checked and merged into a position where its D feature can be checked, and we have so far satisfied only the first of these. Before this spec-mv-connect step, both of these features were unchecked, as indicated by the placement of the "hook" in (D -wh]); this step has the effect of moving the hook leftward past the now-checked -wh feature, hence (D]-wh). The top of the hook "points" towards the remaining unchecked features and (as the parser progresses) moves in that direction, one step at a time, as features are checked. So (D -wh]) indicates that -wh is the next feature looking to be checked, hence the applicability of spec-mv-connect in Step 4, and (D]-wh) indicates that D is the next feature to be checked. Deciding when to check this feature amounts to deciding where to posit a gap site for the now-consumed filler. So although we do now have an obligation to find a place where this D feature can be checked somewhere within the (+wh C, -wh) that has now been predicted, the relationship between this bottom-up unchecked D and this top-down prediction is not the same as, for example, the relationship between the two symbols in the store at Step 5 of Table 6.4 (after consuming *the queen*):

$$(\text{D}])_0 \quad \overline{(\text{V}[})$$

where the linear order in which words have been consumed constrains the positions within the predicted (V) where the D feature may be checked (i.e. it must be some position at the left edge, linearly). Instead, in the present case, we must maintain the obligation to check the remaining D feature somewhere within the (+wh C, -wh), but in a way that gives us free choice regarding when to do so. To record elements with this distinguished status—which are the same as the elements that have some but not all of their features currently checked—I use pre-subscripts, as shown after Step 4 in Table 6.5. I will sometimes refer to these subscripted categories as *bystanders*. Graphically, the intuition is that this category is "there if we want it", but we can also choose to "look over it" and work directly with the (+wh C, -wh) if we wish.

In Steps 5–10, we do exactly that. The complementizer is shifted (Step 5) and connected to the predicted (+wh C, -wh) (Step 6), and the bystander is passed down to the new predicted (V, -wh). In Steps 7–9 the subject is recognized, and it is then connected (Step 10) to the pending prediction to yield the new prediction of a $(=D V, -wh)$, again with the bystander passed down. The store now looks like this:

$$(D]-wh)_0 \overline{(=D V[, -wh)_0}$$

which we can read as saying that we need to fulfill a prediction of a $(=D V, -wh)$, and we have up our sleeve a $(D -wh)$ whose D feature remains unchecked, to use when we wish.

What happens next is the crucial "retrieval" step (Step 11). It is based on the MCFG-style rule

$$(=D V, -wh) \quad \rightarrow \quad (=D =D V) \quad (D -wh)$$

which is an instance of the MG rule nonfinal-merge, because the constituent whose selectee is checked has licensee features (here, $-wh$). Since the left-hand side of this rule corresponds to the category we already have a prediction of, it will be a connect transition (rather than a predict transition). (Notice that the $=D$ selector feature on the left-hand side, and the one that appears in the parser's store at the stage under consideration, is not the one being checked at the (nonfinal-)merge step being discussed.) We connect the daughter we already have—this is when we decide to stop looking over it, and bring it back into the fold—to the predicted parent, and replace that prediction with a prediction of the other daughter category, $(=D =D V)$. This corresponds to drawing the two lines that branch down from the node labeled $(=D V, -wh)$ in Figure 6.4, providing the $(D -wh)$ node with the second dependency that it needs (the other one having already been established earlier, at the step corresponding to drawing the dashed line). The new prediction is straightforwardly fulfilled by scanning *prefers* in the final step.

A perhaps unusual point to note about the nonfinal-merge-connect step is that it treats $(D -wh)$ as the "left" corner of the relevant MCFG-style rule shown just above. This is *not* another instance of a right daughter in the derivation tree linearly preceding its sister due to its being a specifier, of the sort we saw above when the subject *the queen* was connected to top-down predictions in each of the two traces shown above: note that we would usually talk of the "trace" or "gap site" being to the *right* of the verb *prefers* in this sentence, because the vacated position is a complement position. The fact which makes the wh-phrase a left corner in the relevant sense here, however, is the fact that it linearly precedes the verb, due to its having moved to the left periphery of the sentence: of the two derivational children of the $(=D V, -wh)$ node in the derivation tree, the wh-phrase is the one that the parser encounters first. Since movement is always to the left, transitions based on nonfinal-merge and spec-merge will share the property that the selected element precedes the selector and will therefore act as the "trigger" for the rule,[4] whereas transitions based on comp-merge will have the selector as the trigger.

In broad terms, we now have a concrete version of the "active gap-filling" heuristic that humans seem to adopt: it is a heuristic that says to always try nonfinal-merge transitions in preference to other kinds of transitions, in much the same way that

---

[4] This is effectively no longer true in situations involving remnant movement, which I consider in section 6.4.

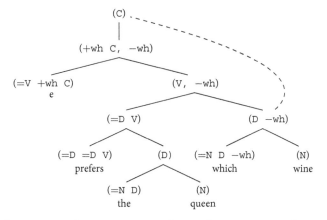

Figure 6.5 A derivation with one movement, from subject position. The parse is shown in Table 6.6.

"late closure" can be seen as a heuristic that says to always try shift transitions in preference to reduce transitions. The particulars of the nonfinal-merge-connect step just discussed, however, of course should be compared with findings from the experimental psycholinguistics literature; I turn to this in section 6.5.

Let us turn now to an example where the parser encounters the same fronted filler (*which wine*) but resolves the dependency with a gap in a different position. Figure 6.5 shows the derivation tree for *which wine prefers the queen*, with the gap in subject position instead of object position. It uses the same lexical items as the previous example.

A trace of the parser's steps on this sentence is shown in Table 6.6. As one might expect, the first three steps are identical to the previous object-gap example (Table 6.5): we recognize the filler wh-phrase, bringing us to the configuration

$$(\text{D -wh}])_0 \quad \overline{(\text{C}[)}$$

after *wine* is scanned. More interestingly perhaps, the next three steps are identical to the previous example as well: we connect this wh-phrase as the specifier of the root CP ("drawing the dotted line") (Step 4), consume the complementizer (Step 5), and connect it to the current top-down prediction (Step 6), leaving us with only the predicted (V, -wh). At this point the parser is committed to analyzing *which wine* as the specifier of the root CP, and has remaining only the task of finding a V projection that contains somewhere inside it a place for the filler's remaining D selectee feature to be checked. Both the object–gap and subject–gap sentences include this same initial portion of work. This is the improvement upon the top-down parser that we set out to achieve.

In Table 6.6, the next step (Step 7) performs the "retrieval", using (the remaining unchecked D feature of) the (D -wh) filler in accord with the nonfinal-merge instance

$$(\text{V, -wh}) \quad \rightarrow \quad (\text{=D V}) \quad (\text{D -wh})$$

Table 6.6 Parsing the subject-movement derivation in Figure 6.5

$_0$ which $_1$ wine $_2$ e $_3$ prefers $_4$ the $_5$ queen $_6$

Step	Rule	Counter	
0		0	$\overline{(C\lceil)}$
1	shift	1	$(=N\ D\ -wh])_1$ $\overline{(C\lceil)}$
2	comp-merge-predict	1	$\overline{(N\lceil)}$ $(D\ -wh])_0$ $\overline{(C\lceil)}$
3	scan	2	$(D\ -wh])_0$ $\overline{(C\lceil)}$
4	spec-move-connect	2	$(D]-wh)_0$ $\overline{(+wh\ C\lceil,\ -wh)}$
5	shift	3	$(=V\ +wh\ C])_1$ $(D]-wh)_0$ $\overline{(+wh\ C\lceil,\ -wh)}$
6	comp-merge-connect	3	$(D]-wh)_0$ $\overline{(V\lceil,\ -wh)}$
7	nonfinal-merge-connect	3	$\overline{(=D\ V\lceil)}$
8	shift	4	$(=D\ =D\ V])_1$ $\overline{(=D\ V\lceil)}$
9	comp-merge-connect	4	$\overline{(D\lceil)}$
10	shift	5	$(=N\ D])_1$ $\overline{(D\lceil)}$
11	comp-merge-connect	5	$\overline{(N\lceil)}$
12	scan	6	ε

to produce a new prediction of category (=D V). Fulfilling this prediction in the remaining steps involves no more movement, and is straightforward.

As in the previous example, the nonfinal-merge step (Step 7) corresponds to drawing the solid line that branches down to the (D -wh) node (and the one branching down to its sister). In the object–gap example, Step 7 (the first step that departs from what we see in Table 6.6) begins the process of consuming the subject *the queen* (specifically, it shifts *the*). So the decision the parser must make about which transition to take from the configuration shown in Step 6 in both tables is precisely the decision of whether or not to take the subject position to be the gap site.

In both of these two cases there is a transition based on a spec-move rule that analyses a wh-phrase as the specifier of a CP; and in particular, in both of these cases it analyses that wh-phrase as the specifier of the *root* CP, a constituent that we already have a prediction for. Things work in essentially the same way if this relevant CP constituent is *not* one that we are already expecting: the difference is simply the choice between spec-move-connect, which we have used in the two examples we have seen so far, and spec-move-predict. The effect of taking this "wrong turn" at Step 4 of Table 6.6 and having a fresh CP constituent be "brought into existence" in addition to the already predicted one (as one might need to do for an input like *[which wine prefers the queen] is an open question*), is shown in Table 6.7. Following the same sequence of steps thereafter, we end up stuck, having recognized the full utterance bottom-up and never connected it to the original prediction of the start category.

A schematic definition of the parsing rules is shown in Figure 6.6. An *item* is a category with or without a bar written over it, and with a "hook" marker indicating the division between checked and unchecked features; a *stack-element* is an item along

Table 6.7 Illustrating spec-move-predict

$_0$ which $_1$ wine $_2$ e $_3$ prefers $_4$ the $_5$ queen $_6$

Step	Rule	Counter	
0		0	$\overline{(\text{C}\lceil)}$
1	shift	1	$(\text{=N D -wh}])_1$ $\overline{(\text{C}\lceil)}$
2	comp-merge-predict	1	$\overline{(\text{N}\lceil)}$ $(\text{D -wh}])_0$ $\overline{(\text{C}\lceil)}$
3	scan	2	$(\text{D -wh}])_0$ $\overline{(\text{C}\lceil)}$
4	spec-move-predict	2	$_{(\text{D}]\text{-wh})_0}$ $\overline{(\text{+wh C}\lceil, \text{ -wh})}$ $(\text{C}])_0$ $\overline{(\text{C}\lceil)}$
	. . .		. . .
11	comp-merge-connect	5	$\overline{(\text{N}\lceil)}$ $(\text{C}])_0$ $\overline{(\text{C}\lceil)}$
12	scan	6	$(\text{C}])_0$ $\overline{(\text{C}\lceil)}$

with zero or more bystander items, written as left subscripts; the parser's store takes the form of a stack of stack-elements. Ellipses in the rules indicate that only the relevant top portion of the stack is shown explicitly. The shift and scan rules are also not shown here. Although not all of the ten rules shown here have been used in the examples above, they fill out a natural array of possibilities: for each of the five MG rules (three cases of merge, two cases of move), there is a predict rule and a connect rule, differing in whether the parent category is introduced as a fresh prediction (predict) or is taken to fulfill an existing prediction (connect). The five MG rules are shown in a tree-based notation on the left, including quasi-daughters for the move rules to bring out the way (the relevant licensee features of) those quasi-daughters play the role of left-corners in the corresponding parsing rules.

6.3.3 Multiple movements

The examples shown so far involve only one movement step. Naturally, there are a variety of potential complications that arise in cases involving more than one movement step. The system as presented here handles some of these complications, but not all of them.

One variation which can be handled straightforwardly is multiple movements of a single constituent. For example, consider a derivation like the one in Figure 6.4 where the wh-phrase moves first to a specifier of the V-projection before going to its surface position. The original steps involved in attaching the filler to its surface position are unchanged. What happens at the intermediate position is something analogous to the "retrieval" steps so far—i.e. establishing a dependency in a nonfinal position— but rather than a nonfinal-merge transition to check a mover's base selectee feature as in Table 6.5 and Table 6.6, this intermediate retrieval is a nonfinal-move transition to check its intermediate licensee feature. A relevant (abstract) example, for the derivation in Figure 6.7 is shown in Table 6.8. The nonfinal-move transition is in Step 5, where the bystander's - f feature is checked.

Grammar Rule	Predict Rule

c-mrg

$$(\alpha, \psi)$$
$$(=f\alpha)_1 \quad (f, \psi)$$

$$(=f\alpha\rceil)_1 \dots$$
$$\vdash \overline{(f\rceil, \psi)} \quad (\alpha\rceil, \psi)_0 \dots$$

s-mrg

$$(\alpha, \phi\psi)$$
$$(=f\alpha, \phi)_0 \quad (f, \psi)$$

$$(f\rceil, \psi) \dots$$
$$\vdash \overline{(=f\alpha\rceil, \phi)_0} \quad (\alpha\rceil, \phi\psi)_0 \dots$$

n-mrg

$$(\alpha, \phi\gamma\psi)$$
$$(=f\alpha, \phi) \quad (f\gamma, \psi)$$

$$(f\rceil\gamma, \psi)\cup\mathcal{B}_1\cup\mathcal{B}_2 \quad \overline{(I)} \dots$$
$$\vdash \quad \mathcal{B}_1(=f\alpha\rceil, \phi) \quad (\alpha\rceil, \phi\gamma\psi)_0 \quad \mathcal{B}_2\overline{(I)} \dots$$

s-mv

$$(\alpha, \phi\psi)$$
$$(+f\alpha, \phi-f\psi) \quad (\beta-f, \chi)$$

$$(\beta-f\rceil, \chi) \dots$$
$$\vdash \quad (\beta\rceil-f, \chi) \overline{(+f\alpha\rceil, \phi-f\psi)} \quad (\alpha\rceil, \phi\psi)_0 \dots$$

n-mv

$$(\alpha, \phi\gamma\psi)$$
$$(+f\alpha, \phi(-f\gamma)\psi) \quad (\beta-f\gamma, \chi)$$

$$(\beta-f\rceil\gamma, \chi)\cup\mathcal{B}_1\cup\mathcal{B}_2 \quad \overline{(I)} \dots$$
$$\vdash \quad (\beta\rceil-f\gamma, \chi)\cup\mathcal{B}_1 \overline{(+f\alpha\rceil, \phi(-f\gamma)\psi)} \quad (\alpha\rceil, \phi\gamma\psi)_0 \quad \mathcal{B}_2\overline{(I)} \dots$$

Grammar Rule	Connect Rule

c-mrg

$$(\alpha, \psi)$$
$$(=f\alpha)_1 \quad (f, \psi)$$

$$(=f\alpha\rceil)_1 \quad \mathcal{B}\overline{(\alpha\rceil, \psi)} \dots$$
$$\vdash \quad \mathcal{B}\overline{(f\rceil, \psi)} \dots$$

s-mrg

$$(\alpha, \phi\psi)$$
$$(=f\alpha, \phi)_0 \quad (f, \psi)$$

$$(f\rceil, \psi) \quad \mathcal{B}\overline{(\alpha\rceil, \phi\psi)} \dots$$
$$\vdash \quad \mathcal{B}\overline{(=f\alpha\rceil, \phi)_0} \dots$$

n-mrg

$$(\alpha, \phi\gamma\psi)$$
$$(=f\alpha, \phi) \quad (f\gamma, \psi)$$

$$(f\rceil\gamma, \psi)\cup\mathcal{B}_1\cup\mathcal{B}_2 \quad \overline{(\alpha\rceil, \phi\gamma\psi)} \dots$$
$$\vdash \quad \mathcal{B}_1\cup\mathcal{B}_2 \overline{(=f\alpha\rceil, \phi)} \dots$$

s-mv

$$(\alpha, \phi\psi)$$
$$(+f\alpha, \phi-f\psi) \quad (\beta-f, \chi)$$

$$(\beta-f\rceil, \chi) \quad \mathcal{B}\overline{(\alpha\rceil, \phi\psi)} \dots$$
$$\vdash \quad (\beta\rceil-f, \chi)\cup\mathcal{B}\overline{(+f\alpha\rceil, \phi-f\psi)} \dots$$

n-mv

$$(\alpha, \phi\gamma\psi)$$
$$(+f\alpha, \phi(-f\gamma)\psi) \quad (\beta-f\gamma, \chi)$$

$$(\beta-f\rceil\gamma, \chi)\cup\mathcal{B}\overline{(\alpha\rceil, \phi\gamma\psi)} \dots$$
$$\vdash \quad (\beta\rceil-f\gamma, \chi)\cup\mathcal{B}\overline{(+f\alpha\rceil, \phi(-f\gamma)\psi)} \dots$$

Figure 6.6 Much of the notation here is carried over from Figure 6.1. I write $\uplus$ for disjoint union, and $x \uplus S$ as a shorthand for $\{x\} \uplus S$; $(\mathbf{I})$ ranges over items (with the parentheses just for visual consistency); $\mathcal{B}, \mathcal{B}_1, \mathcal{B}_2, \dots$ are variables ranging over sets of items ("bystanders"). A subscript 1 indicates lexical; a subscript 0 indicates non-lexical; absence of a subscript indicates unspecified lexicality.

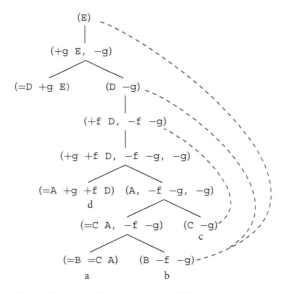

Figure 6.7 A derivation with multiple movements. The parse is shown in Table 6.8.

Table 6.8 Parsing the multiple-movements derivation in Figure 6.7

Step	Rule	Remaining input	
0		b e c d a	$\overline{(E\lceil)}$
1	shift	e c d a	$(B -f -g])_1$ $\overline{(E\lceil)}$
2	spec-move-connect	e c d a	$_{(B -f]-g)_1}$ $\overline{(+g\ E\lceil,\ -g)}$
3	shift	c d a	$(=D +g\ E])_1$ $_{(B -f]-g)_1}$ $\overline{(+g\ E\lceil,\ -g)}$
4	comp-merge-connect	c d a	$_{(B -f]-g)_1}$ $\overline{(D\lceil,\ -g)}$
5	nonfinal-move-connect	c d a	$_{(B]-f\ -g)_1}$ $\overline{(+f\ D\lceil,\ -f\ -g)}$
6	shift	d a	$(C -g])_1$ $_{(B]-f\ -g)_1}$ $\overline{(+f\ D\lceil,\ -f\ -g)}$
7	spec-move-connect	d a	$_{(C]-g)_1, (B]-f\ -g)_1}$ $\overline{(+g +f\ D\lceil,\ -g,\ -f\ -g)}$
8	shift	a	$(=A +g +f\ D])_1$
			$_{(C]-g)_1, (B]-f\ -g)_1}$ $\overline{(+g +f\ D\lceil,\ -g,\ -f\ -g)}$
9	comp-merge-connect	a	$_{(C]-g)_1, (B]-f\ -g)_1}$ $\overline{(A\lceil,\ -g,\ -f\ -g)}$
10	nonfinal-merge-connect	a	$_{(B]-f\ -g)_1}$ $\overline{(=C\ A\lceil,\ -f\ -g)}$
11	nonfinal-merge-connect	a	$\overline{(=B =C\ A\lceil)}$
12	scan	ε	ε

Table 6.9 Parsing the smuggling derivation in Figure 6.8

Step		Input	
0		b a s	$\overline{(C\lceil)}$
1	shift	a s	$(B -g\rceil)_1$ $\overline{(C\lceil)}$
2	spec-move-connect	a s	$_{(B\rceil-g)_1}$ $\overline{(+g\ C\lceil, -g)}$
3	nonfinal-merge-predict	a s	$\overline{(=B\ A\ -f\lceil)}$ $(A -f\rceil, -g)_0$ $\overline{(+g\ C\lceil, -g)}$
4	scan	s	$(A -f\rceil, -g)_0$ $\overline{(+g\ C\lceil, -g)}$
5	spec-move-connect	s	$_{(A\rceil-f, -g)_0}$ $\overline{(+f +g\ C\lceil, -f, -g)}$
6	nonfinal-merge-connect	s	$\overline{(=A +f +g\ C\lceil)}$
7	scan	ε	ε

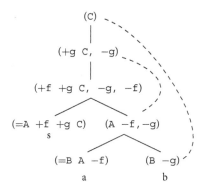

Figure 6.8 A smuggling derivation. The parse is shown in Table 6.9.

Another variation which can be dealt with using the ideas illustrated so far is the "smuggling" configuration, where one phrase moves and a subconstituent of that phrase moves to a yet higher position. An example of a successfully parsed smuggling configuration is shown in Table 6.9, for the derivation in Figure 6.8. This derivation involves fronting of the A-projection, whose yield when it moves is *a b*, to check a -f feature; and then subsequent movement of the contained B-projection to a higher position to check a -g feature. This fronted B-projection is recognized bottom-up and then connected as the highest specifier of the root C-projection (Step 2) in the now-familiar manner. What is distinctive is the next step, Step 3: based on the nonfinal-merge rule

$$(A -f, -g) \quad \rightarrow \quad (=B\ A\ -f)\ (B -g)$$

the bystander's outstanding B feature is used to predict the A-projection that it has moved out of. This leaves the predicted (+g C, -g) unchanged, but introduces other "immediate" (i.e. top of the stack) work to be done, namely fulfilling the newly added prediction of category (=B A -f) which is achieved by scanning *a* (Step 4), at which time we have now recognized the full A-projection bottom-up. This can now be connected as a lower specifier of the C-projection in Step 5, just as the B-projection was connected as its higher specifier earlier in Step 2.

Unfortunately, remnant movement—the "reverse" of a smuggling configuration, where a phrase out of which movement has already taken place itself moves—cannot be handled by the system introduced in this section. I introduce one somewhat tentative extension in the next section which attempts to address this issue.

6.4 Dealing with remnant movement

I will first, in section 6.4.1, try to pinpoint the complications posed by these configurations and build up some intuitions for one way to attempt to tackle these problems, and then in section 6.4.2 I will present one implementation of these ideas that correctly handles at least some cases of remnant movement.[5]

6.4.1 An outline of the challenge

To illustrate, consider the derivation in Figure 6.9. This is minimally different from the smuggling example above, differing just in the order in which the two movements are

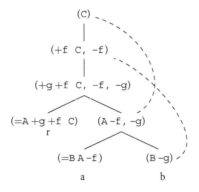

Figure 6.9 A remnant movement derivation

---

[5] It is probably also useful to note that the system presented in the previous section seems closely related to the "MGs with hypothetical reasoning" system in Kobele (2010), which corresponds exactly to MGs with remnant movement disallowed. Specifically, the spec-move transitions here seem to play the role of the discharge rule in Kobele's system, the nonfinal-merge transitions play the role of assume rule, and bystanders play the role of hypothesized constituents (out of which no movement is allowed). (It is possibly natural that a parser might end up emulating something close to this assume/discharge system because the derivation trees in this system put lexical items in essentially their surface word order.) So the task of working out how to enrich the parsing system presented here to deal with remnant movement might be helped by considering the difference between the assume/discharge system and the full MG formalism.

triggered: here the +f licensor, which attracts the larger A-projection, is checked in the higher specifier of C, and the +g licensor, which attracts the smaller B-projection, is checked in the lower specifier of C. (The lexical entries where these orders of licensors are specified have pronunciations *s* for "smuggling" and *r* for "remnant movement".) The derived word order here is therefore *a b r*.

The first symbol in the input is *a*, so we will reach

$$(\text{=B A -f}])_1 \quad \overline{(\text{C}[})$$

after an initial shift step. Following the logic we have been using so far, it seems like the relevant next step should be a predict step on the basis of the nonfinal-merge rule

$$(\text{A -f, -g}) \quad \rightarrow \quad (\text{=B A -f}) \quad (\text{B -g})$$

which we would expect to result in replacing $(\text{=B A -f}])_1$ in our store with the two elements

$$\overline{(\text{B}[\text{ -g}])} \qquad \text{and} \qquad (\text{A -f}], \text{-g})_0$$

in some configuration or other. That is to say, we expect the new state to be somehow constructed out of the following three elements.

- $\overline{(\text{C}[})$ the "underlying prediction"
- $\overline{(\text{B}[\text{ -g}])}$ the "extractee"
- $(\text{A -f}], \text{-g})_0$ the "remnant"

Notice that the extractee here is the first instance we have encountered of a top-down predicted category with multiple "negative polarity" features, i.e. both a selectee B and a licensee -g. The challenge posed by remnant movement appears to be dealing with these kinds of elements, in particular understanding what status they have when they have had some, but not all, of those negative polarity features checked as the extractee has here. (The cases of partially checked negative polarity features that we *have* seen involve constituents that have been found bottom-up and then had a licensee feature checked in a post-movement position, with a selectee feature remaining unchecked.)

To try to isolate out the difficulty that these configurations raise, let us consider how we expect the underlying prediction and the remnant to interact as the parser continues its work, leaving aside the extractee temporarily. The next thing that one would expect to happen would be a spec-move-connect step that puts the remnant in the highest specifier position of the C-projection, of the sort that we have seen many times now. Keeping attention restricted to these two elements (i.e. abstracting away from the fact that the remnant has not, in fact, been completely recognized), we would expect such a transition to look something like this:

(13)   b r $(\text{A -f}], \text{-g})_0 \quad \overline{(\text{C}[})$

spec-move-connect   b r $_{(\text{A}]\text{-f}, \text{-g})_0} (\text{+f C}[, \text{-f})$

As written, this describes the standard situation where what remains is to find some (phonetically null) base position in which the bystander's A feature can be checked, as we work towards fulfilling the prediction of a (+f C, -f). (The presence of the -g mover as part of this bystander category is of course related to the issues that we are temporarily abstracting away from.) At some future point we expect a nonfinal-merge transition to "retrieve" this bystander in the now-familiar manner. Specifically, we expect this to happen when we have worked our way down to a prediction of a (+g +f C, -f, -g), since this is the mother of (A -f, -g) in the derivation tree. Note that by the time this happens, we expect that the extractee *b* has been somehow consumed, since its surface position is to the left of the base position of the A-projection. So we expect the final steps of the parser's actions to be as follows:

(14)   r $_{(A]-f, -g)_0}$ $\overline{(+g +f C[, -f, -g)}$
          nonfinal-merge-connect   r   (=A +g +f C[)
          scan   ε   ε

Note that in this simple, minimal example, "all that happens" between (13) and (14) is the critical (and as yet somewhat mysterious) recognition of the extractee *b* in its base position (where it checks -g): this is what allows the predicted (+f C, -f) in (13) to become (+g +f C, -f, -g) in (14). In remnant movement configurations more generally, however, the state that here exists only while we have a prediction of category (+f C, -f), with both movement dependencies "in progress," will persist over some larger portion of the derivation.

So the question we now wish to ask is what information about (B -g) needs to be added to what is shown in the store in (13), and how should this information bear on the parser's actions as it moves to the configuration shown at the beginning of (14)?

A crucial point to realize appears to be that the availability of the nonfinal-merge-connect step shown in (14), i.e. the "retrieval" of the remnant, should be contingent upon the fact that the extractee *b* has already been consumed. This is indeed the case in (14). But if the string being encountered were, for example, *a r b* (instead of *a b r*), then the following sequence of actions should *not* be possible: process the *a* as a fronted remnant out of which *b* has moved, reaching the configuration shown in (13) but with *r b* as the remaining input, and immediately apply the nonfinal-merge-connect transition shown in (14) ("retrieving" the A-projection and hypothesizing that its gap position is here) and then scan the *r* as the sister of this gap position. The reason this should not be allowed is that it has the consequence of hypothesizing that the surface position of the extractee *b* is further to the right of the base position of the A-projection, since we have not seen *b* by the time we posit the latter's gap; this is incompatible with the assumption we made by analyzing *a* alone (not the string *a b*) as a fronted A-projection. Put differently, when we analyze *a* alone as fronted remnant out of which *b* has moved, we not only commit ourselves to finding a base position for the A-projection and a surface position for *b* further downstream—we commit ourselves to finding the surface position for *b* *before* we find the base position for the A-projection, because the b was extracted (leftwards) out of the base position occurrence of the A-projection.[6]

This suggests an answer to the question of what information about (B -g) is missing from the configuration shown at the end of (13): the bystander $(\text{A -f}], \text{ -g})_0$ must be somehow temporarily inaccessible, its use contingent upon fulfilling the remaining part of the $\overline{(\text{B}[\text{ -g})}$ prediction that we abstracted away from.[7] This suggests a general structure where each stack element is a *tree*, containing not only daughters of the root node as bystanders in the now-familiar sense, but also daughters of those bystanders encoding "conditions" that must be satisfied before those bystanders can be used: each condition is a condition upon the use of one particular bystander (hence the nested structure), and in general there may be more than one condition for any single bystander (e.g. if there are multiple extractees from a moved remnant).

6.4.2 Outline of a candidate solution

Incorporating tree structure into our stack elements in the sense just mentioned allows us to correctly handle the remnant movement derivation in Figure 6.9, plus at least some degree of "iterated remnant movement" of the sort that is necessary for MGs to define non-context-free languages such as the copy language $\{ww \mid w \in \{a, b\}^*\}$ (Kobele 2010).

Three new parsing rules are needed to manipulate these more complex structures: two based on nonfinal-merge, and one based on spec-move. These are shown in Figure 6.10. These rules use essentially the same notational conventions as those presented earlier in Figure 6.6, with the modification that $\mathcal{B}$ now ranges over *sets of trees of items* (rather than simply sets of items). As presented in section 6.3 the system effectively operates on trees that are limited in depth to include at most one level of children (i.e. bystanders); I tentatively take these rules to apply to generalized trees "as is", simply allowing additional surrounding structure to be "carried around" until it is acted upon by the rules in Figure 6.10.[8] I write $I[\mathcal{B}]$ for the tree with root node I and

---

[6] We can imagine more complicated situations involving multiple interacting remnant movement configurations, where this does not hold. I will restrict attention here to situations where any lexical item has at most one licensee feature. Graf et al. (2016) showed that any MG can be converted into an equivalent one obeying this restriction.

[7] One might be tempted to suspect that the -g mover in the bystander category already encodes the relevant dependency, but this will not be sufficient in general: the phrase which is found in the surface -g position must be one that could have had a B feature checked inside the remnant. So if there were some other lexical item with category (D -g), then finding that item somewhere before we posit the gap position of the frontent A-projection remnant would not be sufficient.

[8] There may need to be some restrictions. For example, a bottom-up item with (top-down) bystanders, which will turn out to be what represents a fronted remnant with as-yet-unfound extractees, can be sensibly used as the left-corner trigger of a spec-move or nonfinal-move rule, but *not* as the left-corner trigger of a spec-merge rule, for example, because that is not compatible with this phrase moving. But it may turn out that "incorrectly" using such a phrase in a spec-merge rule would simply lead to dead-ends for the parser.

Grammar Rule	Secondary Predict Rule
n-mrg $(\alpha, \phi\gamma\psi)$ $(=f\alpha, \phi) \quad (f\gamma, \psi)$	$\vdash \dfrac{\mathcal{B}(=f\alpha\rceil, \phi) \dots}{(f\lceil\gamma, \psi)\cup\mathcal{B}} (\alpha\rceil, \phi\gamma\psi) \dots$

Grammar Rule	Secondary Connect Rule
n-mrg $(\alpha, \phi\gamma\psi)$ $(=f\alpha, \phi) \quad (f\gamma, \psi)$	$\vdash \dfrac{\mathcal{B}_1(=f\alpha\rceil, \phi) \quad \overline{\mathcal{B}_2(\alpha\lceil, \phi\gamma\psi)} \quad \mathcal{B}_3(\mathbf{I})\dots}{\overline{(f\lceil\gamma,\psi)} [\mathcal{B}_2]\cup\mathcal{B}_1\cup\mathcal{B}_3} (\mathbf{I}) \dots$

Grammar Rule	Secondary Rule
s-mv $(\alpha, \phi\psi)$ $(+f\alpha, \phi-f\psi) \quad (\beta-f,\chi)$	$\vdash \dfrac{(\mathbf{I}) \left[\overline{(\beta\lceil -f, \chi)}\cup\mathcal{B}_2\right]\cup\mathcal{B}_1 \overline{(\alpha\lceil, \phi\psi)} \dots}{\overline{(\beta-f\lceil, \chi)} \ (\mathbf{I})[\mathcal{B}_2]\cup\mathcal{B}_1 \overline{(\alpha\lceil, \phi\psi)} \dots}$

Figure 6.10 Secondary parsing rules introduced for remnant movement

with child subtrees $\mathcal{B}$.[9] Note that in the system presented in section 6.3, only top-down items had "bystander" children, and those children were always bottom-up elements. In the extended version here, bottom-up items can have children and those children will always be top-down elements. So although the depth of the trees is unbounded, given any two nodes that stand in an immediate dominance relationship there will always be one bottom-up element and one top-down element.

The two rules in Figure 6.10 based on nonfinal-merge allow for cases where the participating selectee occurs further to the right in the input than the selector— this is what occurs in remnant movement configurations, in contrast to the more straightforward cases of nonfinal-merge that are handled by the rules in Figure 6.6 where the selectee (having later moved leftwards) occurs further to the left. Specifically, these two new nonfinal-merge rules hypothesize that the $(=f\alpha, \phi)$ constituent that we have recognized is in fact part of a remnant-moved $(\alpha, \phi\gamma\psi)$ constituent; the rest of this constituent, i.e. $(f\gamma, \psi)$, must be predicted, of course, but we do not expect it to be found immediately. The status of such a constituent is what is encoded by being a top-down bystander. The two new nonfinal-merge rules produce such constituents, and stand to each other in the usual relationship, that a predict/connect pair do. The new rule based on spec-move consumes, or retrieves, such top-down bystanders, and does

---

[9] The notation $_\mathcal{B}\mathbf{I}$ that has been used so far, is therefore equivalent to $\mathbf{I}[\mathcal{B}]$. I am introducing the latter only to avoid the need to iterate subscripts.

Table 6.10 Parsing the remnant movement derivation in Figure 6.9. The crucial remnant movement configuration is established by nonfinal-merge-predict-sec.

Step	Rule	Input	
0		a b r	$\overline{(C\lceil)}$
1	shift	b r	$(\texttt{=B A -f}\rceil)_1$ $\overline{(C\lceil)}$
2	nonfinal-merge-predict-sec	b r	$\overline{(B\lceil -g)}$ $(A \texttt{ -f}\rceil, \texttt{ -g})_0$ $\overline{(C\lceil)}$
3	spec-move-connect	b r	$(A\rceil \texttt{-f}, \texttt{ -g})_0 \left[\overline{(B\lceil -g)}\right]$ $\overline{(\texttt{+f } C\lceil, \texttt{ -f})}$
4	spec-move-sec	b r	$(B \texttt{ -g}\lceil)$ $(A\rceil \texttt{-f}, \texttt{ -g})_0$ $\overline{(\texttt{+g +f } C\lceil, \texttt{ -g}, \texttt{ -f})}$
5	scan	r	$(A\rceil \texttt{-f}, \texttt{ -g})_0$ $\overline{(\texttt{+g +f } C\lceil, \texttt{ -g}, \texttt{ -f})}$
6	nonfinal-merge-connect	r	$\overline{(\texttt{=A +g +f } C\lceil)}$
7	scan	ε	ε

not clearly fit the mould of either predict or connect rules.[10] I will refer to these three rules as "secondary rules," and their abbreviated names used in traces of the parser's actions will have the suffix *-sec*.

A trace of the parser's actions on the simple remnant movement derivation from Figure 6.9 is shown in Table 6.10. The first interesting point is the application of the secondary nonfinal-mrg-predict rule in Step 2. The effect is to hypothesize that the *a* head that we have recognized is in fact all that we are going to see of the A-projection for now. This step therefore takes us into a configuration that has, essentially, a bottom-up recognized A-projection to be put towards fulfilling the underlying (C) prediction—*except that* we still have an obligation to find a (B -g) constituent elsewhere, specifically in a position where its -g feature is checked. At the next step, the A-projection is connected as a specifier of the predicted C-projection. This is an instance of attaching a filler while keeping its gap position unresolved so the bottom-up (A -f, -g) constituent becomes a bystander of the updated top-down prediction, as we have seen many times before (cf. (13)). But in addition now, it brings along its own children which become "embedded" one level further in the tree structure. The resulting tree structure encodes the familiar relationship between (A -f, -g) and (+f C, -f) in the same way as before, but with the additional information that the base position of the (A -f, -g) projection cannot be posited until the predicted (B -g) has been found (based on the logic outlined in the previous subsection). The secondary spec-mv rule, which applies next in Step 4, initiates the satisfaction of this additional requirement: the doubly embedded (B -g) item is "retrieved" and becomes

---

[10] This rule does form a natural class with the other two, in the sense that it deals with movements where a phrase appears to the right of its trace. In the case of the two new nonfinal-merge rules, this coincides with the fact that the selectee appears to the right of its selector (in contrast to the situations dealt with by the simpler nonfinal-merge rules in section 6.3). But the situations to which the new spec-move rule is applicable to not involve a "non-canonical" linear ordering of the mover/licensee and its attractor/licensor.

a top-level top-down prediction, ready to be fulfilled by scanning (at Step 5).[11] The applicability of the familiar nonfinal-merge-connect rule in Step 6, identifying the gap position for the fronted A-projection, is dependent on the fact that the (A -f, -g) item has no more children at this point.

This derivation involved an instance of the secondary nonfinal-merge-predict rule; specifically, this rule corresponds to the application of nonfinal-merge that establishes the relationship between the selecting (=B A -f) head and its evacuated (B -g) complement, and it is an instance of a predict step because the resulting (A -f, -g) parent node is created as a fresh prediction. To illustrate the secondary nonfinal-merge-connect rule, consider the slightly different derivation shown in Figure 6.11. The only difference is that the fronted A-projection contains a (D) specifier in addition to its evacuated (B -g) complement. A consequence of this is that after the shift step that consumes the a (Step 3), there is a predicted A-projection already waiting on the stack, having been created when the initial (D) phrase was analyzed as a specifier (Step 2). This predicted A-projection is the parent (in the derivation tree) of the application of nonfinal-merge that establishes the relationship between the selecting (=B =D A -f) head and its evacuated (B -g) complement, and so the secondary nonfinal-merge-connect rule applies in Step 4. The configuration we reach is identical to the one reached in Table 6.10 after Step 2: an A-projection has been identified bottom-up, but with a gap inside it corresponding to the base position of a (B -g) constituent. In the earlier example in Table 6.10 this bottom-up A-projection was only brought into existence at the point where the remnant-movement configuration was created, so it was brought into existence with the top-down (B -g) prediction as a child[12]; the connect case in Table 6.11 is more complicated because the bottom-up A-projection is already there, so the prediction of the (B -g) constituent whose gap is posited by secondary nonfinal-merge-connect at Step 4 must be added to, or "passed up to," that existing A-projection.[13]

To illustrate that these new rules generalize at least somewhat beyond the specific cases used to motivate them here, Table 6.12 shows how they work on the complex remnant-movement derivation shown in Figure 6.12. This derivation corresponds to the derivation of the string aa in the MG given in Stabler (2011) for the copy language $\{ww \mid w \in \{a, b\}^*\}$, but again writing e for empty lexical items for clarity. Notice

---

[11] One can imagine instead supposing that this is achieved by shifting on the relevant lexical item, and then "matching" the resulting bottom-up item with the doubly embedded (B -g) to cancel the latter out. This seems preferable in the sense that it would avoid spurious predictions about when this element is going to be encountered in the input. I'm opting for the other version only based on an intuition that we should stay in the style of an arc-eager left-corner parser (which the rest of the system has been based on), whereas the cancelling-out alternative seems more in line with the arc-standard versions.

[12] More generally, with reference to Figure 6.10: the bottom-up $(\alpha, \phi\gamma\psi)$ item created by the secondary nonfinal-merge-predict rule gets this new top-down $(f\gamma, \psi)$ bystander *in addition to* any analogous top-down bystanders (denoted by $\mathcal{B}$ in Figure 6.10) that had already been accumulated within the bottom-up $(=f\alpha, \phi)$ item.

[13] More generally, with reference to Figure 6.10: the existing bottom-up item not only gets the new top-down $(f\gamma, \psi)$ bystander, but also inherits any analogous top-down bystanders $(\mathcal{B}_1)$ that had been accumulated within the bottom-up $(=f\alpha, \phi)$ item. In addition, any bottom-up bystanders (i.e. already-processed fillers) for which a gap position was still to be found inside the predicted $(\alpha, \phi\gamma\psi)$ constituent must have their gap position inside the evacuated $(f\gamma, \psi)$ subconstituent, so those are passed down as embedded bystanders $(\mathcal{B}_2)$ for the new top-down item.

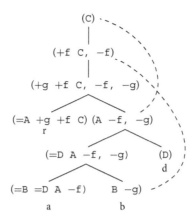

Figure 6.11 Another remnant movement derivation

Table 6.11 Parsing the remnant movement derivation in Figure 6.11. The crucial remnant movement configuration is established by nonfinal-merge-connect-sec this time.

Step	Rule	Input	
0		d a b r	$\overline{(C\lceil)}$
1	shift	a b r	$(D\rceil)_1$ $\overline{(C\lceil)}$
2	spec-merge-predict	a b r	$\overline{(=D\ A\ -f\lceil,\ -g)_0}$ $(A\ -f\rceil,\ -g)_0$ $\overline{(C\lceil)}$
3	shift	b r	$(=B\ =D\ A\ -f\rceil)_1$ $\overline{(=D\ A\ -f\lceil,\ -g)_0}$ $(A\ -f\rceil,\ -g)_0\ \overline{(C\lceil)}$
4	nonfinal-merge-connect-sec	b r	$\overline{(B\lceil-g)}$ $(A\ -f\rceil,\ -g)_0$ $\overline{(C\lceil)}$
5	spec-move-connect	b r	$_{(A\rceil-f,\ -g)_0}\overline{[(B\lceil-g)]}$ $\overline{(+f\ C\lceil,\ -f)}$
6	spec-move-sec	b r	$\overline{(B\ -g\lceil)}$ $_{(A\rceil-f,\ -g)_0}\overline{(+g\ +f\ C\lceil,\ -g,\ -f)}$
7	scan	r	$_{(A\rceil-f,\ -g)_0}\overline{(+g\ +f\ C\lceil,\ -g,\ -f)}$
8	nonfinal-merge-connect	r	$\overline{(=A\ +g\ +f\ C\lceil)}$
9	scan	ε	ε

that when the secondary nonfinal-merge-connect rule applies in Step 4, the new top-down (A -r, -1) bystander inherits the bottom-up (T -r -1) bystander from the prediction that is being completed; since this filler's gap position had not been found in the course of fulfilling this (+1 T -1, -r -1) prediction, its gap site must be in that part of the (+1 T -1, -r -1) which was evacuated, i.e. the (A -r -1) constituent that is hypothesized at this step (as discussed in footnote 13). This means that when the (T -1, -r) constituent is connected as a specifier in Step 5, a tree structure with *three* levels of children is created. When the secondary specifier-move rule applies in Step 6 to "retrieve" the evacuated constituent's prediction, the entire tree structure whose root is the (A -r, -1) item is brought to the top of the stack; from this point on the

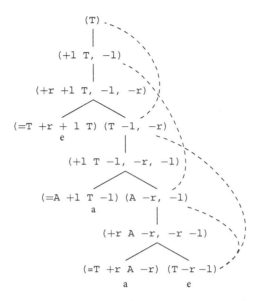

Figure 6.12 A complex remnant movement derivation, corresponding to a derivation from the copy language. The parse is shown in Table 6.12.

Table 6.12 Parsing the complex remnant movement derivation in Figure 6.12

Step	Rule	Input	
0		e a a e	$\overline{(\text{T}\lceil)}$
1	shift	a a e	$(\text{T -r -1}\rceil)_1 \quad \overline{(\text{T}\lceil)}$
2	spec-move-predict	a a e	$_{(\text{T -r}\rceil\text{-1})_1}\ \overline{(\text{+1 T -1}\lceil,\ \text{-r, -1})}\ (\text{T -1}\rceil,\ \text{-r})_0\ \overline{(\text{T}\lceil)}$
3	shift	a e	$(\text{=A +1 T -1}\rceil)_1 \quad _{(\text{T -r}\rceil\text{-1})_1}\ \overline{(\text{+1 T -1}\lceil,\ \text{-r, -1})}$
			$(\text{T -1}\rceil,\ \underline{\text{-r}})_0 \quad \overline{(\text{T}\lceil)}$
4	nonfinal-merge-connect-sec	a e	$\overline{(\text{A}\lceil\text{-r, -1})}\big[_{(\text{T -r}\rceil\text{-1})_1}\big]\ (\text{T -1}\rceil,\ \text{-r})_0\quad \overline{(\text{T}\lceil)}$
5	spec-move-connect	a e	$_{(\text{T}\rceil\text{-1, -r})_0}\big[\overline{(\text{A}\lceil\text{-r, -1})}\big[_{(\text{T -r}\rceil\text{-1})_1}\big]\big]\ \overline{(\text{+1 T}\lceil,\ \text{-1})}$
6	spec-move-sec	a e	$_{(\text{T -r}\rceil\text{-1})_1}\ \overline{(\text{A -r}\lceil,\ \text{-1})}$
			$_{(\text{T}\rceil\text{-1, -r})_0}\overline{(\text{+r +1 T}\lceil,\ \text{-r, -1})}$
7	nonfinal-move-connect	a e	$_{(\text{T}\rceil\text{-r -1})_1}\ \overline{(\text{+r A -r}\lceil,\ \text{-r -1})}$
			$_{(\text{T}\rceil\text{-1, -r})_0}\overline{(\text{+r +1 T}\lceil,\ \text{-r, -1})}$
8	nonfinal-merge-connect	a e	$\overline{(\text{=T +r A -r}\lceil)}\quad _{(\text{T}\rceil\text{-1, -r})_0}\ \overline{(\text{+r +1 T}\lceil,\ \text{-r, -1})}$
9	scan	e	$_{(\text{T}\rceil\text{-1, -r})_0}\overline{(\text{+r +1 T}\lceil,\ \text{-r, -1})}$
10	nonfinal-merge-connect	e	$\overline{(\text{=T +r +1 T}\lceil)}$
11	scan	ε	ε

top-down predictions with bottom-up bystanders behave precisely in accord with the simpler system laid out in section 6.3.

While I take it to be promising that the rules introduced in this subsection naturally extended to this unintuitive case without ad hoc modifications, a proper investigation of the limits of what they can achieve is an ongoing task.

6.5 Empirical connections based on what we have so far

6.5.1 Active gap-filling

As mentioned above, to a good first approximation we can say that the active gap-filling strategy amounts to preferring transitions based on nonfinal-merge in this left-corner MG parser over others. This makes it possible for active gap-filling to be understood as one aspect of a strategy for searching through a search space, much as Late Closure can be understood as a preference for shift transitions over reduce transitions in a bottom-up parser.

Recall that the nonfinal-merge transitions in the examples above occur perhaps surprisingly early. Specifically, in a sentence with a gap in object position (Table 6.5), this transition occurs before the verb is consumed. This was in some ways an arbitrary choice, taking the already-consumed filler to in effect be the left-corner that "triggers" the relevant VP-forming rule. An alternative that is perhaps equally reasonable would be to wait until the verb is consumed, use *that* as the trigger for the VP rule, and add a top-down prediction of an object that is in turn fulfilled by the posited gap. Formally speaking, the question concerns exactly how we should generalize familiar notions such as top-down, bottom-up, and left-corner to a setting where categories have their features checked at different points in time.

Interestingly, however, the choice between the two options just outlined corresponds fairly closely to the distinction Omaki et al. (2015) make between "hyper-active gap-filling" and "conservative active gap-filling." Omaki et al. present some evidence that the strategy humans adopt is in fact the former, more pro-active strategy, where an object-position gap is posited before the verb.

6.5.2 Island sensitivity

Recall from section 6.1 that active gap-filling appears to be island-sensitive: evidence suggests that readers do not posit a gap in the object position of *wrote* in (3). While a satisfying explanation of island constraints remains elusive, it is not difficult to encode the standard generalizations in the MG formalism: for example, we can disallow extraction from within specifiers by disallowing spec-merge in cases where the specifier-to-be is a non-singleton category (i.e. has moving sub-parts).

Given a grammar that enforces island constraints in this way, it may be tempting to suspect that effects such as the absence of a posited gap in the object position of *wrote* in (3) would follow immediately, since the hypothesis space being searched by the parser is precisely the space of possibilities defined by the grammar. (This was my own suspicion before I started writing this chapter.) But things are not quite this simple. It is true that, if a grammar disallows extraction from specifiers, then the parser working with that grammar will not construct filler-gap dependencies where a specifier dominates the gap but not the filler; but this does not yet say anything about *at which point* in the sentence an attempt to construct such a dependency will have to be abandoned.

For example, consider the illicit filler-gap dependency in (6.5.2). (This is a more useful example than (4), since relative clauses are islands irrespective of the position in which they occur.)

(15)   *Who was [a friend of _____] arrested?

We are interested in the question of whether a gap is posited after reading the prefix *Who was a friend of*. Notice that in such a situation, the subject which is in the midst of being processed would eventually play the role of a left corner that triggers a rule positing (say) a TP node with the subject as one daughter and a T′ node as the other. This is to say that the bracketed phrase "is not a specifier yet" at the point where the decision about whether to posit a gap after *of* arises. So a grammatical prohibition on extraction out of specifiers will not prevent the positing of a gap in this position. What it *will* prevent is the use of the bracketed phrase *as a specifier*: at the position marked with a closing bracket, the parser will have recognized an NP with a filler-gap dependency reaching inside it, and will then move on to address the question of how to fit that NP into a larger structure. Only when it reaches this latter question will the specifier-island constraint come into play.

This clearly raises a number of subtle questions about the empirical landscape. At the very least, one would like to know whether there is evidence that readers do not posit island-violating gaps in situations analogous to (15) but with the gap site not at the right edge of the subject island. If humans' positing of gaps is indeed "fully island-sensitive" in this manner, then this would suggest that the parser presented here has departed too far from Stabler's and is not top-down enough: in a fully top-down approach, the current phrase's position in the surrounding structure (e.g. whether it is a specifier or not) is always known.

6.6 Conclusion

I have presented an initial foray into the development of an incremental MG parser that would provide a formal grounding for the growing experimental literature on the formation of long-distance dependencies. The crucial idea is to allow the first link in a dependency (such as a wh-filler) to act as the left-corner which triggers a rule that introduces a prediction of a category that will contain the other link in the dependency (such as a gap). This contrasts with the top-down parser from Stabler (2013b) which requires that all the links in a dependency be identified with particular structural positions before any of the words participating in the dependency are scanned. Remant movement poses distinct challenges, due largely to the fact that they create situations where the parser encounters an element's trace before it encounters the element itself; I have outlined the beginnings of what may turn out to be a solution to these issues. The system does however already provide a solid handle on the robustly attested active gap-filling strategy, which can be seen as a simple search heuristic, preferring a certain kind of transition through the search space over others.

7

Grammatical predictors for fMRI time-courses

Jixing Li and John Hale

7.1 Introduction

There is widespread agreement that a network of brain regions surrounding the Sylvian fissure supports human language comprehension (Stowe et al. 2005; Dronkers et al. 2004; Pallier et al. 2011; Fedorenko et al. 2011). Less clear is what the individual anatomical sites of this network actually do. Towards a more precise functional anatomy of language comprehension, we correlated time-series predictions from a variety of grammar types with fMRI data from several well-known brain regions. The results categorize the types of language-processing these areas carry out. In particular, they confirm a statistically-significant role for a predictor based on Minimalist Grammars (Chomsky 1995b; Stabler 1997).

The blood-oxygen-level-dependent (BOLD) signals that we modeled came from participants listening to a story while in the scanner. The case for such naturalistic stimuli in neuroscience has been made by Hasson and Honey (2012), who argued that findings within a controlled laboratory setup may not be ecologically valid in real-life contexts. We analyzed the freely-available region of interest (ROI) timecourses from Brennan et al. (2016) with two additional regressors not considered before: a memory-based metric "structural distance" and a distributional-semantic metric indicating "conceptual combination." We found that even with these covariates, the predictor based on Minimalist Grammars still significantly improved a regression model of the BOLD signal in the posterior temporal region, roughly corresponding to Wernicke's area.

Our methodology follows Brennan et al. (2016), which itself responds to Sprouse and Hornstein's (2016) exhortation to collaboratively construct a cognitive neuroscience of syntactic structure-building: First identifying the structure-building computations word-by-word, then asking whether there is evidence for those computations in neural signals. This approach allows an investigator to examine cognitive hypotheses about the role of grammar in processing (for foundational discussion of this point, see Stabler 1983).

Minimalist Parsing. First edition. Robert C. Berwick and Edward P. Stabler (eds.) This chapter © Jixing Li and John Hale 2019. First published 2019 by Oxford University Press.

The remainder of the chapter is organized into four sections: Section 7.2 lays out some assumptions about grammar, parsing, and processing complexity in our neuro-computational models; Section 7.3 reviews known effects of word-to-word associations and lexical-semantic coherence in human sentence processing; Section 7.4 details the calculation of the complexity metrics that are used as predictors of fMRI time-courses in this work. This section presents the data, statistical analysis, and presents the results. Section 7.5 discusses the implications of these results for the neurobiology of language more broadly.

7.2 Parameters in neuro-computational models of sentence processing

Under Brennan's (2016) formulation, a neuro-computational model involves an incre-mental parser as well as some kind of linking hypothesis that connects the states visited by that parser to potentially observable neural signals. Table 7.1 identifies the particular combinations that we consider in this work; the fourth column is the linking hypothesis.

Brennan further subdivides the parser into a grammar, a parsing algorithm, and an oracle for resolving the inevitable nondeterminism that attends human language processing. The first and second columns of Table 7.1 specify the grammars and the algorithms respectively. All grammars assume a perfect oracle, and the response function is always the default hemodynamic response function provided by the SPM software package (see Henson and Friston 2007). The following sections demonstrate in more detail how the parameters in Table 7.1 influence the predicted hemodynamic responses of word-to-word processing difficulty.

Table 7.1 Parameters in our neuro-computational models

Model	Grammar	Parsing strategy	Complexity metric
cfg.td	Context-Free Grammar	top-down	node count
cfg.bu	Context-Free Grammar	bottom-up	node count
cfg.lc	Context-Free Grammar	left-corner	node count
mg.td	Minimalist Grammar	top-down	node count
mg.bu	Minimalist Grammar	bottom-up	node count
mg.lc	Minimalist Grammar	left-corner	node count
cfg.surp	Context-Free Grammar		surprisal
struct	Dependency Grammar Context-Free Grammar	bottom-up	nodes between dependencies

7.2.1 Grammar

7.2.1.1 Constituency grammars

We compared models based on Minimalist Grammars (MGs) to simpler Context-Free Grammars (CFGs). The particular CFGs that we considered lack empty categories and have no explicit representation of headedness. As Fong and Berwick (2008) point out, CFGs list related constructions separately. This can obscure linguistically significant generalizations, for instance about argument structure. MGs are a more expressive formalism, inspired by Chomsky's Minimalist Program (for a review see Stabler 2011). Integrating constituency, dependency, and movement information, MG derivations can be viewed as X-bar structures (see e.g. Haegeman 1999). MGs make it convenient to express a variety of well-known analyses, for instance of ditransitives (Larson 1988), relative clauses (Kayne 1994), passives (Baker and Roberts, 1989), head movement, genitives, raising, ECM, control, quantifiers, and Wh-movement (Sportiche et al. 2013).

Much recent work in computational psycholinguistics has applied CFGs in modeling human processing difficulty (see e.g. Demberg and Keller 2008; Roark et al. 2009). Yet, as shown in van Wagenen et al. (2014), the choice of grammar formalism can have a major impact on processing difficulty predictions. Tree (1) and (2) illustrate this difference. They contrast bottom-up node counts based on CFG and MG for the same sentence from *Alice in Wonderland*. At the word *by* the prediction would be 1 under a naive CFG analysis, and 18 under a richer MG analysis.

(1)

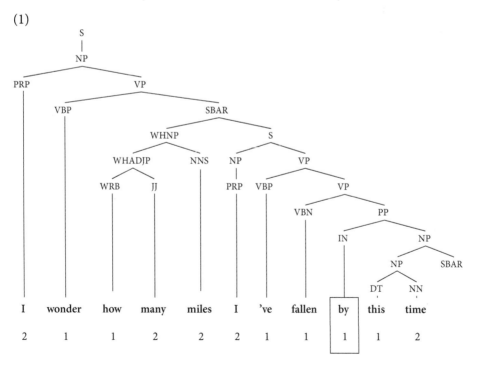

(2)

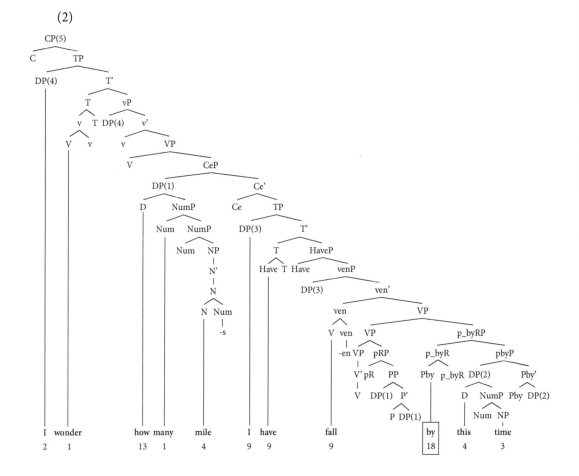

I	wonder		how	many	mile	I	have	fall		by	this	time
2	1		13	1	4	9	9	9		18	4	3

7.2.1.2 Dependency grammars

Apart from the constituency-based hypotheses, we also defined a "structural distance" metric that reflects aspects of both constituency and dependency. This predictor is inspired by earlier work in which linguistic dependency relations correspond to memory retrieval actions that themselves carry a processing cost (Wanner and Maratsos 1978; Gibson 1998; Lewis and Vasishth 2005; Parker et al. 2017). Diagram (3) shows dependency relations, as recovered by the Stanford Parser (de Marneffe et al. 2006).

(3)

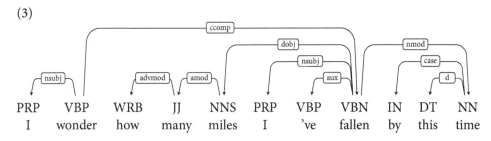

PRP	VBP	WRB	JJ	NNS	PRP	VBP	VBN	IN	DT	NN
I	wonder	how	many	miles	I	've	fallen	by	this	time

To fully specify a complexity metric, it is necessary to quantify how difficult the induced memory retrievals are. A typical approach is to define some function of the distance between words that stand in a dependency relation. This distance could be quantified as the number of intervening discourse referents, the number of intervening words, i.e. "linear distance," or the number of nodes crossed when traversing the syntactic tree structure from a dependent to a head, i.e. "structural distance." Structural distance and linear distance make contrasting predictions on relative clauses in head-final languages, and in fact only structural distance seems to derive the observed "subject preference" pattern (O'Grady 1997; Yun et al. 2010). Indeed, Baumann (2014) compared the three distance measures mentioned above and suggested that structural distance provides the best fit to eye-fixation measures.

Compared to node counts based on phrase structure, structural distance predicts a distinctive pattern of word-by-word processing difficulty. Tree (4) illustrates the structural distance between dependent words in the same sentence in Trees (1) and (2). We considered only the rightmost word in any dependency relation. For words in multiple dependency relations, we summed the structural distances. For instance, the number of non-terminal nodes between *fallen* and *'ve* is 4 (VBP, VP, VP, VBN), between *fallen* and *I* is 6 (PRP, NP, S, VP, VP, VBN), between *fallen* and *I* is 6 (PRP, NP, S, VP, VP, VBN), between *fallen* and *miles* is 7 (NNS, WHNP, SBAR, S, VP, VP, VBN), between *fallen* and *wonder* is 7 (VBP, VP, SBAR, S, VP, VP, VBN), so the summed structural distance at *fallen* is 30. We can see that under the "structural distance" metric, the words *fallen* and *time*, which participate in multiple dependencies, are predicted to induce the most processing effort. This is very different from the bottom-up node count metric based on MG, which predicts *how* and *by* to be the most difficult words to process (see Tree (3)).

(4)

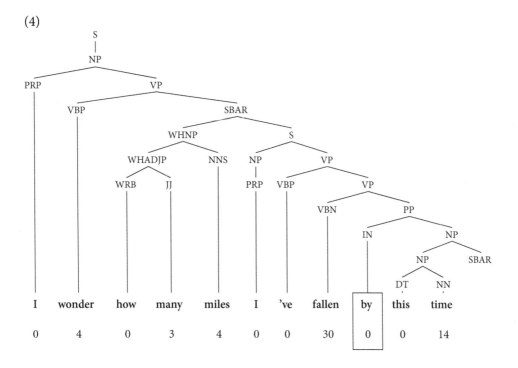

Table 7.2 Steps of top-down, bottom-up, and left-corner parsing for the sentence *John loves Mary*. The numbers below the terminal nodes indicate the node count for that word based on the three parsing strategies respectively.

Tree diagram for the sentence:

```
                S
          _____|_____
         NP           VP
         |        _____|_____
      ProperN    V          NP
         |       |           |
                          ProperN
         |       |           |
       John    loves       Mary
        3        2           2
        2        1           4
        3        2           2
```

Top-Down:		Bottom-Up:		Left-Corner:	
expand by	S → NP VP	shift	John	shift	John
expand by	NP → ProperN	reduce by	ProperN → John	project	ProperN → John
expand by	ProperN →John	reduce by	NP → ProperN	project	NP → ProperN
scan	John	shift	loves	Project + complete	S → NP VP
expand by	VP → V NP	reduce by	V → loves	shift	loves
expand by	V → loves	shift	Mary	project	V→ loves
scan	loves	reduce by	ProperN → Mary	project + complete	VP → V NP
expand by	NP → ProperN	reduce by	NP → ProperN	shift	Mary
expand by	ProperN → Mary	reduce by	VP → V NP	project	ProperN → Mary
scan	Mary	reduce by	S → NP VP	project + complete	NP → ProperN

7.2.2 Parsing strategy

Different parsing strategies lead to different predictions about processing effort on a particular word. A top-down parser starts from a mother node and makes decisions about phrase structure before checking them against the input string. A bottom-up parser starts with the first terminal word and has to check all the evidence before applying a phrase structure rule. A left-corner parser combines both top-down and bottom-up directions, and it applies a grammatical rule after seeing the very first symbol on the right-hand side of the rule (see e.g. Hale 2014: ch. 3). Table 7.2 illustrates the steps of the three parsing strategies for the sentence *John loves Mary*.

7.2.3 Complexity metrics

7.2.3.1 Node count

Node count is the number of parsing steps between successive words under a parsing strategy. This is related to some forms of Yngve's (1960) Depth hypothesis (see also Frazier 1985). As shown in Table 7.2, even for the simple sentence *John loves Mary*, the node counts based on the top-down, bottom-up, and left-corner parsing can be different. We calculated the CFG- and MG-based node counts for the first chapter of *Alice in Wonderland* using the three parsing strategies. The results show very different counts for each parsing strategy based on CFG grammars, as shown in the correlation coefficients between `cfg.bu`, `cfg.td`, and `cfg.lc` in Figure 7.2.

7.2.3.2 Surprisal

The metric "surprisal" is motivated by information theory (see Hale 2016; Armeni et al. 2017: for a review). It quantifies the transition probability from an initial substring to the next word. High surprisal simply means that the next word is improbable on some particular language model.

Surprisals from certain probabilistic grammars predict a "subject preference" for Chinese relative clauses (Jäger et al. 2015). This prediction diverges from an account based on the Dependency Locality Theory (DLT; Hsiao and Gibson 2003). Such controversy makes it more interesting to compare the regression results of the surprisal predictor and the DLT-like predictor structural distance against the fMRI data.

7.2.4 Summary

We formalized syntactic processing during naturalistic comprehension using several different neuro-computational models in an effort to discern their neural bases, if any. The CFG models include both the node count and surprisal metrics. The MG models include only the node count metrics. Surprisal, though well-defined for MGs (Hale 2003), is not available for the current study. The structural distance model is based on both dependency grammar and phrase structure grammar. Its complexity metric is the sum of node counts between dependent words.

7.3 Other factors influencing sentence processing

Apart from the syntactic factors discussed in Section 7.2, other factors such as, word-to-word association, and semantic information also influence processing complexity. We formalize linear order expectancy as trigram surprisal (see Jelinek 1998 for an introduction to n-gram models), and semantic information as cosine similarity between words and its previous context using distributional semantic models (see Lenci 2018 for a review).

7.3.1 Word-to-word associations

Linear, word-to-word, surface dependencies, as reflected in n-gram models, have been shown to influence online sentence comprehension at least at some level of processing (but see Everaert et al. 2015). For instance, Ferreira and Patson (2007) reported that syntactic structure is largely ignored when it conflicts with other information; Christiansen and MacDonald (2009) suggest that some ungrammatical structures can still be processed with ease. Frank and Bod (2011) compared phrase structure grammar models with sequential-structural models, i.e. Markov models and connectionist models in predicting eye-fixation measures, and found better performance for the sequential-structural models. Similarly, Frank et al. (2015) found sequential-structural models fit EEG amplitudes better than does a phrase structure grammar.

This n-gram predictor, based on linear word-to-word relationships, contrasts with the "structural distance" predictor that is based on hierarchical structural dependency.

A number of behavioral studies have shown that violation of hierarchically-based rules leads to increased reading times (e.g. Sturt and Lombardo 2005; Yoshida et al. 2012; Kush et al. 2015), and expectations of word category based on hierarchical grammars predict eye-fixation times (e.g. Boston et al. 2008; 2011). Event-related potential (ERP) studies have also revealed an early negativity for structurally unexpected stimuli (e.g. Xiang et al. 2009). It is therefore interesting to compare the effects of both the linear and hierarchical structural models in sentence processing.

7.3.2 Lexical-semantic coherence

Apart from grammatical information, word meaning also influences sentence processing. As suggested by Landauer (2007), very little of word-order information may actually be used by human readers, perhaps only 10% to 15%. On the other hand, meaning is obviously involved otherwise communication would not be possible. In the famous example *He spread the warm bread with socks*, although *socks* is a well-expected grammatical category "NP," it hinders comprehension and elicits a large N400 effect.

Following Firth's (1957) distributional hypothesis, semantic coherence can be quantified by distributional semantic models, which represent words as high-dimensional vectors based on co-occurrence statistics from a large text corpus (e.g. Baroni et al. 2014; Erk 2012). Similar vectors are assigned to words that usually occur in similar contexts, hence the cosine similarity between two vectors represents the semantic distance between the two words.

Behavioral studies suggest that cosine similarity between word vector and its previous context vector accounts for a certain amount of variance in eye-fixation times (Pynte et al. 2008) and word-pronunciation duration (Sayeed et al. 2015). More recently, Ettinger et al. (2016) showed that similarity distance between the critical word and its context simulates the N400 effect from previous ERP sentence-reading experiments (Federmeier and Kutas 1999).

7.4 Correlating fMRI time-courses with various metrics during natural story listening

7.4.1 Complexity metrics

7.4.1.1 CFG node counts

We first obtained the CFG trees using the Stanford Parser (Klein and Manning 2003), then we counted the number of nodes in the CFG trees that would be visited by a bottom-up, top-down, and left-corner parser respectively.

7.4.1.2 MG node counts

Analogous to the node count predictors based on CFG trees, we also counted the number of nodes in the X-bar trees that would be visited by a bottom-up, top-down, and left-corner parser respectively. The X-bar structures were the derived trees generated by Minimalist Grammars in the sense of Stabler (1997). These structures reflect grammatical analysis by van Wagenen et al. (2014).

7.4.1.3 CFG surprisal

CFG surprisal is a structural notion of expectedness of the next word as described in Section 7.2.3. We used the EarleyX implementation of Stolcke's probabilistic Earley parser to compute surprisal values (Luong et al. 2013; Stolcke 1995). The probabilities of grammatical rules were estimated using the entire *Alice in Wonderland* text.

7.4.1.4 Structural distance

To examine the memory-related complexity metrics sketched earlier in Section 7.2.3, the dependency relations for every sentence were also obtained using the Stanford Parser (de Marneffe et al. 2006). Structural distance is then the number of nodes traversed between the head and the dependent in the phrase-structural tree. We considered only the rightmost word in any dependency relation. For words in multiple dependency relations, we summed the structural distances.

7.4.1.5 N-gram surprisal

As a kind of control (see Section 7.3), we used the freely-available trigram counts from the Google Books project (see e.g. Michel et al. 2011) and restricted consideration to publication years 1850–1900, i.e. the years surrounding the publication of *Alice in Wonderland*. We backed off to lower-order grams where necessary: coverage was 1725/2045 for trigrams and 1640/1694 for bigrams. We then used surprisal of the trigram probabilities to link the probability of a word in its left-context to BOLD signals (see Hale, 2001; 2016).

7.4.1.6 Lexical-semantic coherence

We used latent semantic analysis (LSA; Landauer and Dumais 1997) to build our semantic coherence metric. The training data comprised *Alice in Wonderland* in its entirety. We first built the type-by-document matrix where the rows were all the words in the book and the documents were all the paragraphs. The input vector space was transformed by singular value decomposition (SVD), and truncated to a *100*-dimensional vector space. The context vector was the average of the previous 10 word vectors. We used negative cosine between the target word vector and the context vector to represent lexical-semantic coherence: higher negative cosine value indicates less semantic coherence.

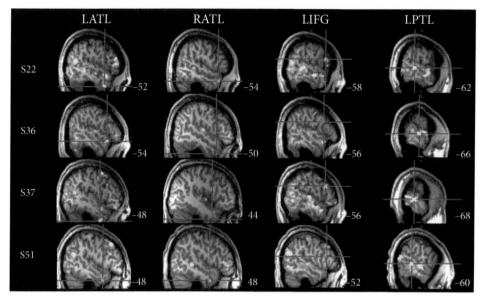

Figure 7.1 ROIs (columns) from four participants (rows). From Brennan et al. (2016).

7.4.2 Data acquisition

We used the freely-available ROI time-courses from Brennan et al. (2016).[1] The data come from 25 native English speakers (17 female, 18–24 years old, right-handed) listening to a story while in the scanner. The story was the first chapter of *Alice in Wonderland*, lasting for about 12.4 minutes. Participants completed twelve multiple-choice questions after scanning to verify their comprehension.

Four regions of interest (ROIs) were used to evaluate the syntactic models, including the left anterior temporal lobe (LATL), the right anterior temporal lobe (RATL), the left inferior frontal gyrus (LIFG), and the left posterior temporal lobe (LPTL). Figure 7.1 shows the ROIs from four participants (from Brennan et al. 2016).

Both functional and anatomical criteria guided the precise positioning of these ROIs. The functional criterion derives from an atheoretical word rate regressor (rate), which has value 1 at the offset of each word in the audio stimulus, and 0 elsewhere. This localizer identified regions whose BOLD signals were sensitive to word presentation. Each ROI sphere (10 mm radius) was centered on a peak t-value of at least 2.0 within the anatomical areas.

Imaging was performed using a 3T MRI scanner with a 32-channel head coil at the Cornell MRI facility; the detailed imaging parameters and preprocessing procedures are described in Brennan et al. (2016).

---

[1] The data can be downloaded at https://sites.lsa.umich.edu/cnllab/2016/06/11/data-sharing-fmri-timecourses-story-listening/.

7.4.3 Data analysis

7.4.3.1 Estimating hemodynamic response

Following Just and Varma (2007), we convolved each complexity metric's time series with SPM12's canonical hemodynamic response function (HRF) to estimate hemodynamic responses for each metric. This estimated response is what should be observed if a brain region were processing the information specified in each neuro-computational model. The time series are made orthogonal to the convolved `rate` vector, since it is our localizer for defining the ROIs.

7.4.3.2 Stepwise regression

We tested the unique contribution of each model by conducting stepwise model comparisons against the ROI time-courses. We used the forward selection approach which starts with no variables in the model, and tests whether adding one variable would give statistically significant improvement of the fit. Our null model included fixed effects for head movements (`dx,dy,dz,rx,ry,rz`) and `rate`; we also included fixed effects for word frequency (`freq`), which were also convolved with the same HRF. The frequency count was estimated using the SUBTLEXus corpus (Brysbaert and New 2009), which contains 51 million words from the subtitles of American films and television series. f0 (`f0`), and root mean square (RMS) intensity (`intensity`) of the speech were also included in our null model. The raw f0 of the 12 minutes speech in the audio was extracted using the fxrapt function from the Voicebox toolbox for Matlab; each contour was further processed by removing any f0 values exceeding 4 *s.d.* from the mean, and filling the gaps by spline interpolation. The RMS intensity for every 20 ms of the audio was calculated to get the intensity vectors. `f0` and `intensity` were also convolved and then sub-sampled to 0.5 Hz to matching the time resolution (TR) of the fMRI measurements. The random effects included a random intercept by participant and a random slope for `rate`:

$$\text{BOLD}_{null} \sim dx + dy + dz + rx + ry + rz + rate + f0 + intensity + frequency\,(1 + rate \mid subject)$$

We then added regressors in the following order: surprisal of lexical trigram probability (`trigram`), negative cosine similarity between word vector and context vector (`lsa10`), structural distance between dependent words based on CFG (`struct`), surprisal of word-category probability based on CFG (`cfg.surp`), node count based on bottom-up parsing on CFG (`cfg.bu`) and node count based on bottom-up parsing on MG (`mg.bu`), namely, `trigram` > `lsa10` > `struct` > `cfg.surp` > `cfg.bu` > `mg.bu`. This order reflects a general direction from predictors with least syntactic information (`trigram`, `lsa10`) to predictors with the richest syntactic information (`mg.bu`).

Model fit was assessed using chi-square tests on the log-likelihood of each regression model. This log-likelihood was the basis of the model comparison. All of the predictors were converted to z-scores before statistical analysis. Statistical significance was corrected for multiple comparisons across four ROIs with the Bonferroni method (the adjusted alpha-level is 0.05/4=0.0125).

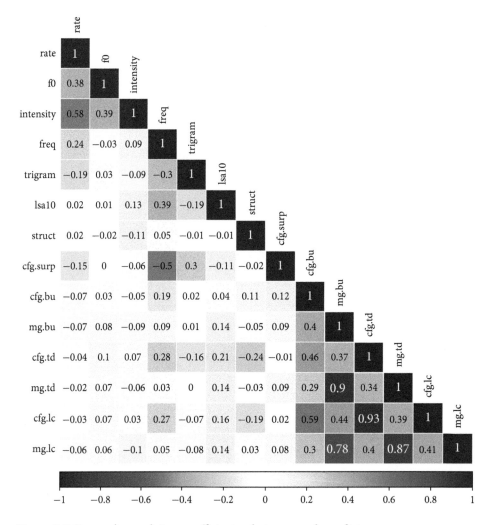

Figure 7.2 Pearson's correlation coefficients r between each predictor

7.4.4 Results

7.4.4.1 Correlations between predictors

As a first step, we checked the correlations between the 14 regressors: rate, f0, intensity, freq, trigram, lsa10, struct, cfg.surp, cfg.bu, mg.bu, cfg.td, mg.td, cfg.lc and mg.lc. The correlation matrix is shown in Figure 7.2. As can be seen, the correlation between rate and intensity is relatively high ($r = 0.58, p < .001$); this is expected because word rate tracks the occurrence of each word in speech, which leads to higher intensity as compared to silence. freq is negatively correlated with cfg.surp ($r(\text{freq}, \text{cfg.surp}) = -0.5, p < .001$).

Among the CFG node count regressors, cfg.td and cfg.lc are highly correlated ($r(\text{cfg.td}, \text{cfg.lc})=0.93, p < .001$), while the correlation coefficients between

Table 7.3 Step-wise model comparison results for all ROIs

	(a) LATL						(b) RATL				
	Parameter	df	LogLik	χ^2	p		Parameter	df	LogLik	χ^2	p
Ø		15	−11659			Ø		15	−11222		
A	trigram	16	−11622	72.9	<.001	A	trigram	16	−11210	22.7	<.001
B	lsa10	17	−11611	22.9	<.001	B	lsa10	17	−11202	16.3	<.001
C	struct	18	−11611	0.7	0.41	C	struct	18	−11195	14.1	<.001
D	cfg.surp	19	−11553	115.6	<.001	D	cfg.surp	19	−11176	37.8	<.001
E	cfg.bu	20	−11553	0.0	0.83	E	cfg.bu	20	−11176	0.5	0.48
F	mg.bu	20	−11551	3.2	0.07	F	mg.bu	21	−11174	3.4	0.07

	(c) LIFG						(d) LPTL				
	Parameter	df	LogLik	χ^2	p		Parameter	df	LogLik	χ^2	p
Ø		15	−10653			Ø		15	−11900		
A	trigram	16	−10648	10.0	0.002	A	trigram	16	−11870	60	<.001
B	lsa10	17	−10646	3.0	0.086	B	lsa10	17	−11853	33	<.001
C	struct	18	−10646	0.0	0.832	C	struct	18	−11842	23	<.001
D	cfg.surp	19	−10633	25.9	<.001	D	cfg.surp	19	−11809	65	<.001
E	cfg.bu	20	−10632	2.0	0.158	E	cfg.bu	20	−11804	11	0.001
F	mg.bu	21	−11630	5.2	0.022	F	mg.bu	21	−11793	22	<.001

cfg.bu and cfg.td (r(cfg.bu, cfg.td)=0.93, $p < .001$) and between cfg.bu and cfg.lc (r(cfg.bu, cfg.lc)=−0.59, $p < .001$) are much smaller.

The MG node counts based on different parsing algorithms are all highly correlated with each other (r(mg.bu, mg.td)=0.9, $p < .001$; r(mg.bu, mg.lc)=0.78, $p < .001$; r(mg.td, mg.lc)=0.87, $p < .001$). To avoid collinearity in hierarchical regression analysis, we included only cfg.bu and mg.bu for comparison between CFG and MG models.

7.4.4.2 Model comparison

Complexity metrics based on each of the neuro-computational models are subsequently added to the four baseline regressions. In the ATLs, an improvement in the goodness of fit is obtained for lexical-semantic coherence, but structural distance is also significant for the RATL. All the parameters are significant for the LPTL, roughly corresponding to the traditional Wernicke's area. Trigram and CFG Surprisal significantly improve model fit in all of the ROIs, but no other regressors are significant in the LIFG except trigram and CFG surprisal. The statistical details for the model comparisons are shown in Table 7.3.

Figure 7.3 shows the estimated coefficients and 95% confidence intervals for each of the predictors when added to the null model. The signs of the coefficients suggest that: (1) higher trigram and CFG surprisal are correlated with more activation in all the ROIs; (2) changes in distributional meaning correlate with more activation in

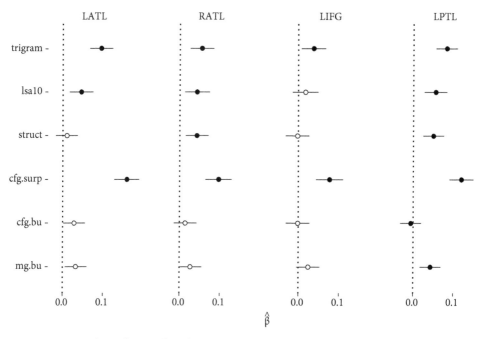

Figure 7.3 Fitted coefficients for all linguistic predictors across six ROIs. Coefficients show the estimated change in BOLD signal per unit change in the linguistic predictor (x-axis). Error bars show 95% confidence intervals. Filled points indicate models that made a statistically significant contribution in step-wise comparison.

the ATLs and LPTL; (3) greater structural distances between heads and dependents are associated with increased activation in the RATL and LIPL; (4) higher bottom-up node counts based on CFG and MG both correlate with increased activity in the LPTL.

7.5 Towards a functional anatomy of sentence comprehension

We found a significant effect for MG and CFG bottom-up node count in the LPTL on top of trigram probability. *Contra* suggestions in Frank and Bod (2011) and Frank et al. (2015), this is evidence for sensitivity to hierarchical syntactic structure, at least in the posterior temporal lobe. Node counts from MG-derived structures are also significant over and above node counts based on CFGs—suggesting that the LPTL is also involved in the processing of long-distance dependency.

Structural distance is significant in the RATL and LPTL. This result aligns well with Baumann's (2014) finding based on eye-tracking corpus that structural distance predicts eye-fixation times in reading, supporting a role for "integration cost" in memory-based models of sentence processing.

The lexical-semantic coherence metric is a significant predictor in the ATLs. This is consistent with previous findings implicating the ATLs in conceptual combination

(Rogalsky and Hickok 2009; Wilson et al. 2014; Pylkkänen 2015). However, we also found a significant effect of CFG surprisal in the LATL, and a significant effect of structural distance in the RATL. This suggests that the ATLs may be involved in syntactic processing as well (Humphries et al. 2006; Brennan et al. 2012; Brennan et al. 2016).

The LPTL activity is highly correlated with all the syntactic and semantic complexity metrics. As suggested by Wehbe et al. (2014), multiple regions spanning the bilateral temporal cortices may represent both syntax and semantics. Our results are consistent with their suggestion that syntax and semantics might be non-dissociable at the level of neurobiology.

No semantic or syntactic metric is significantly correlated with the LIFG except for CFG surprisal. The failure to find effects of grammar has led to reevaluations of deficit-lesion studies that have long associated syntactic computation with the "Broca's area" (e.g. Ben-Shachar et al. 2003; Caplan et al. 2008; Just et al. 1996; Stromswold et al. 1996). However, both this study and Brennan et al. (2016) found significant effects of n-gram models in the LIFG. It is possible that this region is not particularly strained by stimuli that are easy to understand.

To sum up, our correlational results from fMRI suggest that the temporal lobes perform a kind of computation that is both syntactic in the classical sense of phrase structure, and semantic in the sense of distributional word-embeddings. One set of questions this work leaves open is the precise relationships between these two predictors—for instance, temporal precedence. Other methods, such as MEG, may provide further insight here.

Acknowledgements

The authors are grateful to John Brennan for his help in various stages of the work. This material is based upon work supported by the National Science Foundation under Grant No. 1607441. Any opinions, findings, and conclusions or recommendations expressed in this material are those of the author(s) and do not necessarily reflect the views of the National Science Foundation.

References

Aczel, P. 1988. *Non-Well-Founded Sets*. Stanford, Calif.: CSLI.

Adger, D., and P. Svenonius. 2011. Features in minimalist syntax. In Cedric Boeckx (ed.), *Oxford Handbook of Linguistic Minimalism*. Oxford: Oxford University Press, 617–41.

Ahn, B. 2016. Syntax–phonology mapping and the Tongan DP. *Glossa* 1(1): 4.1–36.

Aho, A. V., and Jeffrey D. Ullman. 1972. *The Theory of Parsing, Translation, and Compiling*, vol. 1: *Parsing*. Englewood Cliffs, NJ: Prentice Hall.

Armeni, K., R. M. Willems, and S. L. Frank. 2017. Probabilistic language models in cognitive neuroscience: promises and pitfalls. *Neuroscience and Biobehavioral Reviews* 83: 579–88.

Baker, M., K. Johnson, and I. Roberts. 1989. Passive argument raised. *Linguistic Inquiry* 20: 219–51.

Bar-Hillel, Y., M. Perles, and E. Shamir. 1961. On formal properties of simple phrase structure grammars. *Zeitschrift für Phonetik, Sprachwissenschaft und Kommunikationsforschung* 14: 143–72. Repr. in Y. Bar-Hillel, *Language and Information: Selected Essays on their Theory and Application* (New York: Addison-Wesley, 1964).

Baroni, M., R. Bernardi, and R. Zamparelli. 2014. Frege in space: a program of compositional distributional semantics. *Linguistic Issues in Language Technology* 9: 241–346.

Barton, G. Edward, Robert C. Berwick, and E. S. Ristad. 1987. *Computational Complexity and Natural Language*. Cambridge, Mass.: MIT Press.

Batliner, A., A. Feldhaus, S. Geißler, A. Kießling, T. Kiss, R. Kompe, and E. N. Biggsöth. 1996. Integrating syntactic and prosodic information for the efficient detection of empty categories. In *Proceedings of the 16th Conference on Computational Linguistics*, vol. 1, COLING'96, 71–6.

Baumann, P. 2014. Dependencies and hierarchical structure in sentence processing. In *Proceedings of CogSci 2014*, 152–7.

Beckman, M. E. 1996. The parsing of prosody. *Language and Cognitive Processes* 11(1/2): 17–67.

Beckman, M., and G. A. Elam. 1997. Guidelines for ToBI labelling. Technical report, Ohio State University. http://www.ling.ohio-state.edu/~tobi/ame tobi/.

Beckman, M., and J. Pierrehumbert. 1986. Intonational structure in Japanese and English. *Phonology Yearbook* 3: 255–309.

Beesley, K. R., and L. Karttunen. 2003. *Finite State Morphology*. Stanford, Calif.: CLSI.

beim Graben, P., and S. Gerth. 2012. Geometric representations for minimalist grammars. *Journal of Logic, Language and Information* 21(4): 393–432.

Bellik, J., O. Bellik, and N. Kalivoda. 2015. Syntax-prosody for OT. Technical report, University of California, Santa Cruz. JavaScript application, https://github.com/syntax-prosody-ot.

Ben-Shachar, M., T. Hendler, I. Kahn, D. Ben-Bashat, and Y. Grodzinsky. 2003. The neural reality of syntactic transformations: evidence from fMRI. *Psychological Science* 14: 433–40.

Bennett, R., E. Elfner, and J. McCloskey. 2016. Lightest to the right: an apparently anomalous displacement in Irish. *Linguistic Inquiry* 47(2): 169–234.

Berwick, R. C., and N. Chomsky. 2011. The biolinguistic program. In A. M. Di Sciullo and C. Boeckx (eds), *The Biolinguistic Enterprise*. Oxford: Oxford University Press, 19–41.

Berwick, R. C., and N. Chomsky. 2017. *Why Only Us: Language and Evolution*. Cambridge, Mass.: MIT Press.

Berwick, R. C., and A. S. Weinberg. 1984. *The Grammatical Basis of Linguistic Performance: Language Use and Acquisition*. Cambridge, Mass.: MIT Press.

Bever, T. G. 1970. The cognitive basis for linguistic structures. In J. R. Hayes (ed.), *Cognition and the Development of Language*. New York: Wiley, 279–362.

Bianchi, V. 2000. The raising analysis of relative clauses: a reply to Borsley. *Linguistic Inquiry* 31: 123–40.

Bimbó, K. 2015. The decidability of the intensional fragment of classical linear logic. *Theoretical Computer Science* 597: 1–17.

Bittner, M., and K. Hale. 1996. Ergativity: Towards a theory of a heterogeneous class. *Linguistic Inquiry* 27: 531–604.

Blache, P. 1995. *Towards an Integration of Speech and Natural Language Processing*. Sophia Antipolis, France: CNRS.

Bobaljik, J. D. 2008. Where's ϕ? Agreement as a post-syntactic operation. In D. Harbour, D. Adger, and S. Béjar (eds), *Phi-Theory*. Oxford: Oxford University Press, 295–328.

Boeckx, C. 2012. *Syntactic Islands*. Cambridge: Cambridge University Press.

Boston, M., J. Hale, R. Kliegl, U. Patil, and S. Vasishth. 2008. Parsing costs as predictors of reading difficulty: an evaluation using the Potsdam sentence corpus. *Journal of Eye Movement Research* 2(1): 1–12.

Boston, M. F., J. T. Hale, and M. Kuhlmann. 2010. Dependency structures derived from Minimalist Grammars. In C. Ebert, G. Jäger, and J. Michaelis (eds), *Mathematics of Language* 10/11, vol. 6149 of Lecture Notes in Computer Science. Berlin: Springer, 1–12.

Boston, M., J. Hale, S. Vasishth, and R. Kliegl. 2011. Parallel processing and sentence comprehension difficulty. *Language and Cognitive Processes* 26: 301–49.

Bošković, Ž. 2016. On the timing of labeling: deducing comp-trace effects, the subject condition, the adjunct condition, and tucking in from labeling. *Linguistic Review* 33(1): 17–66.

Brennan, J. 2016. Naturalistic sentence comprehension in the brain. *Language and Linguistics Compass* 10: 299–313.

Brennan, J., Y. Nir, U. Hasson, R. Malach, D. J. Heeger, and L. Pylkkänen. 2012. Syntactic structure building in the anterior temporal lobe during natural story listening. *Brain and Language* 120(2): 163–73.

Brennan, J. R., E. P. Stabler, S. E. Van Wagenen, W.-M. Luh, and J. T. Hale. 2016. Abstract linguistic structure correlates with temporal activity during naturalistic comprehension. *Brain and Language* 157–8: 81–94.

Brown, M., L. C. Dilley, and M. K. Tanenhaus. 2012. Real-time expectations based on context speech rate can cause words to appear or disappear. In *Proceedings of the 34th Annual Conference of the Cognitive Science Society*, 1374–9.

Brysbaert, M., and B. New. 2009. Moving beyond Kučera and Francis: a critical evaluation of current word frequency norms and the introduction of a new and improved word frequency measure for American English. *Behavior Research Methods* 41: 977–90.

Büring, D. 2003. On D-trees, beans, and B-accents. *Linguistics and Philosophy* 26: 511–45.

Cable, S. 2007. The grammar of Q: Q-particles and the nature of wh-fronting, as revealed by the wh-questions of Tlingit. Cambridge, Mass.: MIT doctoral dissertation.

Caplan, D., E. Chen, and G. Water. 2008. Task-dependent and task-independent neurovascular responses to syntactic processing. *Cortex* 44: 257–75.

Cecchetto, C., and C. Donati. 2015. *(Re)labelling*. Cambridge, Mass.: MIT Press.

Chafe, W. L. (ed.) 1980. *The Pear Stories: Cognitive, Cultural, and Linguistic Aspects of Narrative Production*. Norwood, NJ: Ablex.

Charniak, E., and M. Johnson. 2001. Edit detection and parsing for transcribed speech. In *Proceedings of the North American Chapter of the Association of Computational Linguistics Annual Meeting*, NAACL, 1–9.

Cheng, L. L.-S., and L. J. Downing. 2016. Phasal syntax = cyclic phonology? *Syntax* 19: 156–91.

Cho, P. W., M. Goldrick, and P. Smolensky. 2017. Incremental parsing in a continuous dynamical system: sentence processing in gradient symbolic computation. *Linguistics Vanguard* 3(1): https://www.scholars.northwestern.edu/en/publications/incremental-parsing-in-a-continuous-dynamical-system-sentence-pro.

Chomsky, N. 1955. *The Logical Structure of Linguistic Theory*. Cambridge, Mass.: MIT Humanities Library (microfilm edn).

Chomsky, N. 1957. *Syntactic Structures*. The Hague: Mouton.

Chomsky, N. 1965. *Aspects of the Theory of Syntax*. Cambridge, Mass.: MIT Press.

Chomsky, N. 1970. Remarks on nominalization. In R. A. Jacobs and P. S. Rosenbaum (eds), *Readings in English Transformational Grammar*. Waltham, Mass.: Ginn. Repr. in Chomsky's *Studies on Semantics in Generative Grammar* (The Hague: Mouton, 1972), 184–221.

Chomsky, N. 1977. On wh-movement. In P. Culicover, T. Wasow, and A. Akmajian (eds), *Formal Syntax*. New York: Academic Press.

Chomsky, N. 1981. *Lectures on Government and Binding*. Dordrecht: Foris.

Chomsky, N. 1986. *Barriers*. Cambridge, Mass.: MIT Press.

Chomsky, N. 1995a. Bare phrase structure. In G. Webelhuth (ed.), *Government and Binding Theory and the Minimalist Program*. Cambridge, Mass.: MIT Press, 383–439.

Chomsky, N. 1995b. *The Minimalist Program*. Cambridge, Mass.: MIT Press.

Chomsky, N. 2000. Minimalist inquiries: the framework. In R. Martin, D. Michaels, and J. Uriagereka (eds), *Step by Step: Essays on Minimalism in Honor of Howard Lasnik*. Cambridge, Mass.: MIT Press, 89–155.

Chomsky, N. 2001. Derivation by phase. In M. Kenstowicz (ed.), *Ken Hale: A Life in Language*. Cambridge, Mass.: MIT Press, 1–52.

Chomsky, N. 2002. *On Nature and Language*. Cambridge: Cambridge University Press.

Chomsky, N. 2005. Three factors in language design. *Linguistic Inquiry* 36(1): 1–22.

Chomsky, N. 2008. On phases. In R. Freidin, C. P. Otero, and M. L. Zubizarreta (eds), *Foundational Issues in Linguistic Theory: Essays in Honor of Jean-Roger Vergnaud*. Cambridge, Mass.: MIT Press, 89–156.

Chomsky, N. 2013. Problems of projection. *Lingua* 130: 33–49.

Chomsky, N. 2015a. Preface. In *The Minimalist Program: 20th Anniversary Edition*. Cambridge, Mass.: MIT Press.

Chomsky, N. 2015b. Problems of projections: extensions. In E. Di Domenico, C. Hamann, and S. Matteini (eds), *Structures, Strategies and Beyond: Studies in honour of Adriana Belletti*. Amsterdam: Benjamins, 1–16.

Chomsky, N., and M. Halle. 1968. *The Sound Pattern of English*. Cambridge, Mass.: MIT Press.

Christiansen, M., and M. MacDonald. 2009. A usage-based approach to recursion in sentence processing. *Language Learning* 59: 129–64.

Chung, S. 1978. *Case Marking and Grammatical Relations in Polynesian*. Austin: University of Texas Press.

Cinque, G. 1999. *Adverbs and Functional Heads: A Cross-Linguistic Perspective*. Oxford: Oxford University Press.

Clemens, L. E. 2014. *Prosodic Noun Incorporation and Verb-Initial Syntax*. PhD thesis, Harvard University.

Clifton Jr., C., K. Carlson, and L. Frazier. 2002. Informative prosodic boundaries. *Language and Speech* 45: 87–114.

Cole, J., and S. Shattuck-Hufnagel. 2016. New methods for prosodic transcription: capturing variability as a source of information. *Laboratory Phonology* 7(1): 1–29.

Collins, C., and E. Stabler (2016). A formalization of minimalist syntax. *Syntax* 19(1): 43–78.

Collins, J. N. 2014. The distribution of unmarked cases in Samoan. In *Argument Realisations and Related Constructions in Austronesian Languages: Papers from 12-ICAL*, 93–110.

Collins, J. N. 2015. Diagnosing predicate fronting in Samoan. In *Proceedings of the 32nd West Coast Conference on Formal Linguistics*.

Collins, J. N. 2016. Samoan predicate initial word order and object positions. *Natural Language & Linguistic Theory* 35: 1–59.

Comon, H., M. Dauchet, R. Gilleron, C. Löding, F. Jacquemard, D. Lugiez, S. Tison, and M. Tommasi. 2007. Tree automata techniques and applications. Technical report, INRIA, ENS Cachan, France. http://tata.gforge.inria.fr.

Constant, N. 2014. *Contrastive Topic: Meanings and Realizations*. PhD thesis, University of Massachusetts Amherst.

Deal, A. R. 2009. The origin and content of expletives: evidence from selection. *Syntax* 12: 285–323.

Deal, A. R. 2015. Ergativity. In A. Alexiadou, and T. Kiss (eds), *Syntax—Theory and Analysis: An International Handbook*. Berlin: Mouton de Gruyter, 654–707.

Demberg, V., and F. Keller. 2008. A psycholinguistically motivated version of TAG. In *Proceedings of the 9th International Workshop on Tree Adjoining Grammars and Related Formalisms* (TAG+9), Tübingen, 25–32.

den Dikken, M., and A. Lahne. 2013. The locality of syntactic dependencies. In M. den Dikken (ed.), *The Cambridge Handbook of Generative Syntax*. Cambridge: Cambridge University Press, 655–97.

Dillon, B. 2014. Syntactic memory in the comprehension of reflexive dependencies: an overview. *Language and Linguistic Compass* 8(5): 171–87.

D'Imperio, M., F. Cangemi, and M. Grice. 2016. Introducing advancing prosodic transcription. *Laboratory Phonology* 7(1): 1–3.

Dobashi, Y. 2004. Multiple spell-out, label-free syntax, and PF-interface. *Explorations in English Linguistics* 19: 1–47.

Downing, L. J. 2010. An edge-based approach to the alignment of syntactic phases and prosodic phrases. *Transactions of the Philological Society* 108: 352–69.

Dreyer, M., and I. Shafran. 2007. Exploiting prosody for PCFGs with latent annotations. In *Proceedings of INTERSPEECH*, 450–53.

Dronkers, N. F., D. P. Wilkins, R. D. Van Valin, B. B. Redfern, and J. J. Jaeger. 2004. Lesion analysis of the brain areas involved in language comprehension: towards a new functional anatomy of language. *Cognition* 92: 145–77.

Elfner, E. 2012. *Syntax–Prosody Interactions in Irish*. PhD thesis, University of Massachusetts Amherst.

Elfner, E. 2015. Recursion in prosodic phrasing: evidence from Connemara Irish. *Natural Language & Linguistic Theory* 33: 1169–208.

Elordieta, G. 2008. An overview of theories of the syntax–phonology interface. *Journal of Basque Linguistics and Philology* 42: 209–86.

Epstein, S. D., H. Kitahara, and D. Seely. 2016. Phase cancellation by external pair-merge of heads. *Linguistic Review* 33(1): 87–102.

Erk, K. 2012. Vector space models of word meaning and phrase meaning: a survey. *Language and Linguistics Compass* 6: 635–53.

Ettinger, A., N. Feldman, P. Resnik, and C. Phillips. 2016. Modeling N400 amplitude using vector space models of word representation. In *Proceedings of the 38th Annual Conference of the Cognitive Science Society*, 1445–50, Austin, Tex.: Cognitive Science Society.

Everaert, A., M. Huybregts, N. Chomsky, R. Berwick, and J. Bolhuis. 2015. Structures, not strings: linguistics as part of the cognitive sciences. *Trends in Cognitive Sciences* 19: 729–43.

Federmeier, D., and M. Kutas. 1999. A rose by any other name: long-term memory structure and sentence processing. *Journal of Memory and Language* 41: 469–95.

Fedorenko, E., Behr, M. K., & Kanwisher, N. 2011. Functional specificity for high-level linguistic processing in the human brain. *Proceedings of the National Academy of Sciences*, 108: 16428–33.

Ferreira, F., and H. Karimi. 2015. Prosody, performance, and cognitive skill: evidence from individual differences. In L. Frazier and E. Gibson (eds), *Explicit and Implicit Prosody in Sentence Processing*. Berlin: Springer, 119–32.

Ferreira, F., and N. D. Patson. 2007. The "good enough" approach to language comprehension. *Language and Linguistics Compass* 1: 71–83.

Féry, C. 2017. *Intonation and Prosodic Structure*. Cambridge: Cambridge University Press.

Féry, C., and H. Truckenbrodt. 2005. Sisterhood and tonal scaling. *Studia Linguistica* 59: 223–43.

Firth, J. 1957. A synopsis of linguistic theory, 1930–1955. In *Studies in Linguistic Analysis*. Oxford: Philological Society, 1–32.

Flack, K. 2007. *The Sources of Phonological Markedness*. PhD thesis, University of Massachusetts Amherst.

Fodor, J. D. 1978. Parsing strategies and constraints on transformations. *Linguistic Inquiry* 9(3): 427–73.

Fodor, J. D. 1985. Deterministic parsing and subjacency. *Language and Cognitive Processes* 1: 3–42.

Fong, S. 2014. Unification and efficient computation in the minimalist program. In F. Lowenthal and L. Lefebvre (eds), *Language and Recursion*. Berlin: Springer.

Fong, S., and R. Berwick. 2008. Treebank parsing and knowledge of language: a cognitive perspective. In *Proceedings of the 30th Annual Conference of the Cognitive Science Society*.

Fong, S., and J. Ginsburg. 2012a. Computation with doubling constituents: pronouns and antecedents in phase theory. In A. M. Di Sciullo (ed.), *Towards a Biolinguistic Understanding of Grammar: Essays on Interfaces*. Amsterdam: Benjamins, 303–38.

Fong, S., and J. Ginsburg. 2012b. Modeling of coreference relations in multi-object constructions. In *Proceedings of the 13th Tokyo Conference on Psycholinguistics*. Tokyo: Hituzi, 61–80.

Fong, S., and J. Ginsburg. 2014. A new approach to tough-constructions. In *Proceedings of the 31st West Coast Conference on Formal Linguistics* (WCCFL 31). Somerville, Mass.: Cascadilla, 180–8.

Fong, S., and J. Ginsburg. In preparation. The Minimalist Machine. University of Arizona and Osaka Kyoiku University.

Fowlie, M. 2017. *Slaying the Great Green Dragon: Learning and Modelling Iterable Ordered Optional Adjuncts*. PhD thesis, UCLA.

Fowlie, M., and A. Koller. 2017. Parsing minimalist languages with interpreted regular tree grammars. In *Proceedings of the 13th International Workshop on Tree Adjoining Grammars and Related Formalisms*, TAG+13, 11–20.

Frank, R., and G. Satta. 1998. Optimality theory and the generative complexity of constraint violability. *Computational Linguistics* 24: 307–15.

Frank, S., and R. Bod. 2011. Insensitivity of the human sentence-processing system to hierarchical structure. *Psychological Science* 22: 829–34.

Frank, S., L. Otten, G. Galli, and G. Vigliocco. 2015. The ERP response to the amount of information conveyed by words in sentences. *Brain and Language* 140: 1–11.

Frazier, L. 1985. Syntactic complexity. In D. R. Dowty, L. Karttunen, and A. Zwicky (eds), *Natural Language Parsing*. Cambridge: Cambridge University Press.

Frazier, L., and C. Clifton. 1996. *Construal*. Cambridge, Mass.: MIT Press.

Frey, W., and H.-M. Gärtner. 2002. On the treatment of scrambling and adjunction in minimalist grammars. In *Proceedings, Formal Grammar'02*, Trento.

Gaifman, H. 1965. Dependency systems and phrase-structure systems. *Information and Control* 8(3): 304–37.

Gallego, Á. J. 2006. T-to-C movement in relative clauses. In J. Doetjes and P. González (eds), *Romance Languages and Linguistic Theory 2004*. Philadelphia, Penn.: Benjamins, 143–70.

Gärtner, H.-M., and J. Michaelis. 2003. A note on countercyclicity and minimalist grammars. In G. Jäger, P. Monachesi, G. Penn, and S. Wintner (eds), *Proceedings of Formal Grammar 2003*. New York: Springer, 103–14.

Gärtner, H.-M., and J. Michaelis. 2007. Some remarks on locality conditions and minimalist grammars. In U. Sauerland and H.-M. Gärtner (eds), *Interfaces + Recursion = Language? Chomsky's Minimalism and the View from Syntax-Semantics*. New York: Mouton de Gruyter, 161–96.

Gärtner, H.-M., and J. Michaelis. 2010. On the treatment of multiple wh-interrogatives in minimalist grammars. In T. Hanneforth and G. Fanselow (eds), *Language and Logos: Studies in Theoretical and Computational Linguistics*. Berlin: Academie, 339–66.

Gerth, S., and P. beim Graben. 2009. Unifying syntactic theory and sentence processing difficulty through a connectionist minimalist parser. *Cognitive Neurodynamics* 3(4): 297–316.

Gibson, E. 1998. Linguistic complexity: locality of syntactic dependencies. *Cognition* 68: 1–76.

Ginsburg, J. 2016. Modeling problems of projection: a non-countercyclic approach. *Glossa* 1(1): 1–46.

Goldsmith, J. 1976. *Autosegmental Phonology*. PhD thesis, MIT.

Goldsmith, J. 1990. *Autosegmental and Metrical Phonology*. Oxford: Blackwell.

Graf, T. 2011. Closure properties of minimalist derivation tree languages. In *Logical Aspects of Computational Linguistics*, LACL'11, LNCS 6736. Berlin: Springer, 96–111.

Graf, T. 2012. Movement-generalized minimalist grammars. In *Logical Aspects of Computational Linguistics*, LACL, LNCS 7351. Berlin: Springer, 58–73.

Graf, T. 2013. *Local and Transderivational Constraints in Syntax and Semantics*. PhD thesis, UCLA.

Graf, T., and N. Abner. 2012. Is syntactic binding rational? In *Proceedings of the 11th International Workshop on Tree Adjoining Grammars and Related Formalisms*, TAG+11, 189–97.

Graf, T., A. Aksënova, and A. De Santo. 2016. A single movement normal form for minimalist grammars. In *Formal Grammar: 20th and 21st International Conferences, Revised Selected Papers*, LNCS 9804. Berlin: Springer, 200–15.

de Groote, P. 2001. Towards abstract categorial grammars. In *39th Annual Meeting of the Association for Computational Linguistics*, 148–55.

de Groote, P., and S. Pogodalla. 2004. On the expressive power of abstract categorial grammars: representing context-free formalisms. *Journal of Logic, Language and Information* 13: 421–38.

Gussenhoven, C. 2016. Analysis of intonation: the case of MAE ToBI. *Laboratory Phonology* 7: 10.

Haegeman, L. 1999. X-bar theory. In *The MIT Encyclopedia of the Cognitive Sciences*. Cambridge, Mass.: MIT Press.

Hagstrom, P. 1998. *Decomposing Questions*. MIT doctoral dissertation.

Hale, J. 2001. A probabilistic Earley parser as a psycholinguistic model. In *Proceedings of the Second Meeting of the North American Chapter of the Asssociation for Computational Linguistics*, 159–66.

Hale, J. 2003. *Grammar, Uncertainty, and Sentence Processing*. PhD thesis, Johns Hopkins University.

Hale, J. 2014. *Automaton Theories of Human Sentence Comprehension*. Stanford, Calif.: CSLI.

Hale, J. 2016. Information-theoretical complexity metrics. *Language and Linguistics Compass* 10: 397–412.

Hale, J., I. Shafran, L. Yung, B. Dorr, M. Harper, A. Krasnyanskaya, M. Lease, Y. Liu, B. Roark, M. Snover, and R. Stewart. 2006. PCFGs with syntactic and prosodic indicators of speech repairs. In *Proceedings of the 21st International Conference on Computational Linguistics and the 44th Annual Meeting of the Association for Computational Linguistics*, 161–8.

Hale, J., and P. Smolensky. 2006. Harmonic grammars and harmonic parsers for formal language. In P. Smolensky and G. Legendre (eds), *The Harmonic Mind: From Neural Computation to Optimality-Theoretic Grammar*, vol. 1: *Cognitive Architecture*. Cambridge, Mass.: MIT Press, 393–416.

Hale, J., and E. P. Stabler. 2005. Strict deterministic aspects of minimalist grammars. In *Logical Aspects of Computational Linguistics*, LACL' 05. New York: Springer, 162–76.

Halle, M., and J.-R. Vergnaud. 1987. *An Essay on Stress*. Cambridge, Mass.: MIT Press.

Halpern, A. L., and A. M. Zwicky (eds) 1996. *Approaching Second: Second Position Clitics and Related Phenomena*. Stanford, Calif.: CSLI.

Hammond, M. 1984. *Constraining Metrical Theory: A Modular Theory of Rhythm and Destressing*. PhD thesis, University of California, Los Angeles.

Hankamer, J., and I. A. Sag. 1976. Deep and surface anaphora. *Linguistic Inquiry* 7: 391–426.

Hao, Y. 2017. Harmonic Serialism and finite-state Optimality Theory. In *Proceedings of the 13th International Conference on Finite State Methods and Natural Language Processing*, 20–9.

Hardt, D. 1993. *Verb Phrase Ellipsis: Form, Meaning and Processing*. PhD thesis, University of Pennsylvania.

Harkema, H. 2000. A recognizer for minimalist grammars. In *Sixth International Workshop on Parsing Technologies*, IWPT'00, University of Trento, 251–68.

Harkema, H. 2001. *Parsing Minimalist Languages*. PhD thesis, University of California, Los Angeles.

Harper, M., B. Dorr, J. Hale, B. Roark, I. Shafran, M. Lease, Y. Liu, M. Snover, L. Yung, A. Krasnyanskaya, and R. Stewart. 2005. *Summer Workshop Final Report on Parsing and Spoken Structural Event Detection*. Baltimore, Md.: Johns Hopkins University.

Hasson, U., and C. Honey. 2012. Future trends in neuroimaging: neural processes as expressed within real-life contexts. *Neuroimage* 62: 1272–8.

Hayes, B. 1988. Metrics and phonological theory. In F. J. Newmeyer (ed.), *Linguistics: The Cambridge Survey*. Cambridge: Cambridge University Press, 220–49.

Hayes, B. 1989. The prosodic hierarchy in meter. In P. Kiparsky and G. Youmans (eds), *Rhythm and Meter*. New York: Academic Press, 220–49.

Hayes, B. 1995. *Metrical Stress Theory: Principles and Case Studies*. Chicago: University of Chicago Press.

Heinz, J. 2018. The computational nature of phonological generalizations. In L. M. Hyman and F. Plank (eds), *Phonological Typology*. Berlin: Mouton de Gruyter, 126–95.

Hellmuth, S. 2009. The (absence of) prosodic reflexes of given/new information status in Egyptian Arabic. In J. Owens and A. Elgibali (eds), *Information Structure in Spoken Arabic*. Abingdon: Routledge, 165–88.

Hellmuth, S. J. 2006. *Intonational Pitch Accent Distribution in Egyptian Arabic*. PhD thesis, School of Oriental and African Studies, University of London.

Henson, R., and K. Friston. 2007. Convolution models for fMRI. In K. Friston, J. Ashburner, S. Kiebel, T. Nichols, and W. Penny (eds), *Statistical Parametric Mapping*. New York: Academic Press, 178–92.

Himmelmann, N. P. 2014. Asymmetries in the prosodic phrasing of function words: another look at the suffixing preference. *Language* 90: 927–60.

Hirsch, A., and M. Wagner. 2015. Rightward movement affects prosodic phrasing. In *Proceedings of the Northeast Linguistic Society* 45.

Hsiao, F., and E. Gibson. 2003. Processing relative clauses in Chinese. *Cognition* 90: 3–27.

Hualde, J. I., and P. Prieto. 2016. Towards an International Prosodic Alphabet (IPrA). *Laboratory Phonology* 7: 5.

Huang, Z., and M. Harper. 2010. Appropriately handled prosodic breaks help PCFG parsing. In *Proceedings of NAACL-HLT*, 37–45.

Hulden, M. 2017. Formal and computational verification of phonological analyses. *Phonology* 34: 407–35.

Humphries, C., J. Binder, D. Medler, and E. Liebenthal. 2006. Syntactic and semantic modulation of neural activity during auditory sentence comprehension. *Journal of Cognitive Neuroscience* 18: 665–79.

Inkelas, S. 1989. *Prosodic Constituency in the Lexicon*. PhD thesis, Stanford University.

Ito, J., and A. Mester. 1992. Weak layering and word binarity. Technical report, University of California, Santa Cruz.

Itô, J., and A. Mester. 2003. Weak layering and word binarity. In T. Honma, M. Okazaki, T. Tabata, and S. Tanaka (eds), *A New Century of Phonology and Phonological Theory*. Tokyo: Kaitakusha, 26–65.

Itô, J., and A. Mester. 2013. Prosodic subcategories in Japanese. *Lingua* 124: 20–30.

Itô, J., and A. Mester. 2015. The perfect prosodic word in Danish. *Nordic Journal of Linguistics* 38: 5–36.

Jackendoff, R. S. 1972. *Semantic Interpretation in Generative Grammar*. Cambridge, Mass.: MIT Press.

Jäger, L., Z. Chen, Qiang Li, C. Lin, and S. Vasishth. 2015. The subject-relative advantage in Chinese: evidence for expectation-based processing. *Journal of Memory and Language* 79–80: 97–120.

Jelinek, F. 1998. *Statistical Methods for Speech Recognition*. Cambridge, MA: MIT Press.

Joshi, A. 1985. How much context-sensitivity is necessary for characterizing structural descriptions? In D. Dowty, L. Karttunen, and A. Zwicky (eds), *Natural Language Processing*. Cambridge: Cambridge University Press, 206–50.

Jun, S.-A. 1996. *The Phonetics and Phonology of Korean Prosody*. New York: Garland.

Jun, S.-A. 1998. The accentual phrase in the Korean prosodic hierarchy. *Phonology* 15(2): 189–226.

Jun, S.-A. 2005a. Prosodic typology. In S.-A. Jun (ed.), *Prosodic Typology: The Phonology of Intonation and Phrasing*. Oxford: Oxford University Press, 430–58.

Jun, S.-A. 2005b. *Prosodic Typology: The Phonology of Intonation and Phrasing*. Oxford: Oxford University Press.

Jun, S.-A. 2014. *Prosodic Typology II: The Phonology and Phonetics of Intonation and Phrasing*. Oxford: Oxford University Press.

Just, M., P. Carpenter, T. Keller, W. Eddy, and K. Thulborn. 1996. Brain activation modulated by sentence comprehension. *Science* 274: 114–16.

Just, M., and S. Varma. 2007. The organization of thinking: what functional brain imaging reveals about the neuroarchitecture of complex cognition. *Cognitive, Affective, and Behavioral Neuroscience* 7: 153–91.

Kahn, J. G., M. Lease, E. Charniak, M. Johnson, and M. Ostendorf. 2005. Effective use of prosody in parsing conversational speech. In *Proceedings of Human Language Technology Conference and Conference on Empirical Methods in Natural Language*, 233–40.

Kaisse, E. M. 1985. *Connected Speech: The Interaction of Syntax and Phonology*. New York: Academic Press.

Kallmeyer, L., and W. Maier. 2015. LR parsing for LCFRS. In *Human Language Technologies: The 2015 Annual Conference of the North American Chapter of the ACL*, 1250–5.

Kanazawa, M. 2007. Parsing and generation as datalog queries. In *Proceedings of the 45th Annual Meeting of the Association of Computational Linguistics*, 176–83.

Kanazawa, M. 2016. Formal grammar: an introduction. Online lecture notes: http://research.nii.ac.jp/kanazawa/FormalGrammar/index.html.

Kandybowicz, J. 2015. On prosodic vacuity and verbal resumption in Asante Twi. *Linguistic Inquiry* 46: 243–72.

Karttunen, L. 1998. The proper treatment of optimality in computational phonology. In *Proceedings of the International Workshop on Finite-State Methods in Natural Language Processing*, FSMNLP'98, 1–12.

Karttunen, L. 2006a. A finite-state approximation of Optimality Theory: the case of Finnish prosody. In *FinTAL, LNAI 4139*. Berlin: Springer, 4–15.

Karttunen, L. 2006b. The insufficiency of paper-and-pencil linguistics: the case of Finnish prosody. In M. Butt, M. Dalrymple, and T. H. King (eds), *Intelligent Linguistic Architectures: Variations on Themes by Ronald M. Kaplan*. Stanford, Calif.: CLSI, 287–300.

Kayne, R. S. 1984. *Connectedness and Binary Branching*. Dordrecht: Foris.

Kayne, R. S. 1994. *The Antisymmetry of Syntax*. Cambridge, Mass.: MIT Press.

Kayne, R. S. 2002. Pronouns and their antecedents. In *Derivation and Explanation in the Minimalist Program*. Oxford: Blackwell, 133–66. Repr. in R. S. Kayne (ed.), *Movement and Silence* (Oxford: Oxford University Press, 2005).

Kenstowicz, M. 1995. Cyclic vs. non-cyclic constraint evaluation. *Phonology* 12: 397–436.

Kentner, G., and C. Féry. 2013. A new approach to prosodic grouping. *Linguistic Review* 30(2): 277–311.

Kiparsky, P. 1982. Word formation and the lexicon. In *Proceedings of the 1982 Mid-America Linguistics Conference* (Hanshin, Seoul), 47–88.

Klein, D., and C. D. Manning. 2003. Accurate unlexicalized parsing. In *Proceedings of the 41st Meeting of the Association for Computational Linguistics*, 423–30. 'Stanford Parser' code: at http://nlp.stanford.edu/software/lex-parser.html.

Kobele, G. M. 2005. Features moving madly: a note on the complexity of an extension to MGs. *Research on Language and Computation* 3(4): 391–410.

Kobele, G. M. 2006. *Generating Copies: An Investigation into Structural Identity in Language and Grammar*. PhD thesis, University of California Los Angeles.

Kobele, G. M. 2010. Without remnant movement, MGs are context-free. In *Proceedings of Mathematics of Language 10/11*, volume 6149 of LNCS. Berlin: Springer, 160–73.

Kobele, G. M. 2011. Minimalist tree languages are closed under intersection with recognizable tree languages. In *Logical Aspects of Computational Linguistics*, LACL'11, 129–44.

Kobele, G. M. 2012a. Eliding the derivation: a minimalist formalization of ellipsis. In *Proceedings of the 19th International Conference on Head-Driven Phrase Structure Grammar*, 307–24.

Kobele, G. M. 2012b. Ellipsis: computation of. *WIREs Cognitive Science* 3(3): 411–18.

Kobele, G. M. 2015. LF-copying without LF. *Lingua* 166B: 236–59.

Kobele, G. M., and J. Michaelis. 2005. Two type 0 variants of minimalist grammars. In *Proceedings of the 10th conference on Formal Grammar and the 9th Meeting on Mathematics of Language*, FGMOL05, 81–91.

Kobele, G. M., and J. Michaelis. 2009. Locality, late adjunction and extraposition. Presented at the European Summer School for Logic Language and Information, ESSLLI'09; available at: http://wwwhomes.uni-bielefeld.de/jmichaelis/esslli2009/ slides/4-2_Late_Adjunction_and_Extraposition.pdf.

Kobele, G. M., and J. Michaelis. 2011. Disentangling notions of specifier impenetrability. In M. Kanazawa, A. Kornai, M. Kracht, and H. Seki (eds), *The Mathematics of Language*, Berlin: Springer, 126–42.

Kobele, G. M., C. Retoré, and S. Salvati. 2007. An automata-theoretic approach to minimalism. In *Model Theoretic Syntax at 10: ESSLLI'07 Workshop Proceedings*, 71–80.

Koopman, H. 1983. ECP effects in main clauses. *Linguistic Inquiry* 14: 346–51.

Koopman, H. 2012. Samoan ergativity as double passivization. In L. Brug, A. Cardinaletti, G. Giusti, N. Monera, and C. Poletto (eds), *Functional Heads*. Oxford: Oxford University Press, 168–80.

Kratzer, A., and E. Selkirk. 2007. Phase theory and prosodic spellout: the case of verbs. *Linguistic Review* 24: 93–135.

Krivokapić, J. 2014. Gestural coordination at prosodic boundaries and its role for prosodic structure and speech planning processes. *Philosophical Transactions of the Royal Society* B, 369: 20130397.

Krivokapić, J., and D. Byrd. 2012. Prosodic boundary strength: an articulatory and perceptual study. *Journal of Phonetics* 40: 430–42.

Kügler, F. 2015. Phonological phrasing and ATR vowel harmony in Akan. *Phonology* 32: 177–204.

Kuhlmann, M., and M. Möhl. 2007. The string-generative capacity of regular dependency languages. In *Proceedings of the 2007 Conference on Formal Grammar* (FG'07), 160–67.

Kush, D., J. Lidz, and C. Phillips. 2015. Relation-sensitive retrieval: evidence from bound variable pronouns. *Journal of Memory and Language* 82: 18–40.

Kusmer, L. 2019. Optimal linearization: prosodic displacement in Khoekhoegowab and beyond. PhD thesis, University of Massachusetts Amherst.

Ladd, D. R. 1986. Intonational phrasing: the case for recursive prosodic structure. *Phonology Yearbook* 3: 311–40.

Ladd, D. R. 1996. *Intonational Phonology*. Cambridge: Cambridge University Press.

Ladd, D. R. 2014. *Simultaneous Structure in Phonology*. Oxford: Oxford University Press.

Landauer, T. 2007. LSA as a theory of meaning. In T. Landauer, D. McNamara, S. Dennis, and W. Kintsch (eds), *Handbook of Latent Semantic Analysis*. Mahwah, NJ: Erlbaum, 1–34.

Landauer, T., and S. Dumais. 1997. A solution to Plato's problem: the latent semantic analysis theory of acquisition, induction, and representation of knowledge. *Psychological Review* 104: 211–40.

Larson, R. K. 1988. On the double object construction. *Linguistic Inquiry* 19: 335–91.

Lazić, R., and S. Schmitz. 2014. Non-elementary complexities for branching VASS, MELL, and extensions. In *Proceedings of the Joint Meeting of the 23rd EACSL Annual Conference on Computer Science Logic and the 29th Annual ACM/IEEE Symposium on Logic in Computer Science*. New York: ACM, 61:1–61:10.

Leermakers, R. 1993. *The Functional Treatment of Parsing*. Amsterdam: Kluwer.

Lees, R. B. 1960. *The Grammar of English Nominalizations*. The Hague: Mouton.

Legate, J. A. 2008. Morphological and abstract case. *Linguistic Inquiry* 29(1): 55–101.

Lenci, A. 2018. Distributional models of word meaning. *Annual Review of Linguistics* 4: 151–71.

Lewis, R., and S. Vasishth. 2005. An activation-based model of sentence processing as skilled memory retrieval. *Cognitive Science* 29: 375–417.

Liberman, M. 1975a. *The Intonational System of English*. PhD thesis, MIT.

Liberman, M. 1975b. On conditioning the rule of subj–aux inversion. In *Proceedings of the Northeast Linguistic Society* 5, 77–91.

Liberman, M., and A. Prince. 1977. On stress and linguistic rhythm. *Linguistic Inquiry* 8: 249–336.

Lin, C. K., and L. S. Lee. 2009. Improved features and models for detecting edit disfluencies in transcribing spontaneous mandarin speech. *IEEE Transactions on Audio, Speech, and Language Processing* 17: 1263–78.

Lincoln, P. 1995. Deciding provability of linear logic formulas. In J.-Y. Girard, Y. Lafont, and L. Regnier (eds), *Advances in Linear Logic*. Cambridge: Cambridge University Press, 109–22.

Lobeck, A. 1995. *Ellipsis: Functional Heads, Licensing, and Identification*. Oxford: Oxford University Press.

Luong, M., M. Fran, and M. Johnson. 2013. Parsing entire discourses as very long strings: capturing topic continuity in grounded language learning. *Transactions of the Association for Computational Linguistics* 1: 315–23.

Marantz, A. 1991. Case and licensing. In *Proceedings of the Eighth Eastern States Conference on Linguistics*, ESCOL'91, 234–53.

Marcus, M. 1980. *A Theory of Syntactic Recognition for Natural Language*. Cambridge, Mass.: MIT Press.

de Marneffe, M.-C., T. Dozat, N. Silveira, K. Haverinen, F. Ginter, J. Nivre, and C. D. Manning. 2014. Universal Stanford dependencies: a cross-linguistic typology. In *Proceedings of the Ninth International Conference on Language Resources and Evaluation*, LREC-2014.

de Marneffe, M.-C., B. MacCartney, and C. D. Manning. 2006. Generating typed dependency parses from phrase structure parses. In *Proceedings of the Fifth International Conference on Language Resources and Evaluation*, LREC-2006. CD. Paris: European Language Resources Association.

Massam, D. 2001. Pseudo noun incorporation in Niuean. *Natural Language and Linguistic Theory* 19: 153–97.

Massam, D. 2006. Neither absolutive nor ergative is nominative or accusative. In A. Johns, D. Massam, and J. Ndayiragije (eds), *Ergativity: Emerging Issues*. Dordrecht: Springer, 26–46.

Massam, D. 2012. The structure of (un)ergatives. In *Proceedings of the Austronesian Formal Linguistics Association* 16, 125–35.

McCarthy, J. 1982. Nonlinear phonology: an overview. *GLOW Newsletter* 8, 63–77.

McCarthy, J., and A. Prince. 1995. Prosodic morphology. In J. A. Goldsmith (ed.), *The Handbook of Phonological Theory*. Oxford: Blackwell, 318–66.

McPherson, L., and J. Heath. 2016. Phrasal grammatical tone in the Dogon languages: the role of constraint interaction. *Natural Language & Linguistic Theory* 34: 593–639.

Merchant, J. 2001. *The Syntax of Silence: Sluicing, Islands, and the Theory of Ellipsis*. Oxford: Oxford University Press.

Michaelis, J. 1998. Derivational minimalism is mildly context-sensitive. In *Proceedings, Logical Aspects of Computational Linguistics*, LACL'98. New York: Springer, 179–98.

Michaelis, J. 2001. *On Formal Properties of Minimalist Grammars*. PhD thesis, Universität Potsdam.

Michaelis, J. 2005. An additional observation on strict derivational minimalism. In *Proceedings of the 10th Conference on Formal Grammar and the 9th Meeting on Mathematics of Language*, FGMOL'05, CSLI, Stanford. Available at: https://web.stanford.edu/group/cslipublications/cslipublications/FG/2005/.

Michel, J., et al. 2011. Quantitative analysis of culture using millions of digitized books. *Science* 331: 176–82.

Miller, P. H., and G. K. Pullum. 2014. Exophoric VP ellipsis. In P. Hofmeister and E. Norcliffe (eds), *The Core and the Periphery: Data-Driven Perspectives on Syntax*. Stanford, Calif.: CSLI, 5–32.

Miller, T. 2009. Word buffering models for improved speech repair parsing. In *Proceedings of the 2009 Conference on Empirical Methods in Natural Language Processing*, EMNLP'09, 737–45.

Moyle, R. 1981. *Fāgogo: Fables from Samoa in Samoan and English*. Auckland: University Press.

Munn, A. 1994. A minimalist account of reconstruction asymmetries. In *Proceedings of NELS 24*, 397–410.

Myrberg, S. 2013. Sisterhood in prosodic branching. *Phonology* 30: 73–124.

Myrberg, S., and T. Riad. 2015. The prosodic hierarchy of Swedish. *Nordic Journal of Linguistics* 38: 115–47.

Nespor, M., and I. Vogel. 1986. *Prosodic Phonology*. Dordrecht: Foris.

Nijholt, A. 1980. *Context Free Grammars: Covers, Normal Forms, and Parsing*. New York: Springer.

Ochs, E.. 1982. Ergativity and word order in Samoan child language. *Language* 58: 646–71.

Odden, D. 1987. Kimatuumbi phrasal phonology. *Phonology Yearbook* 4: 13–36.

O'Grady, W. 1997. *Syntactic Development*. Chicago: University of Chicago Press.

Omaki, A., E. F. Lau, I. Davidson White, M. L. Dakan, A. Apple, and C. Phillips. 2015. Hyperactive gap filling. *Frontiers in Psychology* 6, article 384. Available at: https://doi.org/10.3389/fpsyg.2015.00384

Pallier, C., A. Devauchelle, and S. Dehaene. 2011. Cortical representation of the constituent structure of sentences. *Proceedings of the National Academy of Sciences* 108: 2522–7.

Parker, D., and C. Phillips. 2016. Negative polarity illusions and the format of hierarchical encodings in memory. *Cognition* 157: 321–39.

Parker, D., Shvartsman, M., & Van Dyke, J. A. 2017. The cue-based retrieval theory of sentence comprehension: New findings and new challenges. In L. Escobar, V. Torrens, and T. Parodi (eds), *Language Processing and Disorders*. Newcastle: Cambridge Scholars Publishing, 121–44.

Pesetsky, D. 1985. Morphology and logical form. *Linguistic Inquiry* 16: 193–246.

Pesetsky, D. 1995. *Zero Syntax: Experiencers and Cascades*. Cambridge, Mass.: MIT Press.

Pesetsky, D., and E. Torrego. 2001. T-to-C movement: causes and consequences. In M. Kenstowicz (ed.), *Ken Hale: A Life in Language*. Cambridge, Mass.: MIT Press, 355–426.

Phillips, C. 2006. The real-time status of island phenomena. *Language* 82: 795–823.

Pierrehumbert, J. 1980. *The Phonology and Phonetics of English Intonation*. PhD thesis, Harvard University.

Pierrehumbert, J., and M. Beckman. 1988. *Japanese Tone Structure*. Cambridge, Mass.: MIT Press.

Price, P. J., M. Ostendorf, S. Shattuck-Hufnagel, and C. Fong. 1991. The use of prosody in syntactic disambiguation. *Journal of the Acoustical Society of America* 90: 2956–70.

Prince, A., and P. Smolensky. 2004. *Optimality Theory: Constraint Interaction in Generative Grammar*. Oxford: Blackwell.

Pylkkänen, L. 2015. Composition of complex meaning: interdisciplinary perspectives on the left anterior temporal lobe. In G. Hickok and S. Small (eds), *Neurobiology of Language*. New York: Elsevier, 622–9.

Pynte, J., B. New, and A. Kennedy. 2008. A multiple regression analysis of syntactic and semantic influences in reading normal text. *Journal of Eye Movement Research* 2: 1–11.

Rezac, M. 2006. The interaction of Th/Ex and locative inversion. *Linguistic Inquiry* 37: 685–97.

Richards, M. 2007. Object shift, phases, and transitive expletive constructions in Germanic. In P. Pica, J. Rooryck, and J. Van Craenenbroeck (eds), *Linguistics Variation Yearbook 6*. Amsterdam: Benjamins, 139–59.

Richards, M. (2009). Internal pair-merge: the missing mode of movement. *Catalan Journal of Linguistics* 8: 55–73.

Richards, N. 2010. *Uttering Trees*. Cambridge, Mass.: MIT Press.

Ristad, E. S. 1993. The anaphora problem. *Information and Computation* 105(1): 105–31.

Rizzi, L. 1990. *Relativized Minimality*. Cambridge, Mass.: MIT Press.

Roark, B., A. Bachrach, C. Cardenas, and C. Pallier. 2009. Deriving lexical and syntactic expectation-based measures for psycholinguistic modeling via incremental top-down parsing. In *Proceedings of the Conference on Empirical Methods in Natural Language Processing* (EMNLP), 324–33.

Rogalsky, C., and G. Hickok. 2009. Selective attention to semantic and syntactic features modulates sentence processing networks in anterior temporal cortex. *Cerebral Cortex* 19: 786–96.

Sabbagh, J. 2014. Word order and prosodic-structure constraints in Tagalog. *Syntax* 17: 40–89.

Salvati, S. 2011. Minimalist grammars in the light of logic. In S. Pogodalla, M. Quatrini, and C. Retoré (eds), *Logic and Grammar*. Berlin: Springer, 81–117.

Salvati, S. 2015. MIX is a 2-MCFL and the word problem in Z2 is solved by a third-order collapsible pushdown automaton. *Journal of Computer and System Sciences* 81(7): 1252–77.

Sayeed, A., S. Fischer, and V. Demberg. 2015. Vector-space calculation of semantic surprisal for vector-space calculation of semantic surprisal for predicting word pronunciation duration. In *Proceedings of the 53rd Annual Meeting of the Association for Computational Linguistics and the 7th International Joint Conference on Natural Language Processing*, vol. 1, 763–73.

Schachter, P. 1977. Constraints on coordination. *Language* 53: 86–103.

Seidl, A. 2000. *Minimal Indirect Reference Theory: A Theory of the Syntax–Phonology Interface*. PhD thesis, University of Pennsylvania, Philadelphia.

Seki, H., T. Matsumura, M. Fujii, and T. Kasami. 1991. On multiple context-free grammars. *Theoretical Computer Science* 88: 191–229.

Selkirk, E. 1996. The prosodic structure of function words. In K. Demuth and J. Morgan (eds), *Signal to Syntax: Bootstrapping from Speech to Grammar in Early Acquisition*. Hillsdale, NJ: Erlbaum, 187–213.

Selkirk, E. 2009. On clause and intonational phrase in Japanese: the syntactic grounding of prosodic constituent structure. *Gengo Kenkyu* 136: 35–73.

Selkirk, E. 2011. Syntax–phonology interface. In J. A. Goldsmith, J. Riggle, and A. Yu (eds), *The Handbook of Phonological Theory*, 2nd edn. Oxford: Blackwell, 435–84.

Selkirk, E., and S. J. Lee. 2015. Constituency in sentence phonology: an introduction. *Phonology* 32: 1–15.

Selkirk, E. O. 1978/1981. On prosodic structure and its relation to syntactic structure. In T. Fretheim (ed.), *Nordic Prosody II*. Trondheim: TAPIR, 111–40.

Selkirk, E. O. 1984. *Phonology and Syntax: The Relationship Between Sound and Structure*. Cambridge, Mass.: MIT Press.

Selkirk, E. O. 1986. On derived domains in sentence phonology. *Phonology Yearbook* 3: 371–405.

Shattuck-Hufnagel, S., and A. E. Turk. 1996. A prosody tutorial for investigators of auditory sentence processing. *Journal of Psycholinguistic Research* 25: 193–247.

Shriberg, E., A. Stolcke, D. Hakkani-Tür, and G. Tür. 2000. Prosody-based automatic segmentation of speech into sentences and topics. *Speech Communication* 32: 127–54.

Sippu, S., and E. Soisalon-Soininen. 1988. *Parsing Theory*, vol. 1: *Languages and Parsing*. Berlin: Springer.

Sippu, S., and E. Soisalon-Soininen. 1990. *Parsing Theory*, vol. 2: *LR(k) and LL(k) Parsing*. Berlin: Springer.

Sobin, N. 2014. Th/Ex agreement and case in expletive sentences. *Syntax* 17: 385–416.

Speer, S. R., and A. Foltz. 2015. The implicit prosody of corrective contrast primes appropriately intonated probes. In L. Frazier and E. Gibson (eds), *Explicit and Implicit Prosody in Sentence Processing*. New York: Springer, 263–85.

Spilker, J., A. Batliner, and E. Nöth. 2001. How to repair speech repairs in an end-to-end system. In *Proceedings of ISCA Workshop on Disfluency in Spontaneous Speech*, 73–6.

Sportiche, D., H. Koopman, and E. Stabler. 2013. *An Introduction to Syntactic Analysis and Theory*. Oxford: Wiley-Blackwell.

Sproat, R. 1985. *On Deriving the Lexicon*. PhD thesis, MIT.

Sprouse, J., and N. Hornstein. 2016. Syntax and the cognitive neuroscience of syntactic structure building. In G. Hickok and S. Small (eds), *Neurobiology of Language*. Amsterdam: Elsevier/Academic Press, 165–74.

Stabler, E. 1983. How are grammars represented? *Behavioral and Brain Sciences* 6: 391–421.

Stabler, E. P. 1997. Derivational minimalism. In C. Retoré (ed.), *Logical Aspects of Computational Linguistics*. New York: Springer, 68–95.

Stabler, E. P. 1998. Remnant movement and complexity. In *Joint Conference on Formal Grammar, Head-Driven Phrase Structure Grammar, and Categorial Grammar*, FHCG-98, Universität des Saarlandes.

Stabler, E. 1999. Remnant movement and complexity. In G. Bouma, E. Hinrichs, G.-J. Kruijff, and R. Oehrle, eds, *Constraints and Resources in Natural Language Syntax and Semantics*. Stanford, Calif.: CSLI, 299–326.

Stabler, E. P. 2011a. After Government and Binding theory. In J. van Benthem and A. ter Meulen (eds), *Handbook of Logic and Language*, 2nd edn. Amsterdam: Elsevier, 395–414.

Stabler, E. P. 2011b. Computational perspectives on minimalism. In C. Boeckx (ed.), *Oxford Handbook of Linguistic Minimalism*. Oxford: Oxford University Press, 617–41.

Stabler, E. P. 2013a. Computational linguistics: defining, calculating, using, and learning linguistic structure. Technical report, UCLA.

Stabler, E. P. 2013b. Two models of minimalist, incremental syntactic analysis. *Topics in Cognitive Science* 5(3): 611–33.

Stabler, E. P., and E. L. Keenan. 2003. Structural similarity. *Theoretical Computer Science* 293: 345–63.

Steedman, M. 1991a. Parsing spoken language using combinatory grammars. In M. Tomita (ed.), *Current Issues in Parsing Technology*. Berlin: Springer, 113–26.

Steedman, M. 1991b. Structure and intonation. *Language* 67(2): 260–96.

Steedman, M. J. 2014. The surface-compositional semantics of English intonation. *Language* 90: 2–57.

Stern, D. N., S. Spieker, and K. MacKain. 1982. Intonation contours as signals in maternal speech. *Developmental Psychology* 18: 727–35.

Stolcke, A. 1995. An efficient probabilistic context-free parsing algorithm that computes prefix probabilities. *Computational Linguistics* 21: 165–201.

Stowe, L. A. 1986. Parsing wh-constructions: evidence for on-line gap location. *Language and Cognitive Processes* 1(3): 227–45.

Stowe, L. A., M. Haverkort, and F. Zwarts. 2005. Rethinking the neurological basis of language. *Lingua* 115: 997–1042.

Stromswold, K., D. Caplan, N. Alpert, and S. Rauch. 1996. Localization of syntactic comprehension by positron emission tomography. *Brain and Language* 52: 452–73.

Sturt, P., and V. Lombardo. 2005. Processing coordinated structures: incrementality and connectedness. *Cognitive Science* 19: 291–305.

Sundholm, G. 1984. Systems of deduction. In D. Gabbay and F. Guenthner (eds), *Handbook of Philosophical Logic*. Boston, Mass.: Reidel, 133–88.

Szabolcsi, A. 2006. Strong vs. weak islands. In M. Everaert and H. van Riemsdijk (eds), *The Blackwell Companion to Syntax*, vol. 4. Oxford: Blackwell, 479–531.

Taglicht, J. 1994. Syntactic structure and intonational phrasing. Technical report, University of Pennsylvania, Working Papers in Linguistics 1.

Taglicht, J. 1998. Constraints on intonational phrasing in English. *Journal of Linguistics* 34: 181–211.

Thatcher, J. W. 1967. Characterizing derivation trees of context-free grammars through a generalization of finite automata theory. *Journal of Computer and System Sciences* 1(4): 317–22.

Thorson, J., and J. L. Morgan. 2014. Directing toddler attention: intonation and information structure. In *Supplement to the Proceedings of the 38th Annual Boston University Conference on Language Development*. Somerville, Mass.: Cascadilla Press.

Tollan, R. 2015. Unergatives and split ergativity in Samoan. In *Proceedings of the Northeast Linguistic Society* 46, 233–46.

Tomioka, S. 2008. A step-by-step guide to ellipsis resolution. In K. Johnson (ed.), *Topics in Ellipsis*. Cambridge: Cambridge University Press, 210–28.

Torr, J., and E. Stabler. 2016. Coordination in minimalist grammars. In *Proceedings of the 12th Annual Workshop on Tree-Adjoining Grammars and Related Formalisms*, TAG+, 1–17. Available at: http://www.aclweb.org/anthology/W16-3301.

Tran, T., S. Toshniwal, M. Bansal, K. Gimpel, K. Livescu, and M. Ostendorf. 2017. Joint modeling of text and acoustic-prosodic cues for neural parsing. arXiv, 1704.07287v1.

Traxler, M. J., and M. J. Pickering. 1996. Plausibility and the processing of unbounded dependencies: an eye-tracking study. *Journal of Memory and Language* 35: 454–75.

Truckenbrodt, H. 1999. On the relation between syntactic phrases and phonological phrases. *Linguistic Inquiry* 30(1): 219–55.

Truckenbrodt, H., and C. Féry. 2015. Hierarchical organisation and tonal scaling. *Phonology* 32: 19–47.

Valiant, L. G. 1975. General context free recognition in less than cubic time. *Journal of Computer and System Sciences* 10: 308–15.

van Wagenen, S., J. Brennan, and E. Stabler. 2014. Quantifying parsing complexity as a function of grammar. In C. Schütze and L. Stockall (eds), *UCLA working papers in Linguistics* 18. Los Angeles, Calif.: UCLA Linguistics Department, 31–47.

Wagers, M. W., and C. Phillips. 2009. Multiple dependencies and the role of grammar in real-time comprehension. *Journal of Linguistics* 45: 395–433.

Wagner, M. 2005. *Prosody and Recursion*. PhD thesis, MIT.

Wagner, M. 2010. Prosody and recursion in coordinate structures and beyond. *Natural Language and Linguistic Theory* 28(1): 183–237.

Wagner, M. 2012. Locality in phonology and production planning. In *Proceedings of the Montreal–Ottawa–Toronto (MOT) Phonology Workshop 2011: Phonology in the 21st Century: In Honour of Glyne Piggott*, McGill Working Papers in Linguistics 22.

Wanner, E., and M. Maratsos. 1978. An ATN approach to comprehension. In M. Halle, J. Bresnan, and G. Miller (eds), *Linguistic Theory and Psychological Reality*. Cambridge, Mass.: MIT Press, 119–61.

Wehbe, L., B. Murphy, P. Talukdar, A. Fyshe, A. Ramdas, and T. Mitchell. 2014. Simultaneously uncovering the patterns of brain regions involved in different story reading subprocesses. *PLoS ONE* 9: e112575.

Wightman, C. W., S. Shattuck-Hufnagel, M. Ostendorf, and P. J. Price. 1992. Segmental durations in the vicinity of prosodic phrase boundaries. *Journal of the Acoustical Society of America* 91: 1707–17.

Wilson, S., A. DeMarco, M. Henry, B. Gesierich, M. Babiak, M. Mandelli, B. Miller, and M. Gorno-Tempini. 2014. What role does the anterior temporal lobe play in sentence-level processing? Neural correlates of syntactic processing in semantic PPA. *Journal of Cognitive Neuroscience* 26: 970–85.

Wu, C.-H., W.-B. Liang, and J.-F. Yeh. 2011. Interruption point detection of spontaneous speech using inter-syllable boundary-based prosodic features. In *ACM Transactions on Asian Language Information Processing*, TALIP 10, 1–21.

Xiang, M., B. Dillon, and C. Phillips. 2009. Illusory licensing effects across dependency types: ERP evidence. *Brain and Language* 108: 40–55.

Yngve, V. 1960. A model and a hypothesis for language structure. In *Proceedings of the American Philosophical Society* 104: 444–66.

Yoshida, M., M. Dickey, and P. Sturt. 2012. Predictive processing of syntactic structure: sluicing and ellipsis in real-time sentence processing. *Language and Cognitive Processes* 28: 272–302.

Younger, D. H. 1967. Recognition and parsing of context free languages in time O(n3). *Information and Control* 10: 189–208.

Yu, K. M. 2011. The sound of ergativity: morphosyntax–prosody mapping in Samoan. In *Proceedings of the 39th Annual Meeting of the North East Linguistic Society*, 825–38.

Yu, K. M. 2014. The experimental state of mind in elicitation: illustrations from tonal fieldwork. *Language Documentation and Conservation* 8: 738–77.

Yu, K. M. To appear. Tonal marking of absolutive case in Samoan. *Natural Language & Linguistic Theory*.

Yu, K. M. 2018. Advantages of constituency: computational perspectives on Samoan word prosody. In *Formal Grammar: 22nd and 23rd International Conferences*. Berlin: Springer, 105–24.

Yu, K. M., and D. Özyıldız. 2016. The absolutive ia particle in Samoan. In *Proceedings of the Forty-Second Annual Meeting of the Berkeley Linguistics Society*, 387–406.

Yu, K. M., and E. P. Stabler. 2017. (In)variability in the Samoan syntax/prosody interface and consequences for syntactic parsing. *Laboratory Phonology* 8(1): 25.

Yun, J., J. Whitman, and J. Hale. 2010. Subject–object asymmetries in Korean sentence comprehension. In *Proceedings of the Annual Meeting of the Cognitive Science Society*, 2152–7.

Zuraw, K., K. M. Yu, and R. Orfitelli. 2014. The word-level prosody of Samoan. *Phonology* 31: 271–327.

Zwarts, S., and M. Johnson. 2011. The impact of language models and loss functions on repair disfluency detection. In *Proceedings of the 49th Annual Meeting of the Association for Computational Linguistics: Human Language Technologies*, HLT'11, 703–11.

Index